3-27-64
7-24-64

THE TWO SIDES IN NFO'S BATTLE

THE TWO SIDES
IN NFO'S BATTLE

By

GEORGE BRANDSBERG

The Iowa State University Press, Ames, Iowa, U.S.A.

1964

About the Author

GEORGE BRANDSBERG feels that it is the responsibility of all people
to be informed on significant developments. His position as news
editor of a Midwestern daily agricultural newspaper has enabled
him to follow closely the trends of contemporary agriculture. Still
a young man, his background already includes a variety of experiences that help him as he views the changing scene through a journalist's eyes. South Dakota born, he was raised on a diversified ir-
rigated farm where dairy cows, sheep, 4-H, the outdoors, Boy Scouts,
and even taxidermy, were a part of his youth. He was graduated
from the University of South Dakota with a degree in philosophy
and minor work in history, journalism and French. He has worked
as a newspaper reporter-photographer and free-lance correspondent.
His writings have appeared in a variety of publications, from the
Christian Science Monitor and the Minneapolis *Tribune* to the
Bicycle Journal.

Composed and printed by
The Iowa State University Press,
Ames, Iowa, U.S.A.

Library of Congress Catalog Card Number 64–13373

1262859

IN MEMORY

of Mother and Father,
whose lives were spent in agriculture

INTRODUCTION

A BOUT THREE YEARS AGO, my writer's curiosity was aroused by the many and far-differing reports on the activities of the National Farmers Organization. Strong accusations and ugly rumors were circulating among the persons identified with one side or the other of the NFO conflict. Yet, no one seemed to be sure of what he had heard and hearsay was often accepted as factual information. Bent on separating facts from rumors, I decided to investigate the NFO story. The more I learned, the more convinced I became that here was information that deserved permanent recording in book form.

As a story, the history of the NFO had the dramatic elements of conflict; it had its heroes and its villains. But more important, it had a significant cause to fight for, although the merits of the method in dealing with the problem at hand—that fuzzy and vexing, but well-known "farm problem"—was indeed a matter for debate.

At this writing, the NFO story remains unfinished. The movement faces a number of alternatives, including survival and continued growth or remaining at the status quo until some unforeseen change in strength and/or policy. And of course there is always the possibility of extinction. Since this account covers only the beginning of the NFO and its activities through its first eight years, it is difficult to draw any final conclusions or evaluations. Nor is it the author's intent to judge the NFO. This book simply attempts to provide the background so that the reader himself might reach an objective understanding of why the NFO is significant. It is also hoped that those who are not directly involved in agriculture or its related fields of agribusiness might gain a better understanding of the current farm situation through this presentation.

Admittedly, there was some difficulty in obtaining all of the information needed to tell the whole story about the NFO. In some instances, both sides were reluctant to give their views openly. However, after three years of studying the NFO story, seeking out both sides' versions of major developments that are pertinent, and interviewing scores of persons on both sides of the controversy, I am convinced that the major points have not been missed. For this accomplishment, I am deeply indebted to many sources who have cooperated in making this work possible.

Omaha, Nebraska

—GEORGE BRANDSBERG

ACKNOWLEDGMENTS

CORDIAL THANKS to Oren Lee Staley, president, National Farmers Organization, Corning, Iowa, to national directors and former board members of the NFO and a large number of individual members for their cooperation in telling the NFO's side; to livestock market interests at Omaha, Nebraska, Sioux City, Iowa, St. Joseph and Kansas City, Missouri, and Chicago, along with officers of the Boards of Trade at Chicago and Kansas City and to M. E. Neely, executive vice president of the Omaha Grain Exchange; to the editors of the Corn Belt Farm Dailies for their assistance in arranging interviews at three of the major terminal livestock markets; to James C. Thomson, managing editor, *The Prairie Farmer*, Chicago; to Charles B. Shuman, president and Creston J. Foster, news director, American Farm Bureau Federation, Chicago; to Jack Jackson, public relations director, The National Grange, Washington, D.C.; to Perry Eberhart, *National Union Farmer*, The National Farmers Union, Denver; to Don F. Magdanz, executive secretary-treasurer, National Livestock Feeders Association, Omaha; to Lyle Liggett, public relations director, American National Cattlemen's Association, Denver; and to milk marketing interests in Omaha and Kansas City, all for their comments and observations on the NFO; to J. W. Brandsberg and family, Kansas City, and Dick Parker for their faithful assistance in gathering newspaper clippings during the all out holding action of 1962 and sundry events that ensued; to Louise Roach for her excellent assistance in preparing the final manuscript; and to Dee Sedlacek for her help in the meticulous task of reading and correcting page proofs. A vote of special thanks also goes to the host of newsmen and other unnamed informants who contributed to this project.

CONTENTS

1

Cause for Revolt
page 3

2

Background:
Evolution of Enough To Eat
page 20

3

Background:
A Heritage of Agrarian Movements
page 35

4

"Let's Call a Meeting. . ."
page 65

5

The Big Meeting for Action
page 93

6

The All Out Holding Action of 1962
page 103

[*xi*]

7
Background:
A Glance at Marketing
page 138

8
"Sign on the Dotted Line. . ."
page 163

9
Staley's Kind of Organization—Part I
page 174

10
Staley's Kind of Organization—Part II
page 202

11
The NFO's "Big Foe"
page 224

12
The NFO Since 1962
page 237

13
Some Alternative Approaches to the Farm Problem
page 254

14
Review and Guidelines to Evaluation
page 259

Appendices
page 267

Notes
page 283

Index
page 295

THE TWO SIDES IN NFO'S BATTLE

1

CAUSE FOR REVOLT

O<small>N</small> A<small>UGUST</small> 28, 1962, an estimated 20,000 determined farm folks crammed into and around Veterans Memorial Auditorium in Des Moines, Iowa, to stomp, whistle and shout their approval of the first "farmers strike" to gather national attention in thirty years. These people were indignantly determined to "do something" about the difference between their incomes and those of their city cousins.

Statistics revealed that the average farm worker was making about 90 cents an hour while the average urban worker was paid $2.51 per hour. This was but one of the illustrations the National Farmers Organization used to show why the rural population should band together and demand better prices for agricultural products that ended up on American dinner tables.

Under the leadership of a dynamic, husky Missouri cattle and hog raiser, the NFO had gathered discontented farmers in the heavy-producing Corn Belt states to wage a stormy campaign for the influence to ask more for their livestock and grains. If they didn't get what they wanted, they'd tell the buyer of these goods and his customers to go hungry until they were ready to pay the price the NFO demanded.

By the end of 1963, the National Farmers Organization had not attained its ambitious goals, but neither had its efforts been proved a failure.

This, then, shall be an account of the beginning and later events that made the NFO the most controversial farm movement of the mid-twentieth century. At the helm of this effort was Oren Lee Staley, whose magnetic personality and ringing voice captivated thousands of followers and presided over the largest gathering of farmers ever held. Staley preached a gospel of collective bargaining for agriculture and thousands stopped to listen. Some reporters described the movement as adamant, evangelical and militant. From the beginning there were seeds of conflict between the standard-bearers of the NFO and those who opposed its program.

Although the NFO started from wonderings aloud between a farmer and a feed salesman in an Iowa farmyard one day in the late summer of 1955, it wasn't until August of 1962 that the group moved seriously to try to control livestock and grain markets.

Summarized, their plan of action was simple:

Get the rural population organized as one big fist clamped over the supply of animals and grains moving into market channels. This will create a shortage of these goods and the meatpackers and other processors will willingly pay more for farm products they need to conduct their businesses. But before selling to them, the NFO will demand that the processors pay a "fair" price, as specified by the NFO, and they must sign a contract to keep on paying these prices to NFO members.

Since the organization's major area of influence was in the Corn Belt states, spanning from Ohio to Nebraska and from Minnesota to Oklahoma, the food basket of the nation, it claimed it had within its reach 80 per cent of the land's hog production, 75 per cent of the corn grown in the United States and three-fourths of the soybeans. This output came from ten states in the sixteen-state region where NFO waged enthusiastic drives to sign up more members.

Even if the NFO couldn't win the support of every steward of the soil, it felt it could bring enough pressure to bear to give its members the kind of price levels federal farm programs had failed to provide. Also, members believed that if instigated, their policies would stabilize the farm economy and would serve as a shot in the arm for prosperity throughout the Midwest, and perhaps the nation.

This was to be the "farmers' organization of farmers working to solve the farmer's problems." As a growing concern, there were difficulties which could be expected. Many farmers were reluctant to sign a membership agreement which seemed to take over control of the member's selling his animals or grain if and when the NFO national headquarters wanted to.

For a while, membership dues were too low to support the expanding group. The eventual raising of these from a dollar to $25 per year—the highest sum of any American farm organization—didn't help recruit more members.

A scandal of an alleged secret affiliation with a labor union had its play.

Three "test" holding actions or strikes were called, each showing successively more influence but none enough to be effective.

Enthusiasm and spirits ran high as members talked their organization up. In neighborhoods where some farmers stubbornly avoided joining and adamantly disagreed with NFO policy, anger sometimes took over. Hard feelings between neighbors worsened as NFO activity picked up speed in some areas. During the "all-out holding action" of September and early October, 1962, feelings favoring and opposing the plan of action reached as high a pitch as had been known. Threats, scuffles, perhaps some bloody noses and a few gunshots were a part of the more extreme troubles stemming from the NFO campaign. Malicious mischief and some vandalism occurred, but both sides of the controversy had ready denials of being connected with such activities as cutting wire fences and throwing rocks through windows of cattle trucks on the way to market.

This was the kind of sensational activity NFO leadership had hoped to avoid in pressing for better farm prices. Intentions of the leaders of the movement were probably sincere; however, it was questioned whether their feelings were those of a majority of the nation's food producers. Because the situation was volatile, a silent opposition to the NFO grew and both sides claimed that the other fellow was lacking understanding of the issues at hand.

What were these issues?

In short, NFO'ers said they were not getting enough money for what they had to sell. Government programs of price supports and acreage controls on crops had not solved the problem of filling the gap between unchanged or lower prices for the farmer's goods while the farmer definitely was paying more money for what he had to buy in town. The cost of land, of machinery, of gasoline and other petroleum products, of clothing and even of food had gone higher but the folks living in the country hadn't shared the gains of the increased prices. This cost-price squeeze was felt in many pocketbooks in the Midwest, and in all of agriculture for that matter.

Another trend that caused worry was the fact that farm population was shrinking and farms were becoming larger in size and fewer in total number. In 1935 the tally of all farms in the United States had reached a record high of 6.8 million units averaging 155 acres. By 1954, the total had slipped to approximately 4.8 million which averaged 242 acres.

This shift of farm units becoming larger in size and fewer in number meant that the rural population was shrinking in relationship to urban population. For example, when the Colonies were ready to throw off British control in the 1770's, the American population was 95 per cent rural. But by 1910, about 36 per cent of the nation's citizens lived and worked on farms. Punctuating the rapidity of the decline of rural population in more recent years, the census of agriculture for 1930 showed 25.2 per cent on farms, in 1940 the total was 23.4 per cent and it slipped to 16.4 per cent in 1950.[1] The 1959 census—the latest available at this writing—showed the farm population had fallen to a low of eight per cent of the nation's total population. And it continued to shrink.

This trend seemed to threaten the survival of the time-honored and beloved institution of the family farm, the NFO, among other farm organizations, claimed. Basically, the family farm was a farm owned and operated by one family. For many years it had been considered the common and essential unit in the social and economic structure of rural life. Some reasons for cherishing the family farm will appear later in this chapter.

The decline in numbers of people on farms had several implications. Besides having fewer neighbors with which to associate socially, the individual living in a rural area felt that he was losing part of his influence in helping to govern his county because in many instances he and his neighbors were outnumbered by the urban dwellers. The shift of population from the country to urban areas brought quite a visible change in rural school districts, which in many cases were consolidated and reconsolidated with other districts or abandoned to send the few remaining children to the nearest urban schools.

The urban-rural division was cause for alarm in the field of other political influence. Farmers looked to their elected representatives to defend rural interests in state legislatures and in Washington. However, the once-powerful Farm Bloc was dwindling to the point that some observers believed that spheres of interest outside agriculture could tire of appropriating vast sums of federal money for farm programs and, simply by having more influence, could conceivably leave agriculture high and dry.

At a glance, farm programs seemed to have confused the issues of what was wrong with farm production in relation to farm incomes. This, at least, was how some farmers viewed government activity in farming. Nonetheless, price supports had become a source of income many farmers could not be without. To drop such programs all at once would spell chaos for those who depended on them for survival.

The age of farm operators was another changing factor on the farm scene in the years after World War II. The 1959 Census of Agriculture showed that the average age of farm operators was 50.5 years, compared with an average of 48.3 years of age in 1950.[2] Where there had been about 1.6 million farmers in the range of 35 to 44 years of age in 1920, farmers in this bracket dropped to just half of that number in 1959. The largest number of operators in 1959 fell in the 45- to 54-year-old range.

What had contributed to the "aging" of the average farmer also figured in the change of farms becoming fewer and larger.

That people were leaving farms at a fearsome rate was very clear: In the years 1950 to 1958, over 7 million persons moved to urban areas. During these years the number of farm people 18 to 55 years old decreased considerably. By 1959 this age bracket made up less than one-third of the farm population.

Why were people leaving country life? One reason was that less manpower was needed as farm technology advanced. There were increased opportunities for non-farm employment—generally paying better money—nearby or elsewhere. Other factors, such as a search for educational advantages, changes in residence for retired persons and quests for other opportunities, figured in this trend. While at one time a lower standard of living and lack of domestic conveniences were important factors in the movement of farm people to the city, in more recent years job opportunities were more important.[3]

Low prices, shrinking population, an aging work force and "greener pastures" in fields away from the farm were parts of the "farm problem," as it was popularly called. Probably more important than these is the fact that farmers had learned to do their jobs so well that they were suffering from being too proficient. Overproduction, coupled with bungling legislative attempts to repeal or amend the law of supply and demand, was a simple way of explaining the mess agriculture was in at the time NFO was getting started. In part, farmers had been encouraged to produce more. Following the drought years of the mid-thirties, farm output began a sharp climb and continued through World War II and the postwar years. Total volume of farm production climbed 25 per cent in the years from 1937–39 to 1947–49. What with heavy demand for food and fiber during the war years and the subsequent period of rehabilitation, this was not hard to understand. This increase continued through the 1950's, showing a 21 per cent gain from 1947–49 to 1957–59. In 1959 production was 26 per cent above the 1947–49 level. Although output had caught up with the vast demand for farm products during the war years, rapid increase in population and continued high consumer purchasing power provided an expanding domestic market for most farm products in the 1950's.

But with the easing of the Korean conflict in 1953, the farmer's economic situation started into a steady decline which brought the price index of farm products down 11 per cent between 1947–49 and 1957–59. At the same time, prices for services and goods paid by farmers climbed 17 per cent and in 1959 stood at record levels.

In order to try to cope with the price-cost squeeze, farmers found that by producing more, even though prices were declining, they could, as individual operators, increase their net incomes. Change to a more profitable kind of production—a different field crop or from grain production to livestock feeding, for example—often would have been too costly since equipment for one kind of operation is so specialized. The same equipment would have little value or use outside of agriculture. Even though a lower price might be paid per unit, the farmer could increase his earnings by reducing the production cost per unit and by turning out more units. This meant the application of more fertilizer for crops or using specialized feeds for livestock and making use of better breeding techniques. The expanded production would give the individual farmer relief, temporary as it may have been. Although seven million people left the farm during the 1950's,[4] which spelled the loss of about a million farms, the land itself was generally absorbed by surviving farms, so there was no cut in production because of abandoned farms.

Larger farms usually proved more efficient for an operator with plenty of equipment and just his own labor potential. The increased use of commercial fertilizers, pesticides, mechanization of chores that formerly required hand labor and mixed feeds and feed additives were among other technical advances that helped to snowball overproduction of farm products. Better breeding practices of livestock and crops, too, added to the soaring output.

If this seems like a headache, perhaps one should consider more fully what goes into the modern process of growing a single crop. Three general steps or procedures are followed before a farmer is paid for his efforts. These are planning, producing the commodity in question and marketing it successfully.

Imagine you are a farmer who owns his land. In the spring you find you have just enough money in the bank to buy food and other necessities for you and your family through the growing season. You consider growing peanuts as a cash crop, that, is, for sale off the farm. Problems of planning for this crop include deciding how much land to plant and which portion of your land you'll use for the crop, that is, if it is practical and profitable to grow peanuts in your part of the country. Then too, you must decide when to plant them. On the financial side of planning the crop, you probably will have to consult your banker to borrow money for seed and enough extra to cover operation costs through harvest time. Also you must check on what regulations you'll have to abide by under the government program covering peanut raising. Perhaps your peanut acreage allotment is not as large as your plans call for. But if you overplant you'll be penalized and possibly even fined.

What are peanuts worth and what are the prospects for a good price at harvest time? Is there a ready market for them nearby? These are other questions you must investigate while planning your peanut crop. Maybe what you learn will discourage you and you'll have to consider a different crop.

Suppose that you have decided to put in peanuts. Once they are in the ground you assume risks which you considered during your planning stage. Perhaps there was a risk of spring frosts killing the crop soon after it sprouted and began to grow. Maybe rains would fail to fall at the needed time and the plants would wilt and die in the hot sun. Or maybe rains would come and keep coming until the crop was drowned out or washed away. Or perhaps all went well and prospects for a bumper crop were good until a hailstorm struck and quickly wiped out the entire investment. Or perhaps weather or labor problems arose at harvest time and the crop wasn't gotten out of the ground in time. Such are some of the risks of raising a crop.

Seeding, of course, would have been the first step in the process of production. Techniques with crops would include cultivation to control weeds and keep the soil conditioned. Insecticides and other disease control measures to keep the plants healthy might be in order. Irrigation, if available and if needed, might be another procedure you would need to use to assure a successful crop. While sweating out the hard work of getting water to your peanut crop, you would be thankful that you had fertilized your land and treated the seed with special preparations 'way back last spring.

As harvest time approaches, your judgment on how far the crop has progressed will determine when to start using specialized machinery to get the peanuts out of the ground. Once the plants have been dug they have to be raked and left a few days to dry before the peanuts in their hulls can be separated from the plants. Throughout the harvest, special equipment is needed and you would have to know how to run it and keep it in operation.

Once out of the field, the crop has to be sold. It is unlikely you would set up a roadside stand near the front gate of your farm to sell raw peanuts. This would be ridiculously impractical since you have tons of the raw crop for sale. In preparation for reaping the crop, you would have contacted the usual buying agencies to take your crop off your hands when it was ready. Part of your marketing arrangements were probably made early in the spring—a processor may have agreed to buy your crop even before the seed was in the ground. If your peanuts are of good quality they will be sold as potential peanut butter or nuts for someone to munch after processing, packaging and moving along channels to the consumer. Roughly 95 per cent of the nation's peanuts end up as food. Or your peanuts may be routed to an oil mill where the vegetable oil would be removed and used in a number of ways.

If you were selling another kind of farm product, you might consign your goods to a commission man who, for a fee, would handle the deal of selling it to a processor at a central market. There are several general methods of marketing farm products, each of which will be examined later. However, as a peanut farmer, the way you do your marketing depends on your past experience, how well you know the market possibilities and which one you like best.

If this sounds like a complicated way of getting peanuts raised and sold, it probably is an oversimplification of what is actually required between seeding and harvesting of just this one crop. The average farm produces several kinds of field crops—such as corn, soybeans, wheat, alfalfa, sugar beets or tobacco—each requiring some specific skills in horticulture and management.

Then there is the possibility of raising livestock. While many farms are used solely for raising cash grain crops, it is safe to say the average farm has some domesticated animals other than pets on it. In the Corn Belt, hogs and beef cattle are usually found on most farms that raise corn and other feed grains. Livestock farming involves the same general procedures of planning, raising and marketing, but with some differing refinements. If a producer has animals, he must also supply feed for them; he can raise the feed himself if he has the cropland or he can buy it. If he does produce the needed feed on his own land, he can combine two kinds of output into one final form for marketing. Instead of selling corn itself, a farmer may choose to convert it into pork or beef by feeding it and selling it in the form of finished animals.

As a business concern, the farm is a complex operation of many different kinds of endeavor, each having a myriad of problems and risks of its own. The farmer's worries are multiplied by the number of different kinds of production he has. Add to that a dozen or so other perplexities which have temporarily skipped his mind and you have a general picture of what the average farmer gets up to each morning.

And while all farms fall into the general classification of agriculture, no two are exactly alike. Geographic differences give varied kinds of climate and soil and rainfall. These are factors which help determine production capacities and the crops or livestock to be raised on a given farm. Again, no two are alike. This diversity of problems is one reason the so-called farm problem is so complex.

Coping with dozens of kinds of planning, growing and marketing has probably helped to bring about the elimination of the public image of the American farmer as a country hick in bibbed overalls and a battered torn straw hat, a rube with a stem of grass between his teeth.

Considering the migration of people away from the farm, along with the economic ups and downs related to this exodus, it is not unreasonable to assume that those who survived and stayed on farms were generally better operators. Of course there were exceptions; marginal farmers who hung on, barely grubbing out a living on too little land with too little equipment or capital to improve their operations. In general, farming followed the example of successful urban businesses.

A farm is like a huge corporation with only one man to

run it. He may have his wife and family to help, but still one man is usually in charge and has to be able to do every job done in his "firm." As chairman of the board, he must judge when his operation is ready for expansion and he must arrange all of the finances either through loans from a number of available sources or from capital on hand. As president and general manager of his own business, he must select seed and foundation livestock, make purchases and arrange hiring of additional labor and be sure all machinery is in good repair. In expert fields, he has to be an animal scientist, a horticulturist, a bookkeeper and—most time consuming—a seasoned farm laborer. He has to know how to operate and keep in adjustment plows, seeders, cultivators, mowers, rakes, balers, ensilage cutters, binders and harvesters. If his tractor stalls in the field, he has to know enough about its mechanics to get it rolling again. If a part breaks, chances are he will be able to weld the broken part in his own farm shop. Keeping a corn picker or a self-propelled grain combine traveling his land is all in a day's work.

Unlike most kinds of production, the farmer faces the necessity of doing one kind of task for a short while and then moving on to another kind, never returning to the first type of task until the next year. Plowing is followed by harrowing or disking in the preparation of land for seeding. Next comes seeding, perhaps cultivation and finally harvesting. Each step requires a certain implement which can be used only for one purpose for a short time.

Because so many kinds of equipment are needed for efficient diversified farming, there is also the problem of keeping the machinery in repair and eventually replacing it. Meeting these costs is another of the rural man's headaches.

Seeing how many differing types of machines the farmer has to help him with his work, it would seem he has it "easy." Not always. There are forever chores that call for swinging a scoop shovel or throwing hay with a pitchfork. Seed usually comes in sacks, heavy sacks. No machines have been devised for those odd jobs such as the minor carpentry or fence repair that turn up around the farm.

Getting back to the "one-man corporation" simile, the average farmer has to keep track of market trends, prices, costs and changes in supply and demand for his particular crops and livestock production. His skill in the field of marketing is intrinsic to better profits and repays him in the additional satisfaction of knowing that he has done as well as, or better than, his neighbor when the final check is deposited in the bank. If he didn't do as well, he wants to know why. And unless he received prices that he considers extremely good, he'll wonder why he didn't do better.

While the matter of "doing as well as my neighbor" is largely a reflection of a farmer's personal pride, it reflects the fact that every producer of one kind of farm product is competing with others growing the same commodity. That healthy competition is good is hard to dispute. The man who can put out a beef or a truckload of corn that is bigger and better should have the advantage over those who don't match his levels. Often, he does. However, when everyone excels and continues to forge ahead to new records, there obviously will come a time when overproduction will force some of the competitors out of business.

Considering that farmers weren't doing as well as many of them thought they should, were there too many of them in business in the 1950's and 60's? Yes, some observers said. In a later chapter will appear a more detailed account of what happened when a group of American industrial executives recommended that two million farmers leave their land so the remaining ones might prosper. An active protest against the endorsement of this recommendation was started in Nebraska in the summer of 1962 by members of the National Farmers Organization. Stores and auto dealerships were picketed and demands of repudiation of endorsement of the recommendations were made by the indignant NFO'ers.

If agriculture were in such trouble, why wouldn't some of its people want to get out of the business? Particularly the ones who were feeling the pinch of their so-called price-cost squeeze. Asking the man from the country this question would probably evoke a reaction that the inquirer might be somewhat daft. Certainly there are times when farm life is dreary, especially when it comes to working outside in inclement spring weather or during the cold, windy days of winter.

But he'll say that his way of life can't be beat, despite some disadvantages. To feel the warm moistness of a handful of loam from your own land just plowed in the springtime is a feeling no one else can understand unless he, too, works the soil. Plenty of fresh air and no trouble with smog, the Midwest farmer will say. There is never a problem of having to force himself off to the golf links or the downtown gymnasium for needed exercise, the farmer might add with a slightly condescending wink.

Working with the miracles of living things—seed germinating and growing into food for the nation's, no, the world's millions—is an experience that gives a deeper meaning to the farmer's life. His livestock, as he gets to understand them, become literally among his friends; it's part of knowing his business.

Although modern machinery has taken some of the sharing of farm work between neighbors, such as the gala old-fashioned threshing crews, the farmer takes pride in knowing most all of his neighbors and being able to depend on them for help if it is needed. With this kind of relationship between himself and his neighbors, he isn't hesitant to help when he is needed either.

Where else can a father's son roam fields and fish in a pond or a stream unbothered by many others? This, not some cramped city apartment, is the place for a boy to have a dog.

"I'm my own boss," most farmers will reply when asked what they like best about their way of life. However, the presence of milk cows on the farm will dictate that the operator get up early in the morning every day to "do chores" and be home at "milking time" every evening. Or it is time to plow. Without recourse, every competent farmer must get this necessary job out of the way. It may appear at times that the farm is the farmer's boss, but in the final analysis, the operator is the one who decides how to make use of his farm.

The "joys of country living" are not all that hold a farmer, deep in economic trouble, to his land. Some ties are emotional. "I am a farmer and proud of it." Others feel "farming is all I know how to do." The variety of work and relative freedom of farming make some suspicious of laboring in factories or on construction crews. Besides, jobs elsewhere often seem to consist of doing one task and one boring task only. Other kinds of work don't appeal. "Executive positions look like too much sitting around, all dressed up with nowhere to go. Besides, who wants to be overbearing, always telling everyone else what to do?" The prospect of changing vocations, as with anyone who likes his work, seems unthinkable to some.

"With hundreds of thousands of skilled urban workers out of a job, what chance has an outsider of finding a good job? If we left the farm, we'd probably just add to the unemployment rolls. Here, at least, we've a cow to milk and a few chickens laying eggs. We can always butcher one of our own hogs. How could we do that if we sold out and moved to town?"

But not all persons were happy with their life on the farm. For those who were dissatisfied, there were two general alternatives: 1) Leave the farm for other work; or 2) stick with farming and hope prosperity would come along; if it didn't come soon, those remaining on farms should seek ways to correct what was wrong.

Operators who were truly unhappy with farming and realized they might do better in another line of work did leave. Many who loved farming were forced to leave because of low incomes.

How about the ones who sought to change the picture? Specifically, how about the NFO's ideas?

In an exclusive interview in May, 1961, NFO president

Oren Lee Staley explained to the author his organization's view of the farm problem:

"We feel that there are many factors involved, of course, in the farm problem. The overriding factor is the lack of price. The farmers are caught in a situation where the price of everything they buy has continued to move upward while the price of everything they sell has moved down. Consequently, this has caught them in a cost-price squeeze. We feel the basic reason for this is that the farmers have nothing to say about the prices they get for their products. They just deliver them to the market place and say, 'What will you give me?', following the same pattern they have always followed in marketing. By that, I'm not trying to say the existing [market] groups have not performed some important functions, but have become more and more neutralized because they have become weaker proportionately to the marketings instead of gaining strength in comparison to the buying interests. By buying interests, I wouldn't confine buying interests to the processors, but also would include the retail end."

Asked if he thought there were other important trends besides economic factors with which the NFO was concerned, Staley commented:

"Of course, I think that the economics of any situation primarily control your everyday life; it controls the living standard of the nation; it controls your spiritual life to a degree. While these other factors are important, they are usually directly related to or are a direct result of the economic factors."

He went on to point out that the goals of his organization were several. The primary goal was to get farmers in a position to price their products in the market as effectively at the market place as the other segments of the economy priced their products and services. Other objectives included giving producers a voice in grading, weighing, establishing marketing incentives and other marketing stipulations; developing orderly marketing procedures; stabilizing farm prices and in general, placing farmers in an economic position equal to the rest of the American economy.

Persuasive literature was prepared and distributed. One pamphlet ended:

> Mr. Farmer, who do you expect to solve your problems? Stop and think! Who is setting your prices now? You are losing more of your purchasing power each day. No one else is going to solve your problems for you. We pledge that the NFO will not be an organization of promises but that it will be an organization of action![5]

The battle cry had been sounded; however, time was needed before response to the call would be heard, before the movement would attract attention.

A glance at the NFO's general policy and its tactics was enough to start asking questions:

Who are the people in NFO? Who oppose it?

Why hadn't other farm organizations tried NFO's plan of action and, if they had, why hadn't the plans worked?

What kind of persons lead the NFO?

What did this all mean to the man-in-the-street who paid the grocery bill?

Was it all a big joke or would it really help agriculture?

The next two chapters will provide histories of agriculture and of farm organizations in modern times before an effort is made to explore comprehensive answers to the above and more questions about the NFO.

2

Background:

EVOLUTION OF ENOUGH TO EAT

IN MODERN AMERICA, plenty of food is generally taken for granted. The average person in the United States doesn't have to worry about where his next meal is coming from—it may come from a number of sources, but he can be reasonably sure it's on its way. Beyond the realms of the family kitchen, supermarkets, lunch counters, restaurants and a myriad of vending machines, there is little need to be concerned about the availability of the food one eats. As long as one has money, one eats—if he can buy it. And usually he can.

But it hasn't always been that convenient. Even 200 years ago (circa 1763), eating habits and the methods of getting something to eat would have differed greatly from those of today. There would have been little or no assurance that food served at an inn would be safe to eat unless it was freshly taken or unless the meal were prepared from such nonperishable products as dried beans, flour, or pemmican. If one ate at home, chances are he had helped provide part of the meal. He may have milked the family cow or gathered vegetables from the family garden. Perhaps part of his meal was the result of marksmanship with a muzzleloader. Living in the mid-1700's was as good as in any period preceding it, and in most instances better. But it was pretty shoddy by twentieth-century standards.

Historical accounts say that the American Indian showed the white newcomer how to grow "Indian corn," or maize. Although many colonial settlers were not unfamiliar with farming, Indian corn was a new crop to them. This was typical of "new things" agriculture was gaining and will probably continue to gain as long as there is progress.

How did it all start? Beyond the veiled mists of prehistory, scholars can little more than speculate on the origins of agriculture. It would be impossible to say that on a certain day 8,000 or 10,000 years ago a primordial John Doe shoved a stick into the ground, planted his first stand of wheat and the crop thrived. However, it is known that in the so-called cradles of civilization such as Mesopotamia, the Valley of the Nile and southwest Asia, very early kinds of wheat and barley were cultivated. Additionally, the earliest traces of civilization are found in Egypt, Syria, Mesopotamia and the Indus Valley, with extensions over Persia and Baluchistan and as far north as Turkestand, according to Curwen.[1]

Until mankind discovered that he could control the production of the animals and plants of which he ate, he was necessarily a hunter of food. Early man gathered his food from plants and also took what he could from stalking wild animals. He was a *gatherer* rather than a grower of food. Possibly he stored grains for the winter, but he had yet to learn to plant and anticipate harvest. There is evidence that early man enlisted the aid of the ancestors of today's dogs in his hunting expeditions. Keeping dogs was more for gathering food rather than growing it, but it wasn't uncommon to kill and eat one once it was too old and feeble to be useful on a hunt.

H. G. Wells suggests that the first seeding of grains was performed as a ritual of sacrifice to a god the hunters sought to appease.[2] Later, upon returning to the place of sacrifice, the hunter found growing grain. Eventually, this gatherer of food learned that by seeding some of it, he would later find grain in the place where it had been cast to the spirits.

Until man learned to grow his own food, most of his waking hours were spent in hunting shelter and enough to eat for himself and his primitive family. Perhaps the only comparable examples of this kind of civilization in modern times are those of Eskimos—who, until the arrival of Western influences, were constantly preoccupied with hunting—and aborigines in South America and Australia.

It has been estimated that 10,000 years ago there were about 10 million humans on earth,[3] making them indeed rare in a world bustling with savage beasts. It is interesting to note that until the advent of agriculture, man probably was not a good enough provider to feed an increase in population.

Curwen points out that the domestication of certain animals as a means of controlling food supply seems to have occurred about the same time as the first cultivation of cereals.[4] Exactly how the hunter became a herdsman is not known, but one speculation is that as the polar icecap of the Ice Age (about 5,000 B.C.) receded, the mild climatic conditions of areas of northern Africa and other seats of civilization began to change slowly from verdant, temperate areas to the deserts they now are. In the transition, men and animals shared the same water holes or oases. Also, it is known that the primitive hunter followed the animal herds, as some of the Plains Indians of North America moved with the vast herds of bison. It is conceivable that early man at times protected the herds he followed from predators or other tribes of huntsmen.

In the process of protecting the herds he followed, early man probably discovered he could influence animals of the herd, such as turning a stampede toward or away from the disaster of their thundering over the brink of a cliff. Perhaps he first corralled his animals by driving them into a blind canyon or some other natural set of barriers.

It is interesting to note that the first Biblical account of agricultural activity came with the growing of Adam and Eve's sons, Cain and Abel. Cain, the first-born, was a tiller of the soil, and Abel, a herdsman. The story of the rivalry between the two is well known as the origin of the expression "my brother's keeper,"[5] and also gives some indication that even in the earliest periods of agricultural development, there was potential friction between crop farmers and herdsmen.

The tiller of the soil led a sedentary life. He had to stay in one area to tend his crops and protect them from wild animals and other intruders. In contrast, the herdsman was by nature migratory, following the herds as they moved about in search of food and water as the seasons turned. What the herdsman lacked in the way of food or clothing not taken from animals, he supplemented by gathering from plants along the way. The early crop farmer, on the other hand, filled his needs left unmet by crops by some hunting and, too, by the domestication of animals.

Taming an animal was simply capturing and keeping it confined until it could be governed and made useful by the man who had taken it. Domestication, however, involved keeping a number of animals so they could reproduce in captivity, serving as a continuing food supply for their masters.

Sheep, goats, pigs and cattle were domesticated at an early age, preceded, of course, by the taming and eventual domestication of dogs. Oxen, camels and horses came under the yoke later. In Egypt, for example, horses were unknown until about 1400 B.C., when Hyksos horsemen invaded from Asia. The milking of cows was recorded in pictorial accounts in Mesopotamia as early as 3000 B.C.

As farming as a way of life progressed, the domesticator of animals and tiller of soil had more time for thinking and developing a culture. Very slowly, commercial aspects appeared in the two kinds of production of food. The herdsman, for example, might barter a sheep or two for jars of grain. As this kind of intercourse became more urbane, a trader living in a settlement might intervene in the transaction. These first faltering steps were taken even before the dawn of history.

Agriculture in the days of the Roman Empire had reached a degree of sophistication that prospered under the system of slave labor. Cato the Elder (234–149 B.C.) was the author of some of the first connected Latin prose, but more important, his *De Agri Cultura*[6] gives a fairly comprehensive idea of how technical farm practices had become. Cato spent his youth on his father's farm in the Sabine country where he acquired qualities of simplicity, frugality, strict honesty, austerity and patriotism. His agricultural treatise is poorly organized, such as the jottings of a farmer taking notes of his experiences, putting down ideas he found useful. It includes instructions for doing such tasks as mixing medicinal preparations, how to make plaster and bricks, how to make the best use of leaves off trees on the farm, what to look for in selecting land for farming and how to judge the production of a farm you may want to buy. It rambles also about what crops to plant in various kinds of soil and gives practical business hints on borrowing and lending. Fertilizing with manure is a point Cato stresses in several instances.

Among his bits of advice:

"This is the proper equipment for an oliveyard of 240 iugera (about 160 acres): An overseer, a housekeeper, five laborers, three teamsters, one muleteer, one swineherd, one shepherd—a total of thirteen persons; three yoke of oxen, three pack-asses to carry manure; one ass for the mill and 100 sheep. . . ." From there he proceeds to list the numbers of hand tools and containers needed. Included also in this list of essentials are one bathtub and other items of furniture for the house on down to ". . . sixteen cushions, ten table covers, three napkins and six servants' hoods."[7]

According to Cato's standards, the leather-tough, practical western ranch foreman could learn plenty from a Roman overseer:

> The following are the duties of the overseer: He must show good management. The feast days must be observed. He must withhold his hands from another's goods and diligently preserve his own. He must settle disputes among the slaves; and if anyone commits an offense, he must punish him properly in proportion to the fault. He must see that the servants are well provided for, and that they do not suffer from cold or hunger. Let him keep them busy with their work—he will more easily keep them from wrongdoing and meddling. If the overseer sets his face against wrongdoing, they will not do it; if he allows it, the master must not let him go unpunished. He must keep the servants busy and see that the master's orders are carried out. He must not assume that he knows more than the master. He must consider the master's friends his own friends. He must pay heed to anyone to whom he has been bidden to listen. He must perform no religious rites, except on the occasion of the Compitalia at the crossroads, or before the hearth. . . . He must see to it that he knows how to perform all the operations of the farm and actually does perform them often, but not to the extent of becoming exhausted; by so doing he will learn what is in his servants' minds, and they will do their work more contentedly. Also, he will be less disposed to gad about, will be in better health and will enjoy his sleep more. He must be the first out of bed, the last to go to bed. Before then he must see that the farmstead is closed, that each one is asleep in his proper place and that the stock have fodder . . .[8]

In continuing his list of duties for the overseer, Cato adds that the man in charge must watch for sickness among animals and perform certain tasks on the field crops in accordance with a good schedule.

While much of Cato's advice and instruction is far from scientific, it does show that an impressive amount of knowledge and a goodly number of practices were followed in husbandry and cultivation in his day.

His admonishments of caution when dealing with traders shows that commerce was active and that the farm manager had to be able to match wits with any and all comers.

Another Roman, Varro Reatinus (116–27 B.C.), who

also came from the Sabine area of the Roman Empire, lamented in his agricultural discourse:

. . . in these days practically all the heads of families have sneaked within the walls, abandoning the sickle and the plow, and would rather busy their hands in the theatre and in the circus than in the grainfields and the vineyards. We hire a man to bring us from Africa and Sardinia the grain with which to fill our stomachs, and the vintage we store comes in ships from the islands of Cos and Chics.

And so, in a land where the shepherds who founded the city taught their offspring the cultivation of the earth, there, on the contrary, their descendants, from greed and in the face of the laws, have made pastures out of grainlands—not knowing that agriculture and grazing are not the same thing. For the shepherd is one thing and the plowman another; and it does not follow that because cattle can graze in a field the herdsman is the same as a plowman.[9]

It is on this tone that Varro opens his book, written to his wife, on his knowledge of caring for cattle and other skills of the farm.

Varro seems indignant over, and sometimes amused by, his observations that some of the skills of farming were being neglected by countrymen moving to the cities or spending much time in the urban areas. He felt city people more indolent than country folk. Perhaps he regretted this trend which, in short, was the result of a better kind of agriculture that permitted some of the population to live at ease, free to pursue cultural activities rather than solely the duties of producing food. In fact, rather than producing food for their own areas, some foodstuffs were being brought in from great distances as a result of extended commerce. It would be superfluous to say that agricultural progress alone was responsible for the rise of great civilizations such as those of the Egyptians, the Greeks, and the Romans. Nonetheless, it did fulfill a basic need, thus giving them freedom to follow pursuits other than tilling, herding or hunting.

With the fall of Rome came stagnation of European agriculture. From the debris of the fallen Roman dominance, feudalism slowly emerged. In perhaps the fifth century, the feudal system began to come into wide use. It consisted of common ownership of the land farmed, the operators living in a pastoral village dominated by a lord, whose manor house was the center of the town. Also, a mill and a church were usually a part of the community.

The farmland surrounding the feudal village was divided up in patches to the different tillers so each had a share of the better fields, grasslands, dryland and timber. While a system of crop rotation was usually practiced and some cropland was left fallow, the open-field plan was used on the entire layout of land surrounding a village. This meant that at a certain time, all strips of land were expected to be planted; at the close of the growing season, all parcels of cropland had to be harvested so the common herd of livestock could be grazed over the land. Everyone had to do each task at the same time. Woe be to him who tried a different crop and wasn't through with harvest when all of his neighbors had their crops reaped. While this system was partially suitable for the providing of the self-contained medieval village, it stifled efforts for the tiller or the herdsman to improve his own crops or animals. Perhaps it would have been to ancient Varro's satisfaction that most of the populace had returned to sweating a living out of the soil. At any rate, it was not until the Crusades began that agricultural progress was shaken from the lethargy that came with the fall of Rome.

In the latter part of the eleventh century, Europe, which had suffered with the decline of Rome and had survived plundering and strife, was presented a common cause. This, of course, was to wrest Jerusalem from the hands of the infidels. While evaluating the motivations of those who led and participated in the Crusades is not essential to this study, it is well worth considering that with a common cause, the peoples of the Continent were less likely to pursue wrangling among themselves. With conquest—albeit not very successful—being attempted and broadening of trade activities, there arose a need for food production beyond the needs of those in an immediate vicinity. With voyages of discovery and the spread of a textile industry in the fourteenth century, there came early ideas for the commercial farm as we know it today.

Another change that ended with the passing of feudalism (in most cases, at least) was that the distribution of land fell into the system of enclosure rather than the old open-field system. The enclosure movement divided the land with fences, hedgerows or walls and the separate farm was the operator's domain. From the fourteenth to the nineteenth century, the trend toward commercialism gained influence.

And in sixteenth century England, agricultural literature sprouted with Fitzherbert's *Boke of Husbandrie* (1523) which recommended using clover, the adoption of root crops and the folding of sheep.

Two names associated with the beginnings of modern agriculture are Charles Townshend and Robert Bakewell. Lord Townshend's Norfolk "four-course system of husbandry" has endured as a model for crop rotation. This involved a cycle of growing turnips, barley, clover and ryegrass and wheat in successive years. Townshend found that this method of crop planning increased the fertility and productivity of the soil. He also revived the abandoned ancient practice of applying lime to certain soils. One historian said that Townshend's ideas not only contributed fortunes to those who applied them in practice but also contributed as few men had to the feeding of Britain's growing population.[10]

What Robert Bakewell did for livestock is a role similar to Townshend's in field crops. Until Bakewell began his work, selective breeding had been practiced very sparsely in Europe or anywhere, for that matter. In Spain, care had been taken in breeding up what became the fine-wooled Merino sheep, but no particular effort had been made to improve the meat-producing characteristics of animals.

Working with his Leicester sheep, Bakewell set out in 1750 to produce meat animals "weighing the most in the best joints and quickest repaying the feed they consumed."[11] Within a few years, his sheep were ready to be marketed at two years of age, while the average contemporary sheep was three or four years old before butchered. Other breeds were developed following his methods.

As examples of the influence of Bakewell's work are Prothero's statements that in 1710 the average cattle and sheep sold in Smithfield Market were beeves of 370 pounds, calves of 50 pounds, sheep carcasses of 28 pounds and lambs weighing 18 pounds. In 1795, a year after Bakewell's death, these respective averages were revised upward to 800-pound beeves, 148-pound calves, 80-pound sheep and 50-pound lamb carcasses.

Even though these strides had been made in England, farming in general was a long way from being filled with scientific practices. Over half of the country was still being farmed in common, a hangnail of the feudalistic method. Arthur Young is credited with helping to disseminate the findings of Townshend and Bakewell. Although Young's writings sold rapidly, there was no way of telling how effective they were in the actual adoption of new methods of cultivation and breeding.[12]

Noteworthy throughout the history of agriculture to this point is that most of the major tasks of the farm were done by hand, with very simple tools or with crude implements drawn by animals. The sickle, the spade and the hoe were as familiar in the days of Varro and Cato as in the time of Townshend and Bakewell.

In the New World colony of Massachusetts in 1637, there were only 37 plows—crude, wooden affairs drawn by oxen. For twelve years after the landing of the Pilgrims, farmers had had no plows but were compelled to tear up the bushes with their hands or the clumsy hoes and mattocks. It became a custom in Massachusetts colony for some owning plows to go about and do the plowing for farmers over a considerable territory.[13]

Except for surfaces that were covered with pieces of iron to slow down wearing, plows were made predominantly of wood until the late 1700's. In 1797, Charles Newbold was the first to draw a letter of patent for a cast iron plow for use in sandy or gravelly soils. The major disadvantage of this plow was that when the bottom was worn out, the whole plow had to be discarded. In 1813, R. B. Chenaworth patented a plow comprised of a moldboard, landslide and share. When one part became worn, it could be replaced without replacing the entire plow.

About 25 years passed between the invention of and the adoption of the cast iron plow. "Many people thought the plows poisoned the ground and caused weeds to grow."[14]

As the pioneers moved westward, they found that the prairie soil stuck to cast iron plows. Having to stop every few feet to clean the moldboard led some to believe that the land would have to be abandoned because it was too sticky. Blacksmiths experimented and some found shapes of plows that did work satisfactorily in different soils.

In 1837, a blacksmith recently arrived in Illinois from Vermont built a plow from a circular sawblade. Thus, John Deere built the first steel plow, which worked the clinging ground better than others available at the time. Soon many others were turning out steel plows.

Some writers might say that modern agriculture was born with the invention of the reaper. While Cyrus Mc-Cormick is often popularly credited with the invention of the reaper, Obed Hussey patented one in 1833, the year before McCormick took out a patent on his version of the early harvesting machine. Nonetheless, the scythe and cradle were still in use on some farms as late as 1850.

Shortage of labor and high grain prices during the Civil War speeded the adoption of machine methods, especially for harvesting small grains. The numbers of horses and mules rose rapidly during the next half century.[15]

Agricultural productivity soared to new highs as waves of settlers moved onto new fertile lands that were free or cheap to buy, and applied new technology based on the use of horses and mules. This trend seemed to continue through the First World War. At that time, the total of horses and mules was the highest in American history, numbering more than 25 million. However, progress had lost its momentum because there was hardly any good new land available and 25 per cent of the crop was being consumed as feed for power animals.

Steam power had its belching, smoking debut, a colorful but short performance and a permanent exit from the tableau of the history of American farm production. Awkward size and weight of these behemoths seemed to prove that steam engines were meant to stay on railroads or steamships.

The advent of the gasoline engine was something else again. The faltering success of steam power for operating farm machinery seemed to support the premise that farming without horses was inconceivable. So, when the gasoline engine was offered as a means of pulling a plow, farmers reacted with ridicule and derision. Some agreed that gasoline engines would be tried, but they would pass like a fad, once they were proved impractical.

American farmers had 50,000 automobiles in 1910, which was a part of the movement to take horses off the roads. By 1925, farmers commanded a road force of nearly four million cars and trucks. However, gasoline-burning tractors were somewhat slower to gain acceptance. In 1925, only about a half-million tractors were in use, but in the next decade this number doubled and twenty years later it had doubled again. At last man had assembled a working machine that "ate" only while it produced. The coming of the internal combustion engine did indeed spell the beginning of a new era for the man in the country.

Looking back over the history of agriculture, farmers were usually self-sufficient. This meant that whatever was needed by the people living on a parcel of land was produced right on that land. Meat and grains for food were either grown or obtained by hunting. Clothing was made from hides and furs or cloth woven from flax or cotton or wool produced at home. The ancient Roman Cato told how the farmer would make bricks; in American pioneer days, logs or chunks of sod served the farmer as building material. With the exception of a few goods, the farmer sup-

plied his own needs. Salt was an age-old commodity that
often came from an outside source; spices were trade goods
throughout history; gunpowder and small hardware needs
were other items an early American farmer needed which
he usually did not make himself. And while there had
been a tendency for farm operations to move toward commercial production wherever there were urban populations
to be served, none paralleled the kind of production that
came with the development of the farm tractor and the machinery that accompanied it.

At the same time, the farmer moved into a new economic position, leaving the old-fashioned system of producing at home most of the goods he needed and consumed.

Davis and Hinshaw,[16] in their entertaining book, divide
the history of American farming into three general eras—
the earthbound era, a transition period and the agribusiness era. The first period was that during which farmers
were relatively self-sufficient, depending on the land they
worked to provide most of the things they needed. In the
two decades from 1920 to 1940, roughly:

Farmers were overwhelmed by problems and hardships that marked
the beginning of the end of the earthbound era and the start of a
new era in which businesses closely related to agriculture outgrew
farming's contribution to the nation's economy. The new land frontier faded from the scene, and the frontier of economic progress
shifted in such a way that farm families were suddenly and desper-
ately confronted with the necessity of *buying* a modern standard of
living instead of being able to create it to a considerable degree directly from the soil of their farms.[17]

It is impossible to say just when this transition began.
Parts of it started with the development of such equipment
as plows and reapers that were manufactured off the farm
but were important to the expansion of agricultural production. With the advent of the internal combustion engine
as an important source of power in rural areas, the country
dweller came to depend on his urban counterparts to supply
more of his needs. There was gasoline and oil to be bought

to keep the engines running. Then there were repairs that often were best made by skilled workers in towns; even if the farmer chose to make repairs himself, he had to buy parts in order to perform such tasks. Cars and motortrucks helped to change the farmer's area of trade—now he was able to travel to a distant city to get services or merchandise he otherwise would have ordered from a catalog or through one of the dealers in a nearby town. In a later chapter, changes in the methods of marketing farm products will be examined to show how this transition of modernization affected the older systems.

A number of other factors played major roles in this period of change. The popularization of the radio gave the farmer world and market news practically as it was happening. Rural electrification came into wide use in some areas; while electricity brought such luxuries as electric irons, refrigerators and quiet washing machines for the farm housewife and motors, electric heaters and power tools for the man of the house, it also presented the monthly "light bill."

Other purchases made away from the farm included buying improved seed, new fertilizers and possibly better breeding livestock as the farm operator became more conscious of improving his production. By this time, of course, the idea of spinning and weaving cloth for garments had long been forgotten for the more convenient shopping trip to town.

Davis and Hinshaw comment:

The transition from earthbound agriculture to agribusiness was particularly rough because we advanced along a ragged, uneven front. The parts of our advance that ran way ahead of the rest seemed to be making spectacular progress. We mass-produced many things that made farming more efficient and more productive—sometimes altogether too productive—and each thing we accomplished in making this progress seemed of itself to be a very praiseworthy and fortunate achievement. But it was this harum-scarum progress that occasionally devastated agriculture and now gives us reason to plan the development of the agribusiness frontier with a great deal more attention to coordination of its units.[18]

In offering a partial solution to the problems arising during this transition, these writers advocate the application of their concept of "agribusiness," which they say:

. . . challenges individuals and groups to use their initiative in developing successful business operations for every phase of producing and servicing a product that originates on the farm. To make these operations successful, those who engage in agribusiness must be everlastingly in quest of versatile, better and more appealing ways to market agricultural products.[19]

The time had come when a farmer could no longer be "just a farmer." In searching for ways to cope with the problems of his operation, farmers joined various farm movements, each with perhaps a different approach to the difficulties encountered and with differing proposals of actions hoped to give a solution to the situation.

Chapter 3 will recount the rise of and the programs of the major farm organizations that came and went or that rose and survived to the period when the National Farmers Organization became an influence among farm interest groups.

1262859

3

Background:

A HERITAGE OF AGRARIAN MOVEMENTS

A GLANCE at the history of farm organizations in the United States since the Civil War reveals a colorful array of leadership campaigning to satisfy many grievances. Most of them had economic inequities as their causes for action, although the approach to solving such complaints may have followed several different avenues. In many cases, if a farm organization failed in its efforts or if its particular "cause" became less of a crisis, it might die to be replaced by a later movement. Or it might find new reasons for agitation and continue to be an active farm organization.

While the farmer's problems have been largely economic, organized efforts among country folk have not always been directed solely to the betterment of income to the farmer-members. Social and educational functions have also been important activities of farm groups, whether at the county, state or the national level.

An interesting observation of Saloutos and Hicks[1] is that most farm movements have illustrated that in the United States there is a geographic region of farm discontent, a region in which agitation for agricultural reform has often started or had the most influence. This includes the western portion of the Middle West—the Dakotas, Nebraska, Kansas, Minnesota, Iowa, Missouri, Wisconsin and Illinois. The most obvious reason for this area to be the proving ground of such movements is the fact that in it agriculture is the prevailing livelihood. There is less of large industry and high finance here, even though the region can boast of influential centers such as Chicago, St. Louis, Kansas City, Minneapolis, Omaha and Des Moines. That these cities are among the major marketing centers of farm products reflects the fact that the farm industry plays a major role in the economy of the region.

Problems common to a corn-and-hog farmer, for example, would be similar to those of a like operator in any part of the region. Also, residents on farms here have faced common problems such as decreasing population, a farm labor shortage, low prices and adjustment to changes in technology.

What were the specific problems and how were they handled? The recession that hit farmers after the Civil War —a situation not too unlike that following the Korean Conflict in the 1950's—is a good place to begin.

Lindstrom[2] points out that the war, like later wars, brought about a great rise in price levels which virtually collapsed when the war effort was over. Then there were inter-regional differences which contributed to the growing discontent among farmers. The previously prosperous eastern farmers were beginning to feel the influence of western competition as markets such as Chicago grew nearer the source of agricultural production. In the South, some land was nearly exhausted because staple crops including cotton, rice, sugar and tobacco had been used mercilessly without much thought of crop rotation to keep up soil productivity. In addition, there were new problems in Dixie caused by the abolishment of the old slave labor system. Overproduction of cotton and an unfavorable credit system resulting in credit bondage to merchants added to the southern farmer's difficulties.

In the Middle West, demand for wheat and corn

sparked a concentrated effort during the war to produce heavily and to make use of farm implements being developed at this time to help increase production. Many farmers specialized in raising corn or wheat, which brought handsome prices during the Crimean and Civil Wars. These producers blindly believed that nothing could disrupt the good demand for their cash crops. But with the end of the war, the demand wilted. For this situation, many farmers blamed the bankers, the railways, the legislatures, the tariff and the monopolies, at times with just cause.

Large land holdings, great distances to market, the rise of a grain ring which manipulated grain prices and which led to a protest movement were among problems the Far West, especially California, came upon. Also, the free-land frontier was being absorbed by settlers and speculation land holdings added to the prevailing difficulties. The grievances that brought farmers together in protest movements for reform revolved about their problems with transportation, merchandising and manufacturing, credit, prices, legislation and political power.

Up until the Civil War, farm groups were largely social clubs in which both men and women could get together or they were more or less educational societies, meeting to discuss problems and compare notes on better ways of production. In the prewar South, such societies originated the idea of agricultural fairs.

To say that farmers had no troubles before the war broke out would not be true; however, the boom that the Civil War brought about served to temporarily delay the rise of widespread farm movements. One of the first significant efforts of farm people organizing to seek reform was the Centralia Convention in Illinois in 1858. At the close of the meeting, delegates had agreed that more attention should be given to the superior importance of farm production, that secret cost-marks should not be tolerated, that agriculture and commerce could only be considered identical when each has an equal share in regulating trade, that a national agricultural bureau should be established to conduct a census of farm production and to collect and disseminate valuable seeds, plants and information to farmers. The convention also claimed that the election of producers to public office should be the rule and the election of non-producers the exception.[3] In a sense, the Centralia Convention served as a preface to agrarian movements that were to come a decade later.

Two specific targets of farm organizations that rose after the Civil War were the railroads and the businessmen whom the groups called "middlemen." The railroads had ridden roughshod over farmers in general in acquiring land, in selling shares of stock that later proved worthless and in charging what the farm interests felt were exorbitant rates for hauling their products to market. Besides, railroads hid behind the Dartmouth College Decision which said they were private businesses and should not be subjected to governmental controls. In other spheres, railroads represented big money and had big influence over legislation. The practice of offering free passes and the sale of railway stock at special bargain prices to the right people were among ways the railroads had of winning or buying friends in legislatures and in Congress. One of the results of these practices of "greasing palms" was the Credit Mobilier scandal in Congress.

Regarding the middlemen, Lindstrom says:

". . . in summary, the following factors aggravated the [farm discontent] situation: (1) excessive rates of interest charged for loans and mortgages, running as high as 20 per cent; (2) the spread of loan agents, especially in the West; (3) a currency which fluctuated; (4) farmers who were in debt getting into still deeper debt; (5) high tariffs when farmers had to sell on a world market; and (6) the heavy burden of taxes, especially upon farm real estate.[4]

The adage that misery loves company took on added meaning as unhappy farm people got together to "do something" about their plight. Major movements included the Grange, the Farmers' Alliance, the American Society of Equity, the Farmers Union and the Farm Bureau.

THE GRANGE IN ITS EARLY YEARS

In 1866, Oliver Hudson Kelley, a clerk for several years in the recently formed Department of Agriculture, was appointed by the first commissioner of agriculture to make a survey of conditions in the war-torn South.[5] Troubled by what he found, Kelley decided that a fraternal organization composed of farmers from all sections of the country would help heal the scars of war and improve the economic and social position of those engaged in farming.

After returning to Washington, he called on five of his friends in the Department of Agriculture and a vineyardist from New York State, and in a Washington office building on December 4, 1867, the seven men drew up a ritual and constitution of the Patrons of Husbandry.

Kelley's niece, Caroline A. Hall, who long served as his secretary, suggested that women be admitted into the organization on the basis of equality with men. She subsequently became its first woman officer as secretary of the new Grange.

On April 3, 1868, Kelley left his Department of Agriculture job to wage a campaign to organize his Grange throughout rural areas. Less than two weeks later, he started Fredonia Grange No. 1 in western New York. The first State Grange was formed in Minnesota in February, 1869. It was followed by the Iowa State Grange in January, 1871. Before the close of 1872, Kelley's energetic and enthusiastic efforts had paid off in the forming of more than a thousand Granges in more than half of the states of the Union. By January, 1873, Kelley and his family moved back to Washington and the National Grange first met as a representative body with 27 delegates from eleven states.

During December of 1873, some 1,235 Granges were established. The high point came in February of 1874 when 2,239 subordinate units of the parent organization were formed. By 1875, 36 of the existing 39 states had State Granges, along with the Territory of Colorado. Official records showed paid membership at that time to be over 850,000.

When Kelley started organizing the Grange, he was "42 years of age and a man of commanding presence, with full beard tinged with white, a high, broad forehead of a philosopher and the eager eye of an enthusiast. 'An engine with too much steam on all the time' was the characterization given by one of his friends,"[6] Kile says in outlining the organization's history.

Although it was to endure as an influence in agricultural movements through the present day, the Grange in its early years had its ups and downs. Kelley's attempts to get the organization rolling were not always successful at first. Out of money after some organizing in 1868, Kelley went back to his farm in Minnesota and was joined there later in the year by his niece-secretary, who helped him with finances and the dissemination of literature. With the additional help of newspapers and farm magazines, he was able to organize three more units of the Grange by January, 1869. Using the claim that the organization was a means of farmers' defending themselves against the insidious effects of corporations as well as being an opportunity for cooperative buying and selling, the group had selling points which attracted members.

Besides, the years 1870–73 were oddly prosperous for the interests of business, manufacturing and speculation. At the same time, farmers were suffering. The government had given railroads millions of acres and the roads were charging heavy rates to carry farm products. "When an Iowa farmer was obliged to burn corn for fuel, because at 15 cents a bushel it was cheaper than coal, while at the same time corn was selling for a dollar a bushel in the East, he felt, quite naturally, that something was wrong."[7]

When the panic of 1873 hit, creditors pressed farmers to settle their mortgages and other debts at a time when the low value of crops made it virtually impossible. This sparked discontent that helped the Granger movement spread rapidly. At the national convention in 1874, the organization diplomatically declared itself an enemy not of capital but of the tyranny of monopolies; not of railroads, but of their high freight rates and monopoly of transportation. A resolution that the Grange was not to be a political function was passed, but this did not prevent discussion in local meetings of economic issues with political bearings. Members hoped to attain their legislative goals through influence in both major political parties.

When professional politicians shunned supporting the farmers' reform proposals because the action sought was not in line with traditional party policy, farmers decided to start their own party. In different states, various names were used for the political affiliation of farmers: Anti-Monopolists, Reformers, Farmers' Party, and others. Since these parties' goals were the subjection of corporations, especially the railroads, to state controls and the attainment of reform and economy in government, Grangers and other farm groups had causes for which they could fight together.

Battles were fought and won in state legislatures for laws that would regulate rates and services of the railroads; enough of this kind of law was passed in states where agriculture was such an influence that it laid the cornerstone for the eventual establishment of the Interstate Commerce Commission, a federal agency. The opposition had been keen and politicians found themselves in the middle of a clash between farmers, who represented many votes, and railroads, with storehouses of powerful capital.

Although farm organizations at that time were also interested in political questions such as currency inflation, better credit facilities, the tariff, reforms in civil service and economy in government, their victories over the railroads seemed to lessen their ardor for political activity. The professional politicians then took over reform movements and farmers' political activity declined.

With this decline in political agitation, the Grange began to lose some of its power until it ventured into cooperative buying and selling. Cooperative creameries, wool houses and tobacco pools, and even the manufacture of farm implements, were activities which the Grange entered in an effort to serve its members. Mismanagement and unfavorable economic conditions broke the co-ops and the Grange went into a slump. By 1895, membership fell to a low of about 100,000. Though down, the Patrons of Husbandry were not out.

Attaining the reform of unfair practices of the railroads was the most obvious accomplishment of the Grange until the turn of the century. Other efforts in which progress was made included the cleaning up of misuse of Land Grant funds and the inauguration of policies that led to constructive application of the Land Grant Act of 1862 for the establishment of agricultural colleges. Grangers backed the Hatch Act, passed in 1887, for the establishment of experiment stations for agriculture. It also agitated for parcel post and pure food and drug laws during the 1880's, but these were not adopted until after 1900. Its mistakes in the operation of cooperatives were useful in later efforts of this kind of buying and selling.

Socially, the Grange provided a common ground for farmers and their families to visit and to discuss their problems. Organization policy also elevated the social and political position of women to one of equality with men at a time when woman suffrage was yet generally unaccepted.

FARMERS' ALLIANCE AND POPULIST MOVEMENTS

The backbone of the Farmers' Alliance activity was the Southern and Northern branches. In Texas in 1875, the Southern Alliance was founded to wage battle against cattle and horse thieves and land sharks. Its first efforts of organizing evaporated in the heat of dissension over the Greenback Party; however, in 1880, the Texas Alliance started up as a secret and benevolent organization, nonpartisan in policy. Within six years, it claimed to have 2,700 local organizations in 84 Texas counties. While one of its primary purposes was to educate the agricultural classes, it turned back to political issues in its demands for high taxation on lands held for speculative purposes, more adequate taxation of railroads, new issues of paper currency and an interstate commerce law. All of these proposals were presented to the state legislature and Congress. Under the leadership of a blacksmith who was also a Methodist preacher, the Texas order did not allow Negroes to join. A Colored Farmers' Alliance was formed in Houston, Texas, in 1886. It was said that by 1891 it had 1,250,-000 members.

The Northern Alliance was formed in New York in 1877 and followed some Grange ideas for its organizational structure. It, too, was a secret organization which campaigned for railroad and taxation reform and legal recognition of Grange insurance companies. It also was to serve as the political mouthpiece of many Grangers. Led by an Illinois farmer and newsman, it was believed to have more than 100,000 members in 1882 with considerable influence in Iowa, Nebraska, Kansas and Minnesota. Other state farm organizations from Louisiana, Illinois and Arkansas aligned themselves, more or less, with the Alliance movement. Another ally was the Knights of Labor with a membership of 700,000 in 1886.

An effort to consolidate the various segments of the Alliance movement was made at a convention in St. Louis in 1889. Lindstrom says that if this merger could have been effected, the Alliance would have fused more than 3,500,000 members from Florida to North Dakota and from New York to California. However, squabbles between the South and the North developed over the admission of colored members, agreement on a name for the organization, and whether secrecy should be an optional part of the groups' policies.[8]

When efforts to unify the Alliances into a solid national body failed, the membership drifted into the furtherance of a third political party to look out for the welfare of farmers. Illustrating the degree of power farmers had in the Congress of 1873–75 were figures showing 61 per cent of the lawmakers were lawyers, 16 per cent were men of commerce or industry, and only seven per cent were farmers. At the same time, nearly half of the nation's population consisted of farm people.[9]

The result of this third-party ideology brought forth the People's Party or the Populist Party, formed in Cincinnati in 1891. The demands of its original platform included: free and unlimited coinage of silver; the issue of fiat money in sufficient quantity to transact business on a cash basis and the loan of such currency to the people at not more than two per cent interest on non-perishable agricultural products; national ownership of all public transportation and communication; the adoption of a graduated income tax; popular election of United States Senators; adoption of the initiative and referendum in legislation; and the prohibition of alien ownership of land.

In 1892, Populists entered candidates for the Presidency and the Vice Presidency in the national election on the above platform and received 22 electoral votes and 1,055,-424 popular votes in the following November election.

When William Jennings Bryan was nominated to the Presidency by the Populists in 1896, he also won the nomination of the Democratic Party. However, both parties ran their own Vice Presidential candidates. Major points of Bryan's platform included the free coinage of silver at a sixteen to one ratio to gold; reduction of the sale of government bonds which were building up the nation's debt on interest-paying loans and, again, endorsement of a graduated income tax. Bryan received 176 electoral votes while his Democratic running mate won 149 (many Populists supported the Democrats' Vice Presidential candidate) and the Populist running mate won only 17 electoral votes. The defeat of Bryan sounded the death knell of the Populist Party, even though its third party activities continued on a lesser scale through the election of 1908. Many Populists fell in line with the Democratic Party, which eventually ended this particular third group in national politics.

In evaluating these movements, Saloutos and Hicks write:

> Implicit in the Populistic concept of government intervention in economic affairs was the assumption that the government itself should be truly representative of the people, that the long-established control of the "plutocrats" should be broken. The first task that the agrarian leaders set for themselves, therefore, was to capture for the people the machinery of government. It was with this end in view that Farmers' Alliance and Populist candidates sought control of state governments, and that the Populist Party nominated J. B. Weaver in 1892 and William Jennings Bryan in 1896 for the Presidency. . . .[10]

AMERICAN SOCIETY OF EQUITY

Even though the early years of the twentieth century delivered some prosperity to American agriculture—mostly because of the rising price of land—there were those who did not share in this advantage and there remained cause for complaint. To some farmers, the idea of using direct action had appeal. In answer to this discontent, the Society of Equity was formed in Indianapolis in late December, 1902. A feed and seed dealer who also published a farm journal, J. A. Everitt, was the early leader of the movement. He had written an emotional book, *The Third Power*, which argued that if farmers would band together, they could be as influential as the forces of labor and capital. His plan was essentially one of controlling the visible supply of farm products and holding it off the markets until higher prices would be paid. "By devising some simple machinery for setting prices, and by keeping farm produce off the market unless and until these prices could be obtained, Everitt was certain that the farmers could not only secure relief from the ill effects of monopoly; they could themselves, in fact, become the greatest of all monopolists," Saloutos and Hicks write.[11]

While Everitt claimed to be a practical man who spent his every waking hour in deep thought, he generally ignored the importance of controlling the production of farm prod-

ucts. His plan called only for a system of spreading marketings more evenly over the twelve months of a year.

Although the membership figures on record of the
Equity are unreliable, it is believed it may have had about
100,000 members at its peak in 1906. Its greatest strength
was felt in Kentucky, Wisconsin, Minnesota, the Dakotas
and Montana.

"Dollar Wheat Bulletins" which urged farmers to hold
their crop until they received at least a dollar a bushel were
sent out in 1903. A smaller-than-usual wheat crop for that
year, plus this "holding action" strengthened wheat prices
and the next year Everitt urged his followers to hold out
for $1.20 a bushel. The effect was temporary.

In 1906, the Equity led a "40-day whirlwind campaign"
to absorb the tobacco producers' groups so a trust could be
built up for power to negotiate for better prices. In the
event that the American Tobacco Company, the sole major
buyer, failed to buy the 1906 and 1907 crops, the Equity
suggested building their own factories.

Under the name of the Burley Tobacco Society, the
Equity group announced that they would try to corner the
whole 1908 crop. Besides resistance among tobacco processors, many farmers did not favor the Equity plan.

. . . why should one producer join the organization, pay fees, and
endure hardships while another who refused to cooperate sold at a
fancy profit?
    Aroused by this situation, some of the tobacco growers finally de-
cided to employ force in order to achieve conformity. Their "night
riders" used the whip or even the rifle on independents or farmers
who "talked too much"; they brutally assaulted tobacco buyers, they
set fires, sowed plant beds to salt or grass seed, and even dynamited
machinery. One terror-stricken farmer found a grave dug in the
midst of his plant beds.[12]

Under this kind of pressure, the total acreage of tobacco
fell about 18 per cent below normal. After long, arduous
negotiating with the American Tobacco Company, the
Burley Tobacco Society closed the largest tobacco transaction in history. From 60 million to 70 million pounds of

Burley were exchanged for $12 million to $13 million. The transaction in 1908 was the result of pooling three crops of tobacco. In 1909, the Equity was on a decline in Kentucky and Tennessee while tobacco production was on the increase. With bitter memories, many farmers turned their backs on another possible attempt to pool their crop.

Dissension spread among the Equity's officers, especially over a 50-year contract Everitt had secured to publish the official publication of the organization. Also, there were disputes over who was actually the leader of the movement.

Existing in an era when cooperative buying and selling became more popular among farmers, the Equity made noteworthy strides in the grain trade. By 1916 the Equity Cooperative Exchange held two seats on the St. Paul Grain Exchange. It also ventured into the livestock commission business with operations in St. Paul and Chicago. These failed, but in the grain trade, the Equity exchange grew until in 1922 it had 80 elevators, 52 of which were in North Dakota, 26 in Minnesota and two in South Dakota. Mismanagement led to the decline of the exchange, however.

Saloutos and Hicks report:

But in spite of its unfortunate experiences, the Equity left its mark. Under its leadership, numerous local grain- and livestock-shipping associations were created, and the farmers were taught the need for a more efficient handling of their produce. Some of its leaders became identified with the Nonpartisan League and took an important part in the League's work, and men like Myron W. Thatcher and others who later assumed positions of leadership in the strong cooperatives built by the Farmers Union in the upper Mississippi Valley obtained much of their early training with the old Equity Cooperative Exchange.[18]

THE FARMERS UNION

In the Southwest, region where the old Farmers' Alliance had failed to be an influence, another farm group was started in 1902, the same year the Equity was formed in Indianapolis.

At Point, Texas, another newspaperman, who was also a farmer and who had been a member of the Alliance, met with nine of his neighbors in Rains County to form Local No. 1 of the Farmers Union. As leader of the movement, Newt Gresham was to face failure after failure in the next few years before his idea of an organization to help solve the economic ailments of the farmer began to gain acceptance. Originally from Alabama, Gresham was said to have had difficulty using a typewriter—or composing a single sentence, for that matter—but he had a mystic quality which was apparently part of his feeling that he had been preordained to lead a vast agricultural following. He is said to have told a friend of his in the early troubled days of the Farmers Union:

. . . I am sorry you don't understand the principles of the Farmers Union more than you do. I feel that God has endowed me with power to do something for suffering humanity, and I expect to spend the remainder of my life in this work, let it be what it may. I had rather lay down under this tree, die and leave my family in despair than to go on my way to success and let this Union go as the Farmers Alliance did.[14]

Gresham did spend the rest of his life campaigning for his "union."

After two years of organizing, the movement had thousands of members in Texas. However, there was dissension. Some members felt that officers of the movement did not "look like farmers." After three years, the Farmers Union had locals in a dozen states; and in December, 1905, delegates from Texas, Oklahoma, Alabama, Georgia and Mississippi met in Texarkana and named their movement the Farmers Educational and Cooperative Union of America. Growing pains were obvious when at one early convention the presiding officer lost control of the meeting to angry, shouting farmer-delegates. The protest of non-farmer leadership was put into action and for a time Gresham was expelled from the Farmers Union because he was a newspaperman, not a farmer. He was later readmitted as an organizer and continued in that function until his death in 1906.

Forming into a national organization brought new control into the movement. With wide dissension in Texas, outside states elected Charles Barrett of Georgia president.

Barrett, whom the Farmers Union fondly refers to as "the friend of Presidents," spent much of his time in Washington, learning about what went on there and meeting many legislators. During his early years as head of the growing organization, he believed cooperatives and efficient marketing were the key means of bettering the farmer's financial straits:

"To aid each other is the one great aim of the movement, and this aim is being realized to a remarkable degree. To others will be left the duty of instructing the farmer how to grow larger crops . . . the Union will devote its energies and direct its attention towards better prices for that which is already grown."[15]

From his association with politicians and lobbyists, Barrett began to suspect virtually everyone in Washington to be some kind of rascal and he mistrusted them all. He termed the group of lobbyists "the assistant government" and attacked the Secretary of the Treasury as "the man who had never lost his poise though he had caused the farmer to lose his shirt." In time, Barrett said the farmer must become involved in politics, and as the farmer becomes involved, so must the Farmers Union.

"The ballot is the deadliest weapon known to modern history. Handled in the proper way, we can shoot down the hypocrites and demagogues. . . ."[16] he said.

Thus concerned with political activity, Barrett became less of an advocate of cooperative marketing and more of a lobbyist himself. Meanwhile, Farmers Union membership had spread into more of the northern states of the Midwest and its membership had swollen to nearly a million, according to one account. Cooperative business enterprises of the Farmers Union were booming in some areas. Wartime prosperity, poor organization and poor leadership caused these co-ops to dwindle away in Texas, the home of the Farmers Union, by 1920. However, it was a strong organization in some other regions, a fact that eventually led to the challenging of Barrett as its real leader. He was voted out of office in 1928.

Back in the midlands, the movement for the utilization of cooperatives was being pushed by Clarence E. Huff, among others. Huff was head of the Kansas Farmers Union and felt co-ops, along with political influence, were the saviours of farmers. In 1927, he reported that there were in Kansas between 600 and 700 local units: elevators, creameries, livestock shipping associations and retail stores and that the whole group was joined or centralized through state-wide units. Besides having co-ops to buy and sell for the farmer, the Kansas Farmers Union had a cooperative bank that was state wide and served organization members exclusively.

The growth of cooperatives was cause for conflict between some Farmers Union leaders. The editor of the *Farmers Union Herald,* which represented the national group engaged in organizing farmers in the Northwest by spending co-op funds, referred to the Nebraska Farmers Union, very active in cooperation, as a "bunch of prune and vinegar peddlers."[17] Naturally, co-op members preferred having their patronage earnings returned to them instead of watching the money go out of the state for recruiting members a thousand miles away. It was easy cause for squabbling.

With the spread of co-op popularity and Farmers Union membership, the waning Equity Cooperative Exchange was absorbed by the more successful Farmers Union interests in 1926. M. W. Thatcher, who was a member of the Equity exchange, led Farmers Union cooperative elevators to combine to form the Farmers Union Grain Terminal Association in St. Paul in 1940. In 1963 it was handling about 25 per cent of the grain flowing into the Minneapolis-St. Paul terminal grain market, according to Farmers Union figures.

Besides grain marketing facilities, the Farmers Union co-ops also deal in farm supplies and operate livestock commission firms at terminal markets on the Missouri River and in St. Paul. Insurance is also a business conducted under the Farmers Union cooperative program.

While the above account seems to show mostly success in the Farmers Union's history, there was plenty of failure down through the years. Early cooperative enterprises were really no more than experiments, and many suffered from the same kind of mismanagement and economic misfortunes that killed the Equity co-ops. There were legal battles challenging whether such operations were lawful. The Farmers Union claims credit for successfully pressing for passage of the Capper-Volstead Act of 1922, which exempted farm cooperatives from provisions of the anti-trust laws.

As a politically liberal organization, the Farmers Union legislative record has its ups and downs. To recount them at this point is not essential to this study.

Some representative examples of the Farmers Union's agricultural policies come from the organization's policy statement for 1962:

. . . a national agricultural policy should be adopted, paralleling the Employment Act of 1946, providing for an annual determination by the Department of Agriculture, setting forth the desirable national production goals for the major commodities and indicating the price levels needed to assure parity income to farmers and for the agricultural industry to make its maximum contribution to the gross national product and to national economic growth. . . .
This agricultural policy is necessary in order that farmers not be subject to an "auction-hammer" type free market which would be forced on them in the absence of farm programs because of the basic weaknesses of their economic organization. Other segments of the nation's economic structure are not subject to this type of market and could not survive under it. Consumers cannot buy from this kind of a market and they would suffer in the long run if the family farm structure of agriculture should lose ground to factories in this field. . . .[18]

To further its policies, the Farmers Union carries on extensive education programs. It also has an extensive youth program. According to the editor of the *National*

Union Farmer, the organization had about 300,000 farm
family memberships during the summer of 1962.

THE FARM BUREAU

The rise of the American Farm Bureau Federation dif-
fers markedly from other agrarian movements in that it
had no single messiah-like founder and its initial purpose
was educational rather than economic or legislative reform.
Also, instead of emerging as a unified voice of farm discontent, its first activities took place during a period of relative prosperity for agriculture.

While other farm organizations usually trace their
origins to a specific time and place, the Farm Bureau was
formed in the wake of different local and state-wide efforts.
As Kile points out,[19] Land Grant colleges established under
the Morrill Act of 1862 and farm experiment stations authorized under the Hatch Act of 1887 had been conducting
"farmers institutes" and other types of extension work to
"take the campus to the farmer." The New York State Agricultural Society led the trend of holding these itinerant
schools in the 1840's. By the turn of the century every state
in the Union except three was the scene of annual institutes conducted by college professors in sessions that
lasted three to five days. In 1899, it was figured that 2,000
such institutes were held with more than a half million
farmers taking part. After Cornell University at Ithaca, New
York, took the lead, other agricultural colleges began adopting "extension departments" for non-student instruction in
new developments in farm technology. Illinois organized
an extension staff in 1901 and other states followed suit.

Teaching agriculture in country grade schools also became common and as a result, corn clubs, hog clubs,
poultry clubs and the like were formed. An outgrowth of
these clubs was the holding of shows to reward the outstanding student-members. Although the above organizations were "boys" clubs, canning and sewing groups were
started for girls.

Passage of the Smith-Hughes Act in 1917 authorized
the use of federal funds to assist the teaching of vocational

agriculture in high schools. This added to the popularization of educating the farmer with new methods.

In 1902, ravages of the Mexican boll weevil in Texas cotton fields caused an emergency which was acted upon by an advisor of the Secretary of Agriculture. A man who had been active in educational and agricultural activities in New York, Iowa and Louisiana, Dr. Seaman Knapp, investigated the situation and decided to introduce the raising of rice as a method of meeting the boll weevil situation rather than combating it. He believed in teaching by doing rather than by showing. By setting up demonstration farms, he was able to have successful and profitable rice crops grown. Curious farmers were sure to inquire and give the new crop a try. Thus, W. C. Stallings was appointed to be the first "county agent" when he went to work in Smith County, Texas. In 1907, the idea of having hired technical advisors on a county level took roots in other Texas counties and in Louisiana. The Department of Agriculture made arrangements in 1911 to assist in cooperative efforts with state colleges to manage these projects. By 1912, 858 field agents of this type were at work in the South, including 13 state agents, 36 district supervisors, 20 special corn club agents, 639 local county agents and 159 collaborating workers assisting in girls' canning and poultry organizations. Demonstration work was carried on in the fields of farm crops, gardens, pastures and later in breeding and care of livestock.

In the North, similar efforts had been carried on in New York and in the Midwest. In 1910–1911, for instance, Illinois farmers formed clubs for holding institutes for educational purposes. Before long it was not uncommon for counties to organize to hire an agent, usually a graduate of the college of agriculture in their state, to serve as an advisor. The "county agent" movement was gaining favor throughout the major farm states.

By January 1, 1915, there were approximately 1,000 county agricultural agents at work in the United States. Those in the South still adhered rather closely to the original demonstration methods but those in the North soon developed, as we shall see, a distinctive type of organization to serve as a vehicle through which to carry their message to the farmer. These organizations differed in plan in almost every state and were known by a variety of names.[20]

There were four major kinds of organizations: those having members scattered throughout the county and who paid membership dues of one to ten dollars; those who had delegates from townships who participated in a central county group; those having a central organization of delegates from already established community clubs, granges, Farmers Union locals and other organizations; and separate farmers clubs which worked directly with the county agent in a given county. Such groups backed the county agent financially and with moral assistance at the inception of the movement.

The county extension workers found that when they worked through these "County Farm Bureaus," their efforts were usually more effective than when they concentrated their attention on an individual farmer.

The World War I effort played no small part in the spread of the Farm Bureau movement. With war and food shortages, the national government soon had county agents provided in almost all of the 2,500 agricultural counties of the United States in an effort to increase food production.[21] In many cases, the government specified that a county had to have a "Farm Bureau" type organization already started before an extension agent would be assigned to help the local farmers.

As the system of county organizations was set up, it was logical that counties in a given state would have common interests that could be strengthened by forming a State Farm Bureau. After a few states were unified, the national counterpart was in order.

In 1919, at the invitation of the New York State Farm Bureau Federation, delegates from twelve states—Delaware, Illinois, Iowa, Massachusetts, Michigan, Missouri, New Hampshire, New York, Ohio, Pennsylvania, Vermont and West Virginia—assembled in Ithaca to consider the establishment of a national organization. Only nine states had state organizations at the time, but the remaining ones were striving for state-wide unification of their Farm Bureaus.

That first national meeting in Ithaca revealed suspicions and differences of opinion from the various parts of the country. Some delegates felt that the new organization should be an agent to solve their marketing problems through the application of cooperative enterprise. Others felt it should be only the vehicle of knowledge pouring forth from agricultural colleges, and that in the hands of men with limited experience it might fall apart and never be a growing giant among farm movements.[22]

However, when another session was called in Chicago later in the year, these differences seemed to have blown over. The educational leaning and the business inclination, more or less opposing stands until now, were featured in two different keynote speeches. Then a final major address was delivered, favoring a middle-of-the-road stand.

"The East and the West, the North and the South, have agricultural problems which are different only in their external aspects," the speaker said. "These problems are basically similar or identical. We need to create a national spirit in our agricultural life. The Farm Bureaus enabled us to look over our line fences, the state organizations enabled us to work on our state problems, and now we have before us the possibility of a national association to create the national agricultural spirit. . . . I stand as a rock against radicalism, but I believe in an organization which strikes out from the shoulder."[23]

By the close of the conference, the speaker was surprised to find himself, James R. Howard, the first president of the American Farm Bureau Federation. Side-stepping conflict over the definite purposes of the new organization, the delegation did not adopt a clear policy statement. Some attending the meeting were disappointed, believing the new group would be too conservative.

However, Howard led the AFBF into an energetic membership campaign in the next few years and gained many, many new followers. Gathering strength in the South was more of a problem because some extension leaders opposed the movement. In the North, however, county agents favored it. Although extension personnel were instructed not to become involved in Farm Bureau activities, they could recommend it.

Although he was tall, angular and usually clothed in ill-fitting suits and had a head of hair that was usually half-tousled, Howard was in great demand to make appearances before gatherings of businessmen and politicians to state the farmers' case.

He once told a grain marketing conference:

"The most potent cause of our present social unrest and commercial stagnation today [1921] lies in the fact that there is no farm market. The farmer's purchasing power is gone. His prices are far below par. His costs of production are deep in red. His markets are gone."[24]

The costs of organizing posed an obstacle for state Farm Bureaus as well as the national in the early years of the AFBF, but many of the Midwestern states were actively engaged in cooperative marketing—buying and selling. Generally these co-ops were organized at a local level and worked in connection with a state cooperative body or exchange and not directly with the State Farm Bureau organization.[25] Besides providing farmer-members with seed and supplies, the co-op founded a line of auto insurance.

Founding the U.S. Grain Growers, Inc., which eventually incorporated a financing branch with capitalization of $100 million, seemed to put the Farm Bureau on the road to effective marketing. Quibbling over a clause of mandatory pooling of grain, plus adverse publicity distributed by members of the grain trade, eventually led to stirring up enough dissension to bring this experiment to an end before it was really tried.

Cooperative livestock marketing involving the facilities and methods of the central markets, proved more successful and has continued to this day under the management of Farm Bureau-fostered co-ops.

Even in its early days, the Farm Bureau was accused of being a tool of Wall Street and Big Business. This has always been denied by the organization. Probably one of the major reasons outsiders hold this belief is the general conservatism of Farm Bureau policy. Another point which causes some suspicion of the organization having a bureaucratic tie (the word "bureau" in AFBF is as misleading as "union" in Farmers Union) with the current Extension Service is the fact that in some Midwest counties the local Farm Bureau office and the county extension director and home demonstration agent headquarters are sometimes found together in the same building or even the same room, divided only by a slight partition. Federal and state regulations forbid financial or political relationships between extension workers and farm organizations in most states. In addition, a joint memorandum issued in 1921 by the head of the Extension Service and the president of the American Farm Bureau Federation outlined the role of county agents in regard to farm organizational activities. The document forbade extension workers to handle farm organization funds or to solicit membership for any farm group. Although at the time the memorandum was issued and in instances in later years there have been accusations that Farm Bureau and extension personnel were in cahoots, the memorandum of 1921 generally stood as a rule of practice. There were, however, some exceptions to the rule and only in recent years has legislation been completed in most states to separate extension people from local Farm Bureau business and membership activities. At this writing, there were only a few isolated instances where the two groups were working together in such a way as to be vulnerable to criticism from other farm organizations. Naturally, Farm Bureau gives moral support to extension work, but there are virtually no hidden or suspicious connections between the two groups that are objectionable.

As with the earlier section relating some of the history of the Farmers Union, the AFBF's legislative record will be largely omitted here. As has often been the case, however, in recent years when the Farm Bureau took a stand on an issue, it would be opposed by the Farmers Union and vice versa. This follows as a result of their respective conservatism and liberalism. These two organizations, along with the Grange, maintain offices in Washington for legislative purposes.

A sampling of Farm Bureau policy is drawn from its 1963 statement:

> A major objective of Farm Bureau policy is to create conditions whereby farmers may earn and get a high per-family real income in a manner which will preserve freedom and opportunity. We firmly believe that this objective can best be accomplished by preserving the market price system as the principal influence in allocating the use of farm resources and in distributing farm production.
> It is abundantly clear from years of experience that needed adjustments are made more readily and the economic well being of farmers is better served in those areas of agriculture which have not been subject to government control and price support programs. Witness livestock, fruits, and vegetables which have remained free of government programs as contrasted to those commodities where government control and price support programs have been operative for many years. . . .[26]

In 1963, the Farm Bureau claimed to be the largest American farm organization with more than 1,600,000 members in 49 states and in Puerto Rico.

THE GRANGE, 1900 TO TODAY

Oliver Hudson Kelley's dreams of giving farmers an organization that would constantly fight intemperance, injustice, intolerance, monopoly, public extravagance, graft and dishonesty and would champion the cause of good government seem to have come true, or at least have endured for nearly a century.

Still basically a fraternal organization with high moral principles and an active social program for both adults and youths, the Grange continues to proclaim itself non-partisan and unbiased in areas of race and creed.

Many pieces of legislation have been added to the organization's tally of accomplishments and, like the other major lobbying groups, it has sustained its share of disappointments in the field of influencing lawmaking. In some states it is active in cooperative business and supports this kind of enterprise as an aid to the farm economy. Civic projects in which community units compete nationwide in service contests and educational programs play an important part in the Grange's activities. Grange Halls in many parts of the country still serve as social centers for both the farm organization and other local groups.

In terms of legislative policy, its 1963 statement seemed to place the Grange somewhere between the conservatism of the Farm Bureau and the liberalism of the Farmers Union:

> Primary farm program objectives of the Grange are to (a) provide equitable income opportunities to farmers and (b) serve total national welfare.
> Agricultural producers are entitled to an opportunity to earn and receive—from consumers of their products instead of from taxpayers—an equitable return for their labor, management, risk and investment. Such return should be reasonably comparable to that received for those same factors by those engaged in non-agricultural sectors of the U.S. economy. . . .
> Farmers must have the help of government in solving the continued problem of overproduction. To a reasonable degree, the supply of farm commodities must be brought in line with demand or government programs for supporting farm prices should be terminated. A continuation of programs resulting in further buildup of already excessive government-owned stockpiles of farm commodities represents wasteful and unsound public policy. . . .[27]

According to Grange figures in 1962, the organization included a membership of about 750,000 individuals who belonged to 7,000 local units in 40 states.

THE NONPARTISAN LEAGUE

In brief, the Nonpartisan movement began in North Dakota in 1915 under the leadership of Arthur C. Townley, one of the most colorful leaders in the history of agriculture. His brand of radicalism called for such measures as state ownership of virtually all kinds of business and full representation of the farm population in state government. Sometimes associated with the Socialist Party, the league did at one time gain almost complete control of the North Dakota government. While a third-party political organization, it had a wide following—almost exclusively—of farmers. It succeeded to a large part the political influence of the Society of Equity and had some following in neighboring states. By 1922, the established political parties had "stolen their thunder" by making promises similar to the league. Some professional politicians, like Robert LaFollette of Wisconsin, avoided making a stand regarding the movement. This did not help its cause. Eventually, as the organization withered, other farm groups, namely the Farm Bureau and the Farmers Union, served as a different and more vital kind of sounding board for farm troubles.

THE FARM HOLIDAY ASSOCIATION

Mention of the name Milo Reno in some parts of Iowa and Nebraska evokes memories in some older residents to tell the story of the Farm Holiday as though it were akin to Custer's Last Stand and they were there. Because it was a movement filled with deviltry and some downright violence, it was short-lived and sensational.

Early agitation started in 1929 against governmental testing of cows for tuberculosis, although this program of disease control had started in Iowa in 1917, it had been conducted without organized opposition until the percentage of tested animals reached the point where it was legally compulsory for remaining herds to be tested. Mandatory testing began in 1929, and it proceeded fairly well until after 1930. Animals that reacted to the tests were condemned and eliminated, with the federal government assuming one-third, the state government one-third and the owner the remaining third of the loss. Some farmers claimed that the test was meaningless or at least unreliable and the loss of animals was unfair in a time of low prices.

The greatest opposition was growing in southeastern Iowa counties where testers had refrained from proceeding because of the resistance. Many of these farmers opposing the "cow squirters" were members of the Farmers Union and had joined the Farmers' Protective Association to fight the test. Attempts were made to obtain legislation against the test and committees were set up to resist efforts of testers to follow the established program.

When a tester called on a farm to examine the cows, it would not be uncommon for many neighboring farmers to show up innocently enough until the government man was ready to start his work. Then he might find himself surrounded by menacing men who were set against his testing. He could leave peaceably or be thrown off the farm, depending on how expediently he handled himself.

High point of the "cow war" came in the fall of 1931 when armed agents were sent out to finish the testing and 400 farmers resisted in the Tipton, Iowa, area. Martial law was declared on the tail of violence that broke out. Although the farmers threatened to stage taxpayers' strikes and to boycott unsympathetic merchants, the veterinarians completed their work. Most of Iowa's farmers were not sympathetic to this protest group.

Having gained some attention from the so-called cow war, Milo Reno, a president of the Iowa Farmers Union life and auto insurance companies and a board member of its fire insurance company, saw an opportunity to use his leadership. Among his memberships, Reno claimed to be a Mason, an Odd Fellow, a member of the Christian Church and the Republican Party, even though in 1928 he had voted for Al Smith and endorsed Franklin D. Roosevelt in 1932. A powerful speaker, he favored the use of a farm strike similar to that used unsuccessfully by the Society of Equity and Farmers Union in their earlier days. At a time when eggs were quoted at 22 cents a dozen, he said the farmer should get 35 cents. Oats, selling at 11 cents a bushel, should have been worth 49 cents, according to

Reno's thinking. Followers of the movement reasoned that if bankers could have a "holiday," why shouldn't the farmers call one of their own?[28]

The Farm Holiday Association itself was formed in Des Moines, Iowa, in May, 1932 when 1,300 attending the meeting gave their support to a strike to begin on July 4 and end only when corn prices reached 92 cents per bushel and hogs climbed to $11.25 per hundredweight. Hogs were bringing about three dollars per hundredweight at the time.[29]

On August 8, a strike was called at Des Moines but the focal point of the effort moved swiftly to Sioux City and Omaha, where farmers turned out to blockade roads to these major livestock markets. Except for some broken windshields and some fist fighting, there was little violence; truckers simply turned back. Although police were called out to disperse the men causing the blockades, market receipts at Sioux City were reduced by half on August 18.

In Nebraska, Fred Kriege, of South Sioux City, who claimed to have started the movement by himself in his state, stirred up feelings and told a gathering in his hometown:

"It is up to the farmers themselves . . . to go through with this program, nobody will help us. The zero hour has arrived; let's get into action."[30] Into action they went. As in Sioux City, a blockade was thrown up around Omaha. Across the Missouri River from Omaha, Iowans cut off traffic into Council Bluffs. Authorities in Omaha became uncomfortable as a thousand men—tenants, farm boys and unemployed city people, lacking shelter, food and money— established an impromptu camp. Pitched battles between deputies and pickets broke out on the nights of August 30, 31 and September 1.

A mob of 500 marched on the jail in Council Bluffs to break in and release some of their fellow pickets who had been arrested because of their troublemaking. Last minute negotiations secured the release of the prisoners on bail and may have averted a tragedy.

The monster of mob violence seemed to have frightened Farm Holiday leadership and calls to end this activity were sounded. Some diehards stood at blockades, to no avail, until they were forced from their posts by cold weather. While the temporary effect of the blockades pushed prices up, the release of shipments of livestock afterwards was like a dam breaking. The supply became a glut on the market and prices were depressed further.

After their failure at a marketing strike, adherents of the movement turned to a campaign devised to break up mortgage foreclosure auctions of farms. By gathering for an auction sale and surrounding potential bidders menacingly, Farm Holiday members could limit the bidding to ridiculously low prices. At one sale in Nebraska, where these "penny auctions" were most prevalent, chickens, cattle and horses sold at five cents each with no opposing bids. Total proceeds of the farm sale were $5.35, which the mortgagor, the receiver for a bank, reluctantly accepted. The organization returned the farm to the original owner, a young widow. A few days later, a similar sale was attended by 1,500 members of the Holiday movement who paid $7.10 for the total offering before giving it back to its former owner.[31]

An attempt to obtain a court order to call a halt to sheriff's sales sparked the worst violence connected with the anti-foreclosure campaign. In April 1933, some 600 persons broke into a courtroom at LeMars, Iowa, and demanded that the presiding judge issue such a court order. When he refused, he was dragged from the bench, blindfolded and taken to a country crossroads where he was beaten severely and threatened with death. But the judge was adamant and would not sign the agitators' demands. The assailants were arrested and sentenced later. No other like incidents occurred.[32]

Reno and his lieutenants met with politicians and received little satisfaction as the movement went into its decline. With the passage of the Agricultural Adjustment Act in 1933, Reno stormed that it was a "brazen attempt to bribe the farmer to surrender what little independence he has left."[33]

Other than bringing attention to the plight of low prices for farm products and the heavily mortgaged state of farm property, the movement proved little over the long haul.

THE FACT that the "farm problem" continued to exist, except for wartime production and other brief periods of prosperity, might make one wonder if the many farm organizations ever really accomplished very much. Although we have largely skirted the legislative victories of farm groups, a large body of constructive regulation has come about with much of the credit going to these groups. Pure food laws and fair practice measures in the market place—such as the Packers and Stockyards Act, the Perishable Agricultural Commodities Act, or the Commodity Exchange Act—are among the many laws on the books to protect farmer, entrepreneur, and consumer alike.

Recalling the mechanical and economic changes that were made in farming after the Civil War (discussed in Chapter Two), it is easily understood that the American farmer has been a victim of constant change for the past century. However, he has organized, sometimes effectively, to meet some of these changes. Rural electrification, better roads, keeping informed on new production developments and political activity, as well as business advantages of cooperatives are among the services that farm organizations have performed. Nor can the social aspect be ignored.

But even with a selection of farm groups available, it was apparent that that was not enough to satisfy everyone living out in the country back in 1955. As with past movements—either originating in the Midwest or gaining its strongest foothold there—The National Farmers Organization sowed the seeds for a "new" movement in the mid-Fifties to obtain for its members the timeworn goal of economic equality with other segments of the nation.

4

"LET'S CALL A MEETING . . ."

SEPTEMBER, 1955 had its high points. That was the month President Eisenhower was stricken with a heart attack and in Argentina, dictator Juan Peron was toppled from his free-spending grip on the government. Comic strip detective Dick Tracy was on a caper that involved an incredibly obese hoodlum named Oodles, and in the world of real crime, the usual kinds of felonies were reflected in the daily headlines. Israeli troops assaulted and seized the Gaza Strip in Egypt and on another world front, U.S. Secretary of State John Foster Dulles was hopefully negotiating for a summit meeting of the Big Four. He was confident of attaining lasting world peace within a decade. Was this just another month of fast-moving events of the mid-century? Perhaps.

In the Midwest, agriculture was the victim of drought. Some of the specialists at agricultural colleges were advising farmers to salvage the withered remains of their corn crop by chopping it into silage rather than hoping for a harvest of the feed grain. Starting in July, hot, dry weather plagued the western parts of the Corn Belt with little relief. Corn wasn't the only crop that was "burning up," though.

Beef cattle and hog production had reached cyclical peaks that year and market prices went into an alarming slump. The continued pinch of the cost-price squeeze coupled with poor crop prospects painted a dismal future for many farmers. They talked about their problems and some wanted to "do something," but there was no ready means of giving vent to these growing frustrations. Many a hard-pressed farmer felt the established farm organizations weren't getting the immediate results he wanted. For example, the Farm Bureau, the major farm organization in the region where discontent was brewing, had not taken a favorable stand on federal farm policy, other than being generally opposed to price support programs and government controls on agricultural production. By and large, it appeared that the Farm Bureau was dragging its feet on nearly all farm legislation, and in fact, generally favored Secretary of Agriculture Ezra Taft Benson's ultimate goal to get government out of agriculture. Letters-to-the-editor were accusing the Farm Bureau of having become "too commercial" and that it had turned into a big cooperative business rather than being a representative of the farmer. As one Iowan put it: "If it was a choice between higher or lower farm price supports, Farm Bureau voted for the lower ones in Congress. And if it was a choice between the farmer and big business, Farm Bureau sided with big business."

Although the Farmers Union had long been a strong advocate of government controls abetted by price support programs, this organization, as well as the National Grange, had little influence in Iowa and other Corn Belt areas where farmers found themselves in trouble. This left a void in which many farmers could feel unhappy about both the Farm Bureau's policies and Secretary Benson's program and expect little favorable action from their point of view either. The situation was ideal for considering a whole new approach to the entire problem.

One mid-September morning in Adams County in southwest Iowa, a feed salesman called on one of his customers. The talk soon turned to some of the problems confronting agriculture. This conversation was the first striking of flint against steel, and the resulting spark ignited agriculture's tinderbox. A few nights later, neighboring farmers had passed the word along that a meeting would be held in Carl, Iowa, to see if they couldn't find a way to improve the farm situation. About 35 persons showed up. Heartened by the turnout, the feed salesman, Jay Loghry, utilized his regular farm calls to arrange more such meetings. On September 21, the new movement—with officers elected but still without a name—met in Corning, Iowa. Two CIO United Packinghouse Union officials attended.[1] One of them reportedly told the farmers present: "We're all for you." He went on to promise that a union meeting the following week would bring "an expression of support in black and white."

A week later, another meeting was called at an auction salebarn in Creston, Iowa. Despite driving rains, an overflow crowd of 1,200[2] showed up to hear Loghry urge farmers to organize. Also on hand were the group's elected president, Duane Orton, who talked about the farmers' problems, and former Iowa Governor Dan Turner, the state's chief executive at the time Milo Reno's Farm Holiday followers were running rampant. To seek law and order, Turner had called out the state militia. Since his political leanings were with Hoover, his political career had been buried by the victory of Roosevelt and the New Deal.[3]

Pushing 80 years of age, the old-school politician, noted for his wit, called on those present to "stay with this until we get through Congress—that's the only way you can get it. You can't get it through a strike. You can't get it through a holiday." He pointed out that the group could "wander in the wrong direction" and pleaded "with all the earnestness at my command and with 40 years of experience in this sort of thing, not to resort to violence."[4]

An extensive landholder, Turner reiterated his oft-heard call for the incumbent Secretary of Agriculture Ezra T. Benson, "to resign and go back to Utah."

Within two weeks of starting a new farm movement, its instigator, Jay Loghry, was in trouble. For one thing, his wife was not sympathetic toward the venture and urged him to get out before he was in too deep. For another, the feed and seed firm for which he had worked for many years fired him.

"I guess they were afraid I would get them in trouble," he told newsmen.[5]

The movement itself almost exploded into nothingness when Loghry told the farmers that it was his aim to unionize them. A meeting in Corning on September 26 included twelve township delegates from the surrounding Adams County gathered to vote against an "organization that breathes of unionism." Only one delegate disagreed. Consequently, Loghry changed his line and made a public statement to this effect.

By the end of September, Loghry's followers named their group the National Farmers Organization. It was touted as a protest group with the aims of petitioning the U.S. Department of Agriculture to put an immediate floor of $20 per hundredweight under hogs and a $30 floor under beef cattle. Another goal was to get Congress to legislate a long-range program to insure farm price parity.[6]

Meanwhile, Loghry was the movement's only employee, drawing a salary from the one-dollar donations collected at the meetings he was conducting in southwest Iowa and northeast Missouri.

Though one account said Loghry wasn't a speaker or a politician,[7] his talks were "straight from my heart and without a script," and had plenty of effect. Farmers flocked by the hundreds to the meetings he called. Governor Turner's experience and skills in working with the public were also important guiding influences on the spreading movement.

While Loghry was the "common man" leader of the budding NFO, Turner was the colorful old firebrand, arousing a following that was to grow phenomenally. Some said Dan Turner's name was magic. As chief advisor of the NFO, he was a political speaker who quoted the Bible, gave his opponents oratorical hell without reserve and, in general, had farmers eating out of his hands.[8] Witness to the way he attracted listeners was a meeting of Lancaster County farmers in Lincoln, Nebraska. At least nine of those on hand to hear Turner had driven 150 miles. They went home saying it was worth every inch of the trip.

As the movement fanned out from its origin in southwestern Iowa, meetings were held in nearly every county, usually in a local livestock auction barn.

At a meeting in Sioux Falls, South Dakota, on October 6, Loghry told farmers that in less than a month, the embryonic NFO had 9,000 farmers signed up in Iowa, Kansas and Missouri.[9] "We don't want to get into politics in any shape or form . . . we're not tied to anyone. These are the farmers themselves talking," he said. Plans at that time called for a 30-day membership drive and then to hold a "big meeting" to draw up demands to be presented to the U.S. Department of Agriculture.[10] It was not until December 15, however, that the big meeting took place. Assembling in the National Guard Armory in Corning, some 750 followers of Loghry and Turner were ready to sit down and decide just what they wanted to say in their petition to the government and the USDA.

The armory was filled and business was in order when the furnace heating the building went on the blink. The delegates bundled up in their coats and the meeting proceeded. The windows were kept closed against the cold December weather, and tobacco smoke filled the room. These inconveniences didn't seem to bother the audience.

By the end of the convention, some significant developments had taken place. For one, a young, stocky and dark-haired Missouri farmer had been elected president of the NFO. Oren Lee Staley was on his way to a career as the most vociferous farm leader of the day.

Regarding policy, ten resolutions were passed at the meeting.[11] The first was a fairly complicated measure seeking to get the federal government out of the business of storing surplus wheat. It called for farmers' storing at their own expense all wheat over bushel allotments set by the USDA. This surplus could be sold under the allotment program during years of drought and insect infestation that might cut normal yields. It included also a provision that if a farmer felt his excess wheat reserve had been built to the point where it could provide him an adequate income during the drought years, he could thus build his own soil bank.

Another major resolution called for a farm program that would guarantee farmers 100 per cent of parity, the line that Turner had been preaching. Immediate price floors of $20 per hundredweight on butcher hogs and $30 per hundredweight on good to choice slaughter cattle, along with "reasonable controls during periods of farm surpluses," were asked of the USDA. With this was a pledge to support the department in a long-range farm program.

As an organization, the NFO declared that it was non-partisan and non-political. It was opposed to violence. Another resolution pledged that the NFO should become "a legislative group" only.

A request was made that farm commodity market "manipulations" be stopped and that Congress investigate. The group also called for the stopping of expenditures of vast sums of public money for the reclamation of desert lands for agricultural purposes until demand for farm products was increased to justify the increased production.

To express their gratitude for the efforts of Governor Turner, delegates passed a resolution requesting that the former Iowa chief executive be named national farmer of the year for his aid to the NFO.

Business reports at the first national convention revealed that the organization listed 55,659 members in the states of Iowa, Missouri, Nebraska, Colorado and Montana. In its three months of existence, the NFO had raised $41,744.44 and spent $6,251.37.[12]

Apparently inspired by the accomplishments of their meeting, farmers went home and spread the word of the NFO. Membership climbed quickly. By the end of January, 1956, it claimed to have signed up 71,000 farmers,[13] and two months later, an Omaha newspaper listed NFO membership at 140,000.[14]

Briefly, what were some of the problems confronting farmers when the NFO was formed? A member would respond that the troubles were mostly matters of low market prices and the drought. Crops were hit worst in the areas of southwestern Iowa and northwestern Missouri, where the movement made its greatest strides at the outset. Iowa's corn crop forecast was revised downward on September 1 to 43 bushels per acre, the lowest since 1947. Iowa pastures were reported in the poorest condition since 1936, all because of dry heat waves during August, 1955. In Nebraska, drought shrivelled corn prospects of 30 bushels per acre to 15.5 bushels by September 1. The prior estimate had been made on June 1.[15]

As mentioned earlier, livestock prices were in trouble. For example, top prices on fat steers at Omaha had ranged from $30 to $40 per hundredweight from January, 1950 through 1954. In 1955, the year's top price of $35 was paid in February, but by August the top had slipped to $23.50 and in December it was down to $22.50, according to data compiled by *The Stockman's Journal* in Omaha.[16] Hog prices at Omaha in 1955 had a top of $18.75 in January that worked its way up to $22.25 in June before slumping to $12 per hundredweight in December. While these figures do not reflect prices of a bulk of sales made on the central market, they do show how drastic the decline was. The drop was enough to erase any profit and spell additional losses for many operators.

Although it was years later when he made the statement, Duane Orton, the first local president of the NFO and later a congressional candidate in the Seventh Iowa District, blamed politics in Washington for the rise of the farm movement:

"As one of the original NFO workers and organizers and also as first treasurer, I want to explain a few pertinent facts.

"First I want to make the unqualified charge—the reason the NFO was founded was because of the deliberate and intentional disregard of the Republican party's leadership for its own political promises. Oh yes, you can be sure these chief Republicans knew how to go after votes—they were long on promises."[17] He went on to cite several instances where politicians had made campaign promises in 1952 of 100 per cent of parity for farmers. When Republican Representative Clifford Hope of Kansas introduced a full-parity bill, 23 out of 219 Republicans supported the measure, Orton said.

"The Benson farm program, pledged to the lowering of farm prices, was installed instead," he added.[18]

The original NFO goal of organizing farmers to send one of their ranks—or 500, if need be—to the National Capital to get favorable legislation was not very successful. The popular press paid little attention to the Washington trips made by Staley and his cohorts to confer with legislators. Congressmen listened politely to the NFO's desires, but did not fulfill them. One NFO account said that following the organization's first national convention, many delegations were sent to Washington, while out in the country, membership grew to 180,000. "This caused great concern on the part of senators and congressmen and other officials in high authority because farmers were organizing in great numbers," the account claimed.[19]

It pointed out that price supports for the year 1956 were to be reduced from $1.56 to $1.41 per bushel on corn, wheat props lowered from $2 to $1.82 and dairy supports were to be dropped from 82 per cent of parity to 77 per cent, according to plans announced by the Department of Agriculture.

"But because of the fact that 180,000 farmers had put in a dollar along with tremendous effort, this drop in support prices was rescinded by executive order and for the crop year of 1956, these support prices were moved back to their original level. The pressure exerted by the NFO undoubtedly was the cause of the restoration of the previous support price levels," the organization said.[20] It made no mention of like efforts by the other major farm organizations.

If nothing more, the trips to Washington helped to further educate NFO officials on legislative accomplishments of the past. Some members had held on to Jay Loghry's idea of organizing farmers in a body as tight and coercive as a labor union. Thinking along the lines of collective bargaining, some wondered what legislation would be necessary for the NFO to legally take up such a program.

At the 1957 national convention, delegates, determined that they were going to find an answer to the farmers' problems by developing a specific program, introduced and passed a resolution to empower a committee to work out a plan of collective bargaining. Earlier curiosity and interest in this approach to boosting farm prices led to finding on the books the Capper-Volstead Act of 1922, which more or less exempted farm groups from anti-trust laws when they tried to bargain collectively. At the time it was enacted, the measure was aimed at protecting cooperatives rather than a group such as the NFO, which had no intention of being directly involved in business other than as a service organization.

On October 28, 1958, after the proposed collective bargaining program was presented to county organizations for their almost-unanimous approval, it was adopted as a part of official NFO policy. In short, this plan called for members to hang onto their products until processors had to come to them and pay the NFO-demanded prices for livestock and grains. NFO worked out price scales and also had contracts to offer processors. Another demanding aspect of this program was the membership contract which outlined the member's obligations to make the program effective. A later chapter will be devoted to both these and other contracts written by the NFO.

Before recounting the NFO's early experiments with collective bargaining activities, there are two developments that were significant, or at least interesting, that arose in the first three years of the group's growth. Both spelled trouble for the sputtering but determined NFO.

On September 10, 1957, the national secretary and the

national treasurer of the NFO resigned in a huff after other
officers had accepted financial assistance from a labor
union.[21] Part of their complaint was that this move had
jeopardized the $50,000 bonds they had posted as officers
of the organization. They added in a statement released
to the press:

"It is our opinion that recent actions effected by certain
officials of the NFO have apparently been intended to circumvent the duties entrusted to us as secretary and
treasurer of the NFO."[22]

The statement from NFO headquarters in Corning was
considerably more nonchalant:

"The National Farmers Organization has accepted financial assistance from the United Auto Workers (AFL-CIO)
for the purpose of stepping up its program for achieving
prosperity for agriculture, and is prepared to continue negotiations looking to closer cooperation with various friendly
labor organizations during coming months, legislatively
and otherwise."[23]

The financial assistance amounted to three $1,000 checks
which were reportedly used to start the organization's
monthly newspaper, *The NFO Reporter*. Other than Jay
Loghry's abortive suggestion that he was going to "unionize"
farmers during the earliest organizing and the random appearances of labor union officials at local NFO meetings,
there had been no previous cause to link the farm group
with organized labor. However, accepting the money
branded the NFO as suspect by some of its own members
and other business interests who were to oppose its collective bargaining program. Staley admitted that the whole
thing had been embarrassing to the NFO and said that no
more such aid was ever accepted. Nonetheless, many continued to believe there was some kind of clandestine and
sinister alliance between the NFO and labor unions. A
later chapter will examine some further NFO-union activities.

An attempt to merge with the Farmers Union nearly
blew up the NFO in the winter of 1958. Some NFO mem-

bers had advocated such a move in Iowa in the fall of 1957. One reason for wanting this merger with the larger, older farm group was that leaders of the Iowa NFO were discouraged with the results of their membership drive after having raised dues from a dollar to five dollars per member per year. In short, some felt it was the only way to save what was left of their progress and following so far. Once the Iowa NFO and the National Farmers Union agreed to the merger, the Farmers Union printed a special edition of its weekly publication and sent it to all NFO members in Iowa, welcoming them into the Farmers Union fold. For the Farmers Union, it would have been an almost un-believably easy way to pick up members, since it had had some trouble organizing in Iowa. However, on February 19, 1958, Iowa's state NFO president, Corbin Crawford, was expelled for his activities to further such a merger and the Iowa chapter was disbanded and reorganized by NFO national officials in Corning. Crawford was also a member of the Farmers Union and reputedly on its payroll.[24] Few rank and file NFO members favored the move and the NFO's national board opposed the merger and thus broke it up before it was completed.

A newspaper account of the shakeup said that NFO membership at that time stood at 43,000, of which 15,000 were farmers in Iowa, the only state to have a state-level chapter of the organization.

The adoption of a program for collective bargaining for farmers apparently was appealing enough to set the stage for a comeback in size and power from the group's rapid growth and subsequent early decline. Membership dues were higher than the original dollar and the lengthy mem-bership contract posed excuses for some farmers to avoid joining if they did not fully agree with the proposed plan of action.

With the gathering of strength to attempt conducting "farm strikes," NFO began to keep its total membership secret.

The organization's tool for working into a position to

bargain collectively was not called a "strike" but a "holding action" in which members simply kept at home commodities they might otherwise send to market. NFO plans included "test holding actions" to measure the support they had among their own members and sympathetic outsiders. Once test holding actions indicated the organization had the strength to win their objectives, then an "all-out holding action" would be called. If effective, this would cut off the supplies of livestock and grains until buyers of these raw goods would be willing to buy at NFO's prices and sign contracts assuring that like prices would be paid in the future, regardless of total available supply.

Some 4,000 members met in St. Joseph, Missouri, on August 8, 1959, to vote for the organization's first test holding. It was decided that hogs would be used as the "test commodity" since raising swine was so common throughout the Corn Belt. The first such action was called on October 6 of that year. Orange handbills loaded with black print—some of it very small for a poster—sounded this appeal:

> Begin holding your hogs—the day has arrived. This is an initial demonstration of farmers' bargaining power; hog holding actions start Tuesday, October 6, 1959. . . . On this day and until notified that holding actions are off, all members of the National Farmers Organization are advised to hold for $19.60 per hundredweight on No. 1 and No. 2 hogs weighing 190 to 220 pounds. Value of other weight hogs will be based on relative merit. . . .[25]

A rather lengthy explanation why farmers should participate in this attempt followed. It also gave some of the history of NFO's program. It cautioned farmers to look for rising prices while the holding action was on, but declining prices immediately afterward. It asked that farmers do two things following a holding action to help avoid flooding the markets: "Don't overload markets immediately. For example, if they [farmers] intend to ship 40 hogs, ship only 30." Secondly, it suggested: "Ship next load at lighter weights than planned. These steps will mean no more tonnage of pork produced because of holding actions."[26]

As a testing action, it was announced that it would be of short duration. Oren Lee Staley told the author[27] that areas involved in this first action included several areas in Iowa, western Missouri and two or three counties each in eastern Kansas and Nebraska. He added that this was a relatively small total area because it was done at a time when the movement was just getting started and that it was fully an exploratory effort to determine the program's strength.

"Now, in our first one, we found immediately that farmers would support our actions wherever they understood, wherever you had organization. In outside areas there was sympathy but not real support," Staley said.

"We also found that right off they [those opposed to NFO's program] would start shipping livestock from great distances to make it look like our efforts were not having any effect. And we also noticed that they [persons connected with the markets and packinghouses] kept the prices just about steady. Up a little, maybe down a little, but about the same. We reasoned from then that this was about the only thing those opposing our efforts could do, because if they did anything other, if they allowed a price increase, the farmers would hold—they always do when prices are going up—or, on the other hand, if they dropped them severely, it would make the farmers so mad that then you would have a lot more support.

"Or, if they had admitted that the receipts were not normal, they had to keep saying the receipts were normal because if they said they'd dropped, again farmers would hold. This is what we detected early and decided it would be the strategy we would follow."[28]

A second test holding action was held about six months after the first one. According to the NFO, this one covered several times the geographic area of its forerunner. The NFO said that it had gained strength in Missouri, over a much larger area of Kansas, had grown considerably in

Iowa and in Nebraska. Some organizing had reached Illinois, and there was a sprinkling of support in Indiana. While it probably had little influence on the hog market— again only this one test commodity was involved—the action seemed to hearten the organization. Little or no opposition was voiced in most quarters.

If there is anything to the idea that "a third time is a charm," it certainly was evident in the NFO's third holding action which started on April 3, 1961. However, charm itself was a missing quality as the move unfolded. This time, instead of using only hogs, cattle and sheep marketings were also involved. At the time, the NFO claimed to have gained more strength in Iowa, Missouri, Kansas, Nebraska, Illinois and Indiana. It also had picked up members in southern Minnesota, South Dakota and Wisconsin and had some organization in Ohio, Michigan, Kentucky and Idaho. Participants were advised to hold their choice steers for $32.45 per hundredweight and No. 1 and No. 2 butcher hogs weighing 190 to 210 pounds for a price of $22.75. Both figures exceeded average prices of the week before by about $5 per hundredweight.[29] The price the NFO demanded for choice wooled lambs was $29.45 per hundredweight, which was $11 to $13 over the previous week's average prices at Midwestern markets.

The next day, the NFO announced that it was heartened by the response to its call to hold livestock off the market and that its members would keep it up indefinitely. However, reports of the effect of the withholding conflicted. While the USDA's Market News Service reported that Monday's total of market receipts was the smallest in two years, market interests said it was because the run was usually smaller on the Monday following Easter. But Staley maintained, "There's no question but that we had a definite impact on the receipts." He had added it was "better than expected." Market operators at Chicago, Kansas City, Omaha, Louisville, Columbus and Cincinnati insisted that there was no change from the previous year's Easter Monday, as far as the number of market arrivals was concerned.[30]

By the end of the first week of the holding action, the NFO was again charging that market operators were manipulating market receipt tallies by shipping livestock back and forth from various marketing points in order to make it look as though the holding action was having no effect.

"Eventually they are going to have to start killing some of them [animals] if they don't wear them out first," Staley said. However, USDA reports showed that livestock receipts at the major terminal markets for the week, compared with the previous week, were 196,700 cattle against 212,600, 258,500 hogs compared with 298,900 and 89,300 sheep against 104,200 head the previous week.[31] These figures pleased the NFO. Market interests continued to say it was just a matter of receipts being down because of the post-holiday period. The difference between the run the week before Easter and the week following was a decline of 7 per cent for the latter time. Then, too, the latter period showed a 6 per cent increase in arrivals over the same period a year earlier, so who was to say whether the holding action was really being effective?[32]

On Tuesday of the second week of the holding action, the NFO claimed that its withdrawal from Midwestern livestock markets had put the "squeeze" on sales rings and packing plants but the USDA was reporting normal sales and prices.

"All buying interests are frantic as we go into the second week of action," Staley said. He also charged that market operators were juggling shipments and figures to make trading appear normal. The president of the stockyards company in Omaha snapped back at this accusation, saying that if the market men tried to shuffle livestock, it would be known in fifteen minutes. He termed Staley's claim "really ridiculous."[33] Other market leaders made similar statements.

When the holding action was in its tenth day, Staley

announced that the NFO would continue its campaign. He pointed out that cattle receipts at the twelve major Midwestern markets had fallen to their lowest levels in nine years and said this was an indication that the NFO was making itself felt.[34]

"We feel that the pressure is building and our members have requested that we continue putting the squeeze on," he added.[35]

The USDA in Omaha refused to speculate on whether the drop in arrivals was caused even in part by the holding action, but it did say heavy snows in western Nebraska early in the week and abundant rains elsewhere in the state probably depressed shipments to that market.

On April 17, 1961, two weeks after the action was called, Staley reiterated his statement that the NFO would keep holding. He noted that cattle receipts were lower than usual but that hog and lamb arrivals had increased at major markets. "The spirit of the producers is good," he said, adding, "We'll continue the holding action until next week."[36] But on the morning of April 19, the holding action was over and all began to settle down again.

While the "test" action was going on, NFO'ers trooped to the market places to observe what was going on. Some followed trucks loaded with livestock to see where they were being taken. One case was cited where a couple of men followed a truckload of hogs to a railroad loading point and watched them being put on a livestock car in western Iowa. Upon asking where the hogs were being shipped, they were told that these hogs came from the market at St. Joseph, Missouri, and were being "shuffled up to Omaha." The NFO "checkers," as they were called, managed to get aboard the train to verify what they had been told. They got off the train in Colorado, sorely aware of their being the victims of a prank. The hogs were being shipped to the West Coast for slaughter.

Staley commented that "a lot of the boys had a lot of fun" following trucks, some of which they lost and others which they traced from loading to unloading points. It was through these efforts that the NFO interpreted transit activity to include shuffling of receipts. Members interpreted many moves as "unusual."

On the markets themselves, some impressive crowds of members appeared to see what was being done. Trading, of course, was carried on as usual, but some of the NFO'ers felt that the quality of animals was poorer and that the supplies were smaller than usual.

A report issued from Corning[37] said that "in our organized areas, based on the reports from those areas, we held from 25 to 90 per cent [of the livestock that otherwise would have been marketed]. In reviewing receipts as reported by our checkers at all the marketing points, one important point always stood out. If a substantial number of livestock was shipped from any given area, that area was either an unorganized area or one that was weakly organized."

The report pointed out that NFO headquarters had fewer telephone calls from outlying areas from members who wanted to end the action. This, it said, was indication that farmers were becoming more willing to take part in the holding action. In earlier attempts, some farmers learned that while they held their animals, buyers were getting their supplies from areas where there was no NFO influence. Rather than wishing to continue to hold, these NFO members wanted to go to the areas where animals were being shipped to organize and gain strength for a later try.

The largest groups to visit the central markets showed up on April 12 and 13. Although numbers were difficult to establish, estimates indicated that 1,500 came to Sioux City, 1,200 to Omaha, 2,000 to St. Joseph, 2,000 to Kansas City, 3,000 to East St. Louis, 500 to 700 to Chicago, and around 500 to Evansville, Indiana. Sullen and suspicious, most of the groups were men. Perhaps the only point that both the NFO and market interests agreed on was that there had been no violence and by and large the visiting groups had conducted themselves in a gentlemanly fashion.

The wrap-up of NFO's analysis of its third and final test holding action said:

It appears to us, based on the information collected and on the reports of thousands of farmers, that the shuffling of livestock to make receipts appear normal was accomplished primarily in three categories: (1) Shuffling of livestock from market to market which in some instances means double counting; (2) the shipment of live-stock from direct buying points through terminal markets, which also apparently means double counting; and (3) the use of dealers and others for consignments of livestock to commission firms and prob-ably holding this livestock over to be counted in each day's saleable receipts.

We believe an investigation should determine if there was collu-sion between buying and selling interests to make receipts appear normal, and also, to determine if the above practices are used dur-ing holding actions and other periods of market to control the market.

We must remember that markets usually react, at least to some extent, not on the present supply but on what farmers and processors believe the supply to be. In checking with the representatives of the Market News Service we find that they have no direct check in al-most all instances on the receipts, but that they take the information given them by the present marketing system, and that, also, they take the information given them on the kill from the present market-ing system. In reality, what is happening is that the Market News Service takes the figures given them by the present marketing system, accepts them, and gives the stamp of approval of the USDA.

With the information that we have gathered on shuffling, we also find included in these practices some other points which we believe require immediate investigation to determine if:

(1) The livestock handled in packer and chain store feeding oper-ations is used to regulate the supply in such a manner as to regulate price . . .

(2) Contract deliveries of livestock are used to regulate supply in such a manner as to also regulate price.

(3) The pre-market price and receipt information released by the Market News Service to the packers is used to even out prices. (This, in reality, could mean the Market News Service serves as a third party to carry out procedures not otherwise legal between packers.)[38]

The NFO also called for investigations of "the strange lack of interest shown by Market News Service in verifying their receipt figures" and the structure of the market report-ing system to determine "whether it possesses personnel and facilities to adequately carry out their duties under the present marketing conditions."

The established marketing system seemed to be a corrupt combine of conniving opportunists, if one were to believe all the NFO said about it. It was true that market interests were not admitting that the NFO holding action had any influence on livestock receipts when it actually did have some effect, though not an appreciable one.

As for shuffling receipts, it did not make sense for stockyards companies to foot the bill for hauling animals back and forth. There was no tangible evidence that stockyards firms did this. In the case of packinghouse operations, there were normal movements of animals for slaughter that would appear to be incidents of shufflling. For example, if a packer in Sioux City could not buy a desired kind (weight and degree of finish) of animal on the market where his facilities were located, he might have to depend on other outlets to acquire the animals he needed to fulfill his commitments. This meant he might station buyers at Omaha or Sioux Falls or any other market within a reasonable distance to fill his needs. Once the animals were bought at a different market, the packer had to move them to his own plant to process them. Then, of course, they would be loaded up and taken to Sioux City. Only the largest packers have plants at each of the major terminal markets and there are many meat processors who have but one plant.

Another common practice is for a seller (feeder or farmer) to ship his animals to one market to offer them for sale, but if not satisfied with the price he is bid there, he can and sometimes does load them up again and take them to another market in hopes of "doing better." This has nothing to do with intentional "manipulating" of receipts either.

From the buyer's point of view, there is nothing morally or legally wrong with taking advantage of a lower market elsewhere. If he could feasibly and profitably bring them to his own plant for slaughter, it might look like a shuffling of receipts, but in actuality, it would not be. The practice of buying direct from farmers is not much different, except that the packer goes to the farmer rather than another major market away from his own packinghouse.

How much corruption could marketing interests get away with? Not much. The combined rules and regulations of livestock exchanges and federal agencies do an efficient job of protecting all concerned against unfair trading practices. Severe penalties are meted out for infractions. To say that these rules are never broken would be untrue, but the fact that there are occasional misdealings would not be evidence enough to label the whole marketing system as "corrupt."

The idea of distributing misinformation about market receipts and price trends would serve no other purpose than to hurt the central markets themselves, and those working in them realize this. If, for example, the operators of one market got together and attempted to tell the public that receipts on a given day were at lower levels than usual in an effort to attract more business on that day, it would take only until livestock shippers arrived to realize that they had been misinformed. That would lead to dissatisfaction and their taking their business elsewhere. The same is true in the case of lying about prices, especially if the market interests were to say they were higher than prices actually were.

For markets that are competitive both among their own members and with other terminal points, it would be unreasonable for them to balloon the number of receipts since to do so would indicate a possible oversupply of offerings unless extremely good demand could be shown before the trading was actually done. This would require a dependable crystal ball. To falsely advertise an undersupply of livestock could precipitate a glut and consequent lower prices. Customers of a market would not be taken in twice on that kind of deal, either. Since nearly all firms connected with livestock markets have been built on reputations of honesty and integrity, it was most unlikely that they would abandon their foresight to resort to lies which in the long run could only hurt their business.

By and large, market interests did not publicly offer any opinions on the NFO's early holding actions. A silent opposition was growing, however, and many were glad when the third "test holding action" was over.

Exactly what the test holding actions accomplished was debatable. The first two had little effect, but the third one did attract considerable public attention. For the NFO, the added publicity probably helped to recruit some more members. Staley announced at the end of the action that the NFO had two-thirds of the strength it needed to force processors to negotiate and bargain in good faith for fair prices. When he talked about the prices aimed at in the test holding actions, he claimed that these were not just fair prices but that they were the very minimums farmers could accept and still receive their "cost of production and a reasonable profit." The "cost of production" terminology seemed to be borrowed from the Farmers Union. Other than directing attention to the NFO itself, these moves did show that not all farmers were prospering and that in fact many were in serious financial straits.

Those opposed to the movement again were silent on giving an appraisal of the holding actions. Most scoffed that "they just made a lot of noise" and that in the end the NFO did not have enough power to really affect the markets.

Meanwhile, the NFO faded out of newspaper headlines and its members continued to recruit new followers and to call on processors to explain their program. Representatives of packinghouses and other processing firms courteously listened to NFO delegations, but they were not inclined to take action upon NFO suggestions.

When the NFO held its national convention in Des Moines, Iowa, on December 7 and 8, 1961, members were buzzing with stories of their experiences in the third test holding action. Many were confident that the organization was on the brink of an economic revolution that would give the farmer his rightful place in the sun, especially after enduring so many hard times. As with previous conventions of the group, this one was opened with an invocational prayer and singing of the national anthem. A Des Moines city official made his welcoming speech and business was under way. True to form, speeches were optimistic and encouraged members to "hit 'em again, and harder."

A record number of 3,500 voting delegates was on hand in the Veterans Memorial Auditorium to adopt resolutions at the close of business sessions. With a total of sixteen major points, the list was headed by a pledge "to work with all our energies and minds in every honorable way to bring ourselves and our neighbors together to bargain collectively for the sale of our farm products and that we shall hold together, sell together and act together in all ways according to law, to accomplish fair price settlements with processors of our commodities by contract."[39]

Asserting that it was ready to contract with processors, the NFO recommended that all possible efforts be made to promote signing "master contracts" with processors, that "no sell—no buy" campaigns be directed against processors that resisted signing NFO contracts and that an "all-out holding action" be called if all other efforts to bargain with processors failed. Other resolutions supported legislation which NFO believed would be helpful to farmers and demanded investigations of the marketing systems and the Market News Service.

Highlight of the convention was the appearance of Secretary of Agriculture Orville L. Freeman. As the secretary entered the convention hall, the crowd of some 6,000 stood up to hand him a howling, whistling ovation that lasted several minutes. Once the applause subsided, Freeman launched a speech praising the accomplishments in agriculture that had been brought about in the first year of his administration. He pointed out that farm income had increased 9 per cent during 1961 and that government stocks of feed grains would be reduced for the first time in nine years. In exploring methods to help alleviate the farm problem, he dwelled on his plan of "managed abundance" and suggested the use of production adjustment and producer marketing programs which would be designed, administered and financed by farmers themselves.

"If the producers of a commodity want a market program, then the department will provide the technical assistance and advice. It will, at the request of the industry, hold hearings and referendums," the agriculture secretary said.[40]

As the address progressed, Freeman was interrupted seven times by standing ovations that thundered through the auditorium. However, the loudest roar of approval came when he told the enrapt crowd:

"Our greatest problem is that we don't have enough bargaining power in the market place!"*

Freeman had told the delegation exactly what they wanted to hear and they loved him for it. When he left the podium and came down from the platform, farmers eager to shake his hand nearly buried him. It was a welcome he would never forget.

Some months later, when asked by the author what he thought of the agriculture secretary's speech at the national convention, NFO president Staley smiled, "I think he got just a little carried away."

Although the NFO wasn't quite ready for another action, it was apparent that the calling of holding actions wasn't over. Officials of the organization said "the day is getting near" for calling an all-out withholding, which they said would "win the battle." But members were cautioned that it would not be easy and that more strength was needed to really assure a victory. They continued to work toward that goal.

STARTING IN THE FALL OF 1961, an exchange of open letters between NFO president Staley and American Farm Bureau president Charles B. Shuman appeared in Chicago-published semi-monthly *The Prairie Farmer*. The two had once had a difference of opinion on the agricultural problem

---

* At this point in his address, Secretary Freeman departed from the pre-released text of his remarks and in effect personally endorsed the NFO's policies. News media covering the convention evidently overlooked this endorsement.

in an encounter in Washington and the letters they wrote
led to a challenge for a public debate.

> . . . I read the letter from Mr. Shuman in answer to my chal-
> lenge to him to discuss the issues he raised in his first letter to the
> "Readers Say" column. . . .
>   He said in his letter he would accept the challenge but then
> seemed to express reluctance. He said he did not believe that farm-
> ers wanted their leaders fighting and arguing. I did not challenge
> Mr. Shuman to a fight or an argument.[41]

The stipulations that the NFO president asked were
that the debate consist of 30-minute statements by both involved and a question and answer period following these
two talks. He asked that it take place somewhere in central
Illinois in a "meeting place large enough to accommodate
a large number of farmers that I am certain are eager to
attend." Staley ended the lengthy letter:

> Mr. Shuman has said he is willing to appear—but is he really
> willing? He can prove that he is by naming the date, time and place.
> His decision will let it to be known to all farmers whether he is will-
> ing or whether he is afraid.

In a later issue of the farm publication, Shuman wrote:

> Oren Lee Staley, president of the NFO, asked me to set a time and
> place for the "discussion" he proposes. I suggested two such times
> but neither met his approval.
>   He repeats his challenge in the January 6 issue of *The Prairie
> Farmer* and I accept. Since he is concerned that the maximum num-
> ber would hear the discussion, I propose that it be held over radio at
> at time to suit our mutual convenience. [Chicago radio station] WGN
> has offered its facilities. If Mr. Staley will suggest some dates, I
> will be glad to help make the arrangements.[42]

The great debate never materialized. NFO'ers joked that
"Charlie" was afraid to face up to the spellbinder Staley.
There was no doubt that Staley was a powerful speaker who
could arouse a crowd. Shuman, on the other hand, seemed
to be a quiet, fatherly leader who would be out of place de-
bating with a man whose voice often reached a level of
virtual shouting at the peak of a speech.

Staley's comment: "In the end, he declined to debate."
Shuman chuckled before telling the author his version
of the challenge: "Oh, that. Staley wanted the discussion
held before a large crowd to back him up. We couldn't
agree on where to hold it, so it never developed." While
there was some friction between the NFO and the Farm
Bureau, this encounter between the leaders of the two
groups was probably the best-humored of their differences
of opinion evaluating the farm problem and possible solu-
tions.

"THE SHOWDOWN is getting closer. The processors will
either bargain in good faith or they will have to accept the
consequences and responsibility of an all-out holding
action," Staley wrote in his "President's Message" column
of the March 1962 NFO *Reporter*, which in its lead article
said:

Area meat bargaining committees have launched a series of meetings with a number of processors, as activities surrounding the
NFO's whirlwind drive to the bargaining table continues to mount.
This drive is a two-pronged operation which includes offering the
processors an opportunity to bargain in good faith and at the same
time exerting every possible effort to continue strengthening the organization for an all-out holding action in the event the processors
do not choose to bargain in good faith.
Undoubtedly there were many who felt that processors would
never even discuss prices or marketing conditions with the NFO
marketing area bargaining committees. Any idea of this nature already has been proven wrong.
There has not been one refusal on the part of meat processors
to meet with NFO marketing area bargaining committees.
The discussions between NFO committees and processors have
been friendly and businesslike. The processors are businessmen and
they know that the agricultural industry has problems which vitally
affect them as well as producers.
They also recognize the tremendous growing strength of the NFO
and realize the power that will be mustered in an all-out holding
action.

Quoting Staley, the paper said, "It is likely that friendly
conversations with processors will continue, but in the end

it is probable that NFO will have to prove to them through an all-out holding action that they must sign a contract and recognize the farmer's right to price his products."

While enthusiasm and support for an all-out holding action was being whipped up by NFO leadership, another controversy developed, again in the NFO's favor, as far as getting widespread publicity was concerned.

On July 15, 1962, the Committee for Economic Development, which called itself a non-profit, non-political economic research and education organization supported by voluntary contributions from business concerns, offered a program to improve the profits of agriculture without government controls and to establish free markets for farm products. Although the Washington-based committee claimed its purpose was to help determine through objective research those economic policies which would encourage attainment and maintenance of high production and employment within the framework of a free society, it was not long before NFO members were calling it the "Committee for Economic Disaster" and likening its policies to Hitlerism.

The CED statement said the heart of the farm problem was a need for "massive adjustment" of resources, especially human resources, then committed to farm production. It said that the reduction of the farm labor force by about one-third, or two million workers, was needed in the next five years. It also called for the immediate reduction of the prices of wheat, cotton, rice and feed grains so farmers would not be misled by high price supports into retaining excessive resources in agriculture. Noting that production methods on farms had become more efficient and needed less manpower, plus the belief that governmental farm programs had impeded the flow of labor from agriculture to other fields by artificially keeping farm prices up, the CED recommended stressing vocational training other than in farming in predominantly agricultural regions and giving more federal aid to public education.

Also, the CED suggested preparing young people from farms for other careers before they became committed to agriculture. It described its "adaptive program" as one which "seeks to achieve adjustment to economic reality without imposing hardships, by means of programs that promote adjustment but cushion the effects upon people and property. Such an approach calls for action by government working with the free market, and not against it and by permitting full production rather than by limiting production," the CED said.

Despite the good intentions of the committee, its recommendations sparked furor among some farmers.

About a month after the program was announced,[43] some farm groups, especially the NFO, were planning boycotts directed against firms whose executives belonged to the Committee for Economic Development. Among these were Ford Motor Company, John Deere Tractor Company, Sears-Roebuck and Company, Montgomery Ward Company, General Motors and Pillsbury.

A Kansan who was on President Kennedy's agricultural advisory committee said he was personally organizing a boycott in his state. He added he was changing his mind about where he would buy a $25,000 tractor.

"I don't believe Ford and Deere executives realize farmers spend $40 billion a year with American industry . . . but I am sure as hell going to bring it to their attention," he told United Press International in Topeka.

In Kansas and other states, the NFO was planning a boycott of its own. Members of the farm group were collecting the bulky mail order catalogs of Sears and Montgomery Ward stores to take them back and dump them on the stores' front steps as a protest against the firms being connected with the CED.

On August 17, NFO'ers stacked about 200 Sears catalogs in front of that firm's store in Lincoln, Nebraska. A representative of the farm said in Chicago, "This is ridiculous. Sears has been the farmer's friend for years."

Meanwhile, in Corning, NFO officials announced that these demonstrations were not an organized boycott, but spontaneous and simultaneous efforts on the farmers' part to let the firms know how they felt. An officially proclaimed boycott by the NFO was believed illegal in some states, so Corning did not take credit for the picketing that was to follow in several Midwestern cities.

The next day, August 18, 200 NFO members and their wives quietly gathered at a huge Sears store in Omaha to protest. They stacked 150 catalogs at the store's entrance. The president of the Nebraska NFO asked that store officials in Omaha repudiate support of the CED plan, even though a Sears executive was a member of the committee.

A representative of the Omaha store told the gathering, "So far as Omaha is concerned, it is the Sears feeling that we cannot go along with Mr. [Theodore] Houser [a member of CED].[44]

Similar "catalog marches" were held at St. Joseph, Missouri; Kearney, Nebraska; Austin, Minnesota and Corning and Mason City, Iowa. At the same time, parades around Ford Company agencies in twelve Midwest states were planned by NFO members. In Sioux Falls, South Dakota, for example, about 30 farmers drove a caravan of Fords around one agency to show their disapproval of a former Ford Company director being connected with the CED. In Madison, Wisconsin, 92 Ford cars and trucks circled one firm; in Ottumwa, Iowa, between 40 and 50 farmers formed a caravan for the same purpose, and similar demonstrations took place in Kentucky, Missouri and Nebraska.[45]

Eventually, Sears and Ford publicly announced that they did not officially endorse the CED program and that their employees who were members of the committee were advocates of the plan solely as private citizens. That took care of the demonstrations. NFO claimed another victory and certainly scored a vast amount of national publicity for its efforts. Although the demonstrations seemed to indicate that they were being conducted by wrathful and vengeant farmers, they were carried on without incident or unfriendliness between the individual dealers and the NFO'ers involved.

Just as this controversy was calming down, the call went out for an NFO "meeting for action" in Des Moines. In view of Staley's threats to call an all out holding action, there appeared to be more excitement ahead.

5

THE BIG MEETING FOR ACTION

Holding actions called by the National Farmers Organization were usually preceded by "meetings for action." The purpose of these gatherings was for members to vote on whether they wanted to hold. Generally, it was a foregone conclusion that NFO would hold, but the meetings offered a system of democratic process and gave individual members the feeling that they were taking part in the over-all design of policy. Another aspect of these meetings was the opportunity they offered to whip up enthusiasm and to show the public how large a meeting the NFO could muster. It was good for publicity and morale.

The first such gathering was held on August 8, 1959, preceding the October 6 test holding action that year. A year later, on August 9, 1960, another one was called. The third meeting for action came on August 28, 1962, sounding the signal for NFO to call its first "all out holding action." These meetings were larger and louder than the annual national conventions of the organization held usually in December. When the 1961 meeting for action was held in Des Moines, some 13,000 members trooped into town to whoop it up for the NFO's collective bargaining program. At that time the movement boasted it had held "the largest farm meeting in history." [1]

Following on the tail of the protest against the Committee for Economic Development program, the 1962 meeting for action was even larger and louder. Thousands of farmers, some with their wives, converged on Des Moines by carloads and busloads. A smattering came by commercial airlines, but most arrived by buses that carried banners advertising the NFO meeting.[2]

It was a hot, clear Tuesday, a day many Iowans would consider to be "a good corn-growing day" when the throngs of farm folk began filling the mammoth Veterans Memorial Auditorium. Although the CED protest had gotten its results of disavowal of endorsement of the program by Sears and Ford, many NFO'ers brought with them to Des Moines loads of the bulky mail order catalogs to stack on the front steps of the auditorium. The pile mounted to over five feet high, and after people stopped dumping the books someone rigged a small stick gallows at the top of the pile. Dangling from the hanging tree was a rag doll with a hand-printed note pinned on its front.

> **"Mr. 'C.E.D.' (the rat)**
> **He was caught chasing farmers off the farm.**
> **(1 down—199 to go.)"**

The ratio at the bottom of the note referred belatedly to one large firm giving in to NFO's demands of repudiation of the CED plan. The other figure was the remainder of the committee's 200 member firms.

Inside the huge meeting place confusion was king until the meeting was brought to order. Many delegates couldn't find their designated blocks of seats, so farmers manned a public address system to boom out appeals such as, "Saline County, Nebraska, where are you?" Already the hall was becoming too warm for comfort and a tobacco-smoke haze bore down on the crowd. Some groups paraded in picket lines around the sides of the main floor of the auditorium, carrying placards objecting to the CED plan. As delegates filled the main floor and balconies, blocks of seats were identified by banners and signs naming counties and states. Once the main part of the auditorium had reached its capacity of 15,000, the overflow crowd of some

5,000 more was diverted into the basement, where public address speakers were set up so the members could hear the proceedings.

The meeting got underway with requests to clear the aisles and sides of the meeting place in accordance with the fire marshal's regulations. The buzz of the crowd quieted to a murmur and an invocational prayer, followed by the pledge of allegiance to the flag with everyone participating, and the singing of the national anthem by a baritone, started the day's program. A representative of the Des Moines Chamber of Commerce told the NFO'ers they were "always welcome—welcome always. And have a successful day and a safe journey home." President Staley introduced national officers and members of the national board of directors of NFO. Then it was time for speeches.

Offering a 30-minute harangue was Vince Rossiter, the president of a small bank in Hartington, Nebraska. Rossiter had followed the movement's activities closely and appeared at many NFO meetings. He was an ardent supporter of the organization's program for collective bargaining and was duly concerned with economic aspects of the farm problem, both for the farmer and the small-town businessman.

Rossiter praised NFO members for their patience and forbearance in pushing their program. He congratulated them for the response to the call for this meeting for action. Getting on into his message, he cited a conversation with a bank customer who had come into his office to renew his farm loan note.

"I asked him how long he wanted his paper extended," Rossiter recounted. "Without batting an eyelash, he replied, 'Forever.' Then, I asked him, just for the sake of conversation, what he'd do if he had a million dollars. 'Pay my bills—as far as it would go.' "

Remarking how he enjoyed seeing the slogans put up at different NFO meetings, Rossiter said the one he liked best at this gathering was: "It's time we quit farming farmers and started processing processors." Recalling a sign he had seen on a trip through Wyoming, he said he thought its message was appropriate for the NFO: "Kissin' Don't Last—Cookin' Do!" He told the audience it was about time for farmers to "stop kissin'."

He pointed out that in the preceding ten years, the nation's economy had rolled along downhill until it was approaching the day that it would be similar to those of the late 1920's and early 1930's. He warned that if "we run out of credit, we'll regress into another depression."

Saying that agricultural production had increased a predicted 35 per cent for the 1962 crop year, farmers would accept $2.4 billion less for it, compared with 1947–49 production and prices. "Farmers are underpaid and this must be corrected by farmers themselves—no one else, apparently, is going to do it," he said. He added that farmers would have made $250 billion more than they did in the past decade had the prices paid to them followed levels of other segments of the national economy.

"Time is running out," he warned. "Do you think that the consumer or the Congress will tolerate a raise in food prices if 18 million to 25 million heads of families are out of work and feeding 40 million to 50 million mouths on $25 to $30 a week unemployment checks?"

After lauding the NFO members for their protests against the CED plan, Rossiter told them, "When you decide you're going to resolve this [cost-price squeeze] problem, you decide also that you're in for one of the most rugged fights of your life and that you're going to be abused and mistreated and that you're not going to get credit for doing anything. . . . Until you can get just as rugged as these people you're dealing with [processors and buyers of farm products], you don't have a ghost of a chance at attaining your goals."

Asking for the blessing and assistance of Almighty God in NFO's efforts, Rossiter concluded: "Let's stop kissin' and start cookin'."

Oren Lee Staley delivered the only other prepared address at the meeting. Dressed in the usual dark suit, the big Missourian took the podium and soon was hammering down his oratorical points in a loud and angry voice. He began:

"This afternoon we contemplate decisions that we are going to make together, decisions which will very well determine the future of agriculture. . . .

"If not for the NFO, all farmers would have to look forward to is going to the marketplace and asking 'What will you give me?' Here we are, businessmen representing a $211 billion investment, 13 per cent of the nation's total investment, but last year [1961] receiving less than 4 per cent of the national income. I ask you, is that good business? I say it's an insult to the business intelligence of the American farmers!" he shouted.

Saying that he was proud to be a part of the movement that started in Nebraska against the CED proposals, Staley termed the Committee for Economic Development the "Committee for Economic Disaster. It was well planned—oh, yes, well planned to starve you out of business. . . . I say it's time that other people learn to run their own affairs and let them know that the American farmers can run their own affairs without someone else telling them how to do it."

Relating that he had received a telegram from an official of Sears, Roebuck and Company, Staley said this may have been "a little disappointing to you and spoiled a lot of fun, by the looks of the catalogs out front." Sears had divorced itself from the CED policy. Staley then read a telegram from the head of American Oil Company and Standard Oil of Indiana, assuring that "neither participated in preparing this report and have taken no position in its support."

Moving on to the business at hand, Staley reported, "Our bargaining committees have met with processors and not one single processor has refused to meet with us. They have reported that these discussions have been friendly and businesslike. Many committees have visited processors twice. We have given processors sufficient time to make their decisions. . . .

"I don't want you to vote for this battle or to go into this battle unless you're determined to win. And I stand here this afternoon before you as your leader, as your president, but just feeling as though I'm another one of the members, just feeling that we're all in this together, that we're all farmers, whether some of you that live on the Pennsylvania line or some of you that are from the state of Idaho, or some of you, as I see St. Louis County, Minnesota, and some of you are on up toward the Canadian line and into Kentucky and Oklahoma. It doesn't make any difference where we're at, we're farmers, we've got the same problems and we've organized for one thing. . . .

"I'd hate to be on the side that's saying, 'Let it go on as it is.' I'd hate to be on the side that's saying to the American farmers, 'Continue to go to the marketplace and say 'What will you give me?'

"I wouldn't feel that I was representing farmers; I would feel that every member of the NFO should get Staley back to the farm in northwest Missouri just as fast as possible and I'd say you all ought to ride me out of here on a rail if I were saying that to the American farmers. And I'd say that's exactly what you should do and what you'd be entitled to do and I'd say that this is exactly the position that you should take as members when you're out battling for a price and a farmer says, 'No, no, you shouldn't do this.' Just say to him you're mighty proud to be able to have enough backbone to stand up and battle for what you know is right. That's important; and it's very, very important."

As Staley's hour-long tirade progressed, he was interrupted at nearly every pause by applauding. Occasionally some listeners in far parts of the auditorium would shout that they couldn't hear and in one instance Staley had to ask those standing along the sides of the main floor to be quiet so others could hear. Tobacco smoke had accumulated into a denser fog and the August warmth inside the auditorium was still more oppressive. In the press section near the platform, reporters busily scribbled their notes. At the front of the high stage, both professional and amateur talents were attending tape recorders.

One young farmer sitting by his machine grinned at the author and remarked, "I don't much feel like listening to him [Staley] this afternoon, but some cold day next winter when I don't have much to do, I'll play it back and hear what he said."

Staley himself was sweating under the labor of his speech. While some observers cynically remarked that he "sounds like a real hog caller," it was with caution to whom they commented on the leader's energetic use of his powerful lungs.

Back at the podium:

"If all of our members will work, if you will keep contacting the non-members, to get them to join, and if you will work and keep your members informed, and if you will go into this battle with an attitude that you're going to stick until you win, then this afternoon we're ready to recommend full confidence that the battle be waged. *Are you with us or are you not?*" Staley shouted so loud his voice cracked.

The audience cheered and whistled and clapped their enthusiastic approval. This was the "vote" approving the call for NFO's first all out holding action. There was no question offered whether anyone present opposed the move.

He reiterated that NFO had given processors fair opportunity to bargain in good faith and that NFO had also offered a proposal for disposal of surplus commodities and a farm product promotion program.

"If the consumer should run short of food, don't let them blame the farmers; let them put the blame where it is—and that is that the buyers and processors of farm commodities have not recognized the right of the farmers to price their products. That's whose fault it is and no one else's. . . ."

Staley announced the recommendations of the NFO directors:

● That an all out holding action start at midnight, August 31, 1962. The recommended prices to hold for were set at $32.45 per hundredweight on choice beef cattle weighing 800 to 1,000 pounds. The desired price on No. 1

and No. 2 butcher hogs averaging 190 to 210 pounds was listed at $22.75 per hundredweight. Top grade fat wooled lambs were priced at $29.45 per hundredweight. All other grades of these kinds of livestock were to be priced on relative merit.

● It was suggested that members put their livestock on a short-grain ration to avoid an increase in the total meat tonnage while the holding action was in effect.

● Members were advised to carry out plans to store all of the corn and soybeans they possibly could and hold for the established price of $1.49 per bushel for No. 2 or better yellow corn and $2.56 per bushel for No. 1 soybeans. Other grades would be priced according to relative merit.

● The calling of area meetings for dairy members was recommended "sometime after the start of the holding action for them to determine" whether they wanted dairy products included in the all out holding action and based on the decisions reached in these area meetings, leave the final decision of including dairy products in the holding to the national board of directors. If a dairy product holding were called, the recommended asking prices were to be $6.05 per hundredweight for Grade A milk (about 13 cents per quart) and $5 per hundredweight for "manufactured" milk [milk going to powdering plants and other processes outside of direct food uses; this class of milk was often considered "surplus" production].

After additional applause approving these recommendations, Staley opened the floor for discussion. To cope with the massive crowd, eight microphones had been spotted in different areas of the main floor. Unfortunately for those members in the basement of the building, there were no such facilities set up there for them to have their say. Each microphone was manned by NFO members from different states who, were responsible for letting delegations be heard and for keeping eager speakers orderly while waiting their turn at the microphones. The facilities were numbered, 1 through 8, and their use was rotated in order. Delegates wishing to speak had to give their names and identify their home counties before giving their views. While this arrangement would seem potentially very cumbersome with such a large gathering, it worked surprisingly smoothly.

One of the first suggestions to come from the floor was that the all out holding action be started immediately. This idea was put down, however, since the board and most members felt that the three marketing days between the meeting for action and the holding itself would provide members an opportunity to prepare for the action and to sell whatever livestock that was immediately ready for market.

Another member moved that members go to their local grocery stores and buy several pounds of meat to deplete their retail supplies. Staley said this practice would be illegal if the NFO, as an organization, endorsed it. However, he said, individual members might follow that suggestion if they pleased.

Another member suggested that a dairy product holding action be called to coincide with the other holding activities. However, members generally agreed that following the board's recommendations in this area was a better idea.

Much touting of the approaching holding action was made from the floor. As the tone of offerings from the audience turned to simple but ardent messages of encouragement, Staley gave his attention to a press conference. However, stubborn farmers who wanted to have their say to the dispersing crowd had to be quieted by Staley before the session with reporters got successfully under way.

The NFO president told reporters that he believed the organization had between 25 and 30 per cent of the nation's agricultural output under its influence at the outset of the holding action. However, he said that the holding action might require a considerable period of time before its total effect would be felt by processors. He predicted that the first two weeks would serve as a "shake-out" period.

After that, farmers who "really mean business" would hold
for whatever length of time was necessary to force processors to sign contracts.

Market interests and farmers on both sides of the NFO
movement took a "wait-and-see" attitude toward the holding action as the beginning of it approached on Labor Day
weekend, 1962.

6

THE ALL OUT HOLDING ACTION OF 1962

As NFO MEMBERS jubilantly filed out of Des Moines' Veterans Memorial Auditorium, fired up by Staley's vociferous speechmaking, they knew they had many preparations to make in the three days elapsing between their impressive meeting in the Iowa capital and the outset of the holding action at midnight the following Friday. Calling on neighbors to persuade them to support the NFO effort was an issue of paramount importance. Those who had hogs and cattle ready for market needed to dispose of them before the action started.

As for non-farmer market interests, including stockyards firms, livestock commission companies and packers, the predominant attitude was one of alert observation but little concern over the outcome of the declared moratorium. Some of the livestock commission men who traveled the countryside on usual late-in-the-week calls on farmers encountered some unfriendliness and occasional sympathy of non-member farmers who were "going along with the holding action just to see what happens."

Most newspapers looked on with interest as the holding action approached, waiting for the news to happen. A few that didn't believe the move would work, said so on their editorial pages, but not in very harsh terms. A major daily in South Dakota commented editorially:

"We don't think the National Farmers Organization idea

will work—because the American farmer is the most individualistic operator in the world. "Some farmers will not go along with the NFO, and will not hold their grain and livestock from the market. This, too, is their privilege—and the NFO should not attempt to coerce them into doing so."

Near the end of the lengthy editorial, the newspaper pointed out, "Not all American agriculture is flying a distress signal by any means. Prices could be better—but they've been a lot worse than they are right now."[1]

More or less in answer to this, South Dakota's representative on the NFO's national board of directors said: "Farmers can't afford to sit around on their calloused posteriors much longer. They are going to have to take some calculated risks. We are going to stay with this thing until it's solved, that's all there is to it!"[2]

Other critics of the approaching NFO action voiced their opinions politely. The president of the Iowa Farm Bureau said his organization recognized the right of farmers to market their products or not, but insisted that legal action would be used against any threats or intimidation.[3] He added: "To insure this right, we will insist that the proper officials take immediate action to enforce laws if there are any threats, intimidations or any other attempts to interfere with farmers' rights to market their products."[4]

The National Livestock Feeders Association, headquartered in Omaha, issued a statement calling for orderly marketing. "Practically no factor in pricing is any more meaningful than a well-spread and even supply," the statement said. Although it did not mention the NFO by name, it said that "finished livestock and fresh meat are extremely perishable. Neither can be held in storage or in feedlots for any long period without loss."[5] It added that interference with the flow of livestock to market would, when ended, cause bunched shipments and a consequent oversupply that would depress prices.

In Kansas City, Secretary of Agriculture Orville Freeman was on hand for the dedication of a federal agricultural data processing center and spent 45 minutes visiting with NFO president Oren Lee Staley and other leaders of the farm group. Following the session with Staley, Freeman said in a news conference that the NFO action was a "very dramatic example" of frustration among farmers and expressed sympathy with it. However, he added that he was not "expert enough to make a prediction" on the outcome. "The trouble in such actions before was that not enough farmers would participate," he observed.[6]

Nebraska Representative Ralph Beermann, a Republican, blamed unsound government farm policy for the NFO's calling the holding action and added that he was sympathetic to the action but thought that the organization would face difficulties in achieving its objective of higher prices.[7]

Meanwhile, Staley announced in Corning, that NFO checkers would man four posts in each county to observe the flow of livestock to the markets. He revealed that Illinois members were putting finishing touches on temporary storage facilities for soybeans. With confidence, he predicted that the drive would be felt in meat markets within a week. "We are getting enthusiastic response from farmers in general," he reported.[8] Declining to announce the name of the firm involved, Staley also made public that the first processor had signed a contract with the NFO. Whether the processor was a packer or in the grain business was not disclosed. The size of the signer was also left a mystery.[9]

As a part of preparation for the holding action, it was apparent that some NFO'ers were unloading livestock ready for market. Compared with the supply of the week before, arrivals at the twelve major markets numbered 48,000 hogs on Friday, up 11,000 head from the week before. That Friday's cattle receipts were double the number of the previous Friday, totaling 18,000 on the day before the holding action was to start. Sheep and lamb receipts at the major markets were estimated at 6,000, about 2,000 more than the same day a week earlier.[10]

Staley noted that "although receipts were higher than usual for a Friday preceding a holiday [Labor Day], prices were also up. The processors are trying to stock up, even at higher prices, so they can weather out a sudden drop in supplies after our members pull out of the market," he claimed.[11]

Another vote of support came from the president of the Kansas Farmers Union, who sent 500 letters to officers of his organization urging an attitude of "friendliness and co-operation toward the holding action." He termed it "a noble experiment conducted by hard-working, dedicated family farmers."[12]

In an attempt to deplete retail meat supplies at a super-market, more than 100 farmers converged on a store in Kirksville, Missouri, with intentions of buying all the meat on hand.[13] However, the buying spree was not successful, a spokesman for the store said later.[14]

Over the Labor Day weekend, members of the organization began to set up observation posts out in the country and at country buying stations, terminal stockyards and some packinghouses. Under the NFO "minuteman system," these people were to collect data on activity and forward them to state and national offices for tabulation. Reasons for having their own observers went back to the NFO's mistrust of USDA tabulations of livestock market arrivals. Additionally, the members were curious about the quality of animals arriving, where they came from and, of course, how many were actually showing up for market.

At Omaha, for example, members parked a camper-equipped pickup truck at a stockyards' entrance. This was manned by at least two persons 24 hours a day. When a truck swung onto the viaduct leading to the unloading chutes, these checkers would step to the edge of the street to observe the contents of the truck. They also noted the name on the truck and jotted down the license number and home state. These data were taken to local headquarters set up in a motel and the information was then sent on to Corning, where tabulations were prepared and sent out several times a week during the holding action. Any hour of the day visitors or workers in the stockyards area would see NFO members standing around their observation post or sitting in cars, watching any activity. Since the stockyards facilities in the major central markets are private property, these NFO "checkpoints" were established with the permission of the owners of the yards, usually with the stipulation that they could stay as long as there was no interference with usual functions at the marketplace. A majority of members at these checkpoints were careful not to get in the way or cause any disturbances, although there were exceptions as the holding action progressed.

All was relatively quiet in the marketplace over the Labor Day weekend. Since there was no trading on Saturday and Sunday, which was normal, nor on the following holiday Monday, few arrivals were coming into the stockyards and there was little for NFO checkers to see. Meanwhile, the countryside was reportedly bustling with members calling on their neighbors in attempts to get everyone signed up or at least to get assurances of support of the holding action. On Tuesday, September 4, the holding action got underway in earnest.

Staley said, "It will be a big day at the terminal markets," pointing out that receipts were customarily heavy after a holiday. However, he predicted the holding action would succeed, possibly in two or three weeks.[15]

Taking a slightly different approach to making the holding action effective, the Wright County, Iowa, NFO chapter announced that its members had raised $25,000 to take options on hogs in their county at a dollar above the local August 31 market price.[16] The money had been collected by voluntary subscription to divert hogs from normal market channels.

"This is being done to prove to farmers in our county

that we are confident of victory in the all out holding action," the group said in a public statement.[17] Following this announcement and through the holding action, no more news coverage was given the Wright County proposal. To the best of the author's knowledge, none of the money was used for purchasing hogs. In all likelihood, it was returned to the subscribers since the initial announcement of the move had served its purpose of attracting publicity.

Trouble was brewing out in the country. Recalling complaints by truckers who had been followed in earlier test holding actions, it became apparent that someone was taking more drastic action than trailing or simply cursing the drivers who were moving livestock to market. Complaints were made at St. Joseph, Missouri, early in the first week of the holding action, that truckers had encountered groups of men along highways who tried to flag down trucks. In two instances rocks had been thrown through the windshields of the big carriers as they roared by.[18] A Missouri highway patrol spokesman said he was hesitant to connect these incidents with the NFO and suggested that pranksters might have been responsible for the rock throwing.[19]

One trucker told this story:

"We were traveling on Highway 71 south of Maryville, [Missouri] about 35 miles from the St. Joseph market. We drove by a bunch of men at a crossroad—and they didn't try to stop us. I can't say for sure who they were. Then a car passed us, got ahead, turned around and came back toward my truck.

"As this car met us, a bucket of rock was thrown at us. Our windshield was smashed and glass flew all over," the driver said.

"We could have been killed!" a passenger in the vehicle exclaimed. Highway patrolmen found rocks two to three inches in diameter in the truck which was loaded with about 50 butcher hogs and traveling 50 miles per hour when hit by the rocks.[20]

Livestock auction sales were interrupted by NFO backers in two northern Missouri towns.[21] At Palmyra, a sale was called off on the day after Labor Day because a pen of hogs was turned loose, a telephone wire cut and a crowd hooted and clapped hands to interfere with the operation. In Lewiston, 1,500 to 2,000 chanting persons gathered before the sale was scheduled to start and blocked alleys to the sales ring so the auction was delayed for eight hours.[22]

Upon receiving reports of violence, Missouri Governor John Dalton called on local law enforcement agencies to deal with this kind of occurrence. "The State of Missouri will not tolerate any lawbreaking activities by anyone or any group," he warned.[23]

Rock throwing led to shooting at livestock trucks. In the St. Joseph marketing area, two farmers reported that they had been shot at.[24] One incident occurred near an NFO checkpoint on U.S. Highway 275 as an Oakland, Iowa, farmer was returning from St. Joseph with a load of feeder cattle. He said three shots were fired at his truck near Savannah and that one .22 caliber bullet hit a dual tire on his truck. When police questioned men at the checkpoint, they denied knowledge of the shooting.

A Westboro, Missouri, farmer said his truck was shot at, too, on a trip from St. Joseph to his home and that he found two slugs in a tire and a hole in a mud flap on the vehicle.

By Wednesday of the first week of the holding action, reports of threats and more vandalism came from northwest Missouri and Wisconsin. Near Maryville, Missouri, a woven wire fence around a 240-acre pasture and a barbed-wire fence around an 80-acre pasture were cut in 86 places.[25]

"I think I know who did it as well as you do," the owner told a newspaper reporter. The victim was president of a farmer-owned cooperative which operated a hog buying station. The directors of the co-op had voted not to close down its hog buying during the NFO holding action. The owner of the farm planned to offer a reward for the arrest and conviction of the vandals.[26]

A young trucker at Clearmont, Missouri, said he had

been warned by two men who flashed a light into a bedroom window and said that the only way he would be free from interference "would be to travel with an armed escort at both the front and rear" of his truck. He identified the two as NFO members.[27]

In Wisconsin, a newsman and a packinghouse representative reported being threatened by NFO people.[28]

While rowdyism and outright violence colored the NFO holding action with an element of sensationalism even in the first week, there were several developments at the markets that gave NFO officials cause to claim they were winning in their drive to control prices. Significant, but disputed, was the reduction of livestock receipts in all marketing systems.

Ignoring or denying the charges of responsibility for scattered violence, Staley and his lieutenants confidently claimed they were gaining the upper hand in their "battle" for better prices. They announced two more processors had signed their "master contract" and that the trend would continue. Although their claims were to be disputed, the prospects for holding action results looked rosy, if one were to listen only to the militant farm group's side of the story.

Announced hikes in wholesale and retail meat prices caused Staley to charge that the increases had been made too soon by packers and other interests. While it would be logical for dressed meat prices to rise with the climb in liveweight livestock prices, Staley claimed that the boost was being made on meat from animals that were slaughtered before the holding action started.[29] He charged that the processors were taking "unfair advantage" of the consumer. Increased demand for meat was pinned on the holding action and "a fear of a shortage."[30] At Kansas City, a packer said wholesale dressed meat prices went up 4 to 6 cents a pound in the early part of the NFO holding action, during a period when they usually declined.[31] Retail chain stores based in Chicago and St. Louis, along with major packers and the Market News Service, predicted prices would rise, perhaps as much as 10 to 15 cents a pound during the second week of the holding action.[32]

Refuting Staley's charge of "unfair advantage" in raising prices of meat, the president of a major packing firm with a plant in Omaha said that price levels are governed by "the law of supply and demand and what we have to pay for meat determines what we have to charge for it."[33]

In answer to the NFO leader's statement that higher prices were being paid on meat slaughtered before the holding action began, the executive said, "No packer has much of a backlog of meat. It's perishable and we have to get rid of it. This is particularly true of beef.

"Beef shipped Friday probably came from cattle we killed Wednesday. We sell beef daily. We kill it, put it in the cooler, chill it out and ship every day," he added.[34]

Whether or not the NFO holding action was responsible, several packers began laying off workers during the first week of the NFO drive. In Iowa, 200 workers were to be idled in Mason City, but officials at the plant said they could not say if the holding action was the reason for this. They added, however, that livestock receipts were "lower than we anticipated."[35] Another packer said they were laying off 200 workers at their Waterloo, Iowa, plant and closing another packinghouse at Columbus Junction, Iowa, because receipts were so light. Two hundred packinghouse workers were to be furloughed at Ottumwa, Iowa, if reduced livestock supplies continued, another meat processor announced. Similar moves were made at Dubuque, Iowa, and in Marshalltown, Iowa, killing crews at one plant were sent home early one day because there was only half of the normal supply of animals on hand.

Although Staley said, "We're getting an earlier reaction to our holding action than we had expected," processors and market spokesmen generally declined comment on the lower number of livestock receipts.[36]

NFO, of course, proudly claimed the lowering in receipts

was caused by their holding action. Market operators, on the other hand, pointed out that the four-day marketing week, shortened by the Labor Day holiday, was one reason for fewer livestock at the markets. Besides, they argued, recent rains had improved pastures so some stockmen were keeping their animals at home to take advantage of the additional feed. Rains also often reduced shipments of animals to market because of muddy roads, they added. However, the shorter marketing week was ascribed as having the biggest effect on the receipts and not any restrictive movement by the NFO, market interests maintained.

In one case, the count made by NFO checkers was disputed. Members of the farm organization claimed that arrivals on the Sioux Falls, South Dakota, market were reported about 500 head more than actually were on hand.

An executive of the stockyards in Sioux Falls said that the NFO count did not represent the number of animals actually traded. In reply to the NFO claim, he retorted that the stockyards count had to be right in order to comply with the federal Packers and Stockyards Act. He added that the animals were counted as they were hauled into the yards, when they passed through the gate, and again after they had been weighed at the consummation of their selling.[37]

Livestock prices moved upward during the short marketing week and the NFO quickly seized upon the trend as a result of its members' "battle." Market interests, however, were more inclined to say that this was a natural trend following reduced supply. The official USDA market report for the week showed fat steers and heifers selling 25 cents to a dollar higher. The final count of cattle and calf receipts at the twelve major terminal markets was 176,048, compared with 208,133 the year before.[38] The total for the week before the holding action started was reported at 236,608.[39] If one compares the run of cattle and calves the week before the action started with the supply during its first week, the figures seem to show a dramatic reduction. However, it is well to remember that the former week was one of exceptionally heavy market receipts and that the second week was cut short one day by the holiday. At Chicago, the top price on fat cattle was $34 and a bulk of the choice fat steers at the twelve major markets changed hands at $28.50 to $31 while choice fat heifers brought $26 to $28.50.[40] Considering that the NFO was asking $32.45 per hundredweight, for choice steers, it would appear that prices were not too far from the levels the farm organization wanted.

During the first week of the holding action, hogs around the central market circuit gained 75 cents to $1.50 with No. 1 and 2 butchers weighing 200 to 220 pounds cashing at $19.75 to $20 and a few reaching $20.50 at St. Paul, Minnesota.[41] At the central markets, arrivals for the week totaled 183,955 compared with 301,931 the week before and 259,173 for the Labor Day week of the year earlier. On the interior markets of Iowa and southern Minnesota, the USDA reported hog receipts at 155,000 for the week, compared with 297,000 the week earlier and 284,000 for the like period the year before.[42] The price trend on the interior market was 75 cents to 85 cents higher with returns on the animals somewhat lower than those paid at terminal markets.

As the first full week of the holding action came to a close there were more scattered reports of harrassment. A farmer's truck was stopped on a Kansas highway and searched. In Missouri and Iowa, where trouble had already flared, flimsy plastic bags of paint were splattered against passing trucks. More fences were cut.

NFO checkers stood their posts. In Omaha, members' wives took a turn in the cold, drizzly weather, getting splashed on as the big trucks rolled into the stockyards.[43]

Most observers felt it was too early to draw any conclusions about the holding action. However, those opposing it generally avoided commenting and others in favor of it argued that the lower receipts and higher prices were carrying their efforts to the brink of success.

Oren Lee Staley was predicting a shortage of meat in food stores within a week.

"We've got the processors and buyers in a very tight

spot. If they don't get out and buy a lot of livestock in the
next few days, there could be a severe shortage of meat by
the end of the week. We could be over the hump then, but
we expect ups and downs yet, which probably will continue
into the following week," he said. Confidently, Staley added,
"This coming week will be a crucial one."[44]

The second week of the all out holding action opened
with livestock marketings on the increase compared with
the week before. Higher dressed meat prices were still
being anticipated by packers and retailers and Staley took
his protest against this boost one step further by telegram-
ming the Department of Justice to call for a federal investigation of the meat price hike. He maintained that the purpose of the sharp increase was to cause buyer resistance to
slow down consumption of meat, thereby stretching meager
supplies and to rouse public sentiment against the NFO
action. He argued that while the holding action had thus
far increased prices received by farmers for their livestock
by 3 to 5 per cent, the expected meat price increase
amounted to as much as 20 per cent on some cuts.

"If substantiated, this appears to be collusion and price
fixing by a major packer and chain stores and in direct
violation of anti-trust laws," Staley said.[45]

A spokesman for the National Livestock Feeders Association took issue with Staley's charge and also his claims
of the effect of the holding action. The feeders official said
that the action had not influenced the cattle market and
that the attempt was self-defeating. The reduction in cattle
supplies and the resulting increase in beef prices had been
predictable as long ago as the previous July 1 because of
natural supply factors, he pointed out. However, he admitted that the market moratorium "may have had some
effect in a few places" in the case of hogs.

"There is no basis in fact for any charge that meat prices
have been increasing more than necessary," he said, adding,
"There is no need to be alarmed about any shortage of meat
supplies. The consumers are going to continue to be well
fed."[46]

A market spokesman in Kansas City said the holding action was losing its grip but Staley dismissed this claim as "wishful thinking."

Early in the second week of the action, Staley announced that NFO members might start holding feeder cattle off the market. This class of cattle generally consists of younger stock at lighter weights which are sold to feeders who put growth and finish on them before they are ready for slaughter. At Omaha, an NFO official claimed that there were "lots of two-way cattle in the yards." He went on to say that his organization would be watching to see if all of these were slaughtered or if some were bought for feeding purposes.

"There's no doubt that if large numbers of feeders are slaughtered, a serious meat shortage will develop," the NFO spokesman claimed.[47]

"That doesn't make a bit of sense," a Midwest market authority said in reply to the accusation that feeder cattle were being bought for slaughter. "Feeders have been selling two to three dollars higher than fat cattle. It's an absurd charge."[48]

Meanwhile, in Omaha, a stockyards official conceded that the NFO effort could have been partly responsible for the 20 per cent dip in hog receipts. "If the NFO weren't in the picture, we'd be wondering what was happening to hogs," he said. He also pointed out that the volume of market arrivals reflects "thousands of independent decisions" by farmers and that a number of non-NFO members also could be holding hogs to see what happened to the market.[49]

As arrivals of cattle and calves at the major markets increased, Staley maintained that his followers were not discouraged. The action would go on, he said, and should reach the crucial stage at the middle of the next week.[50]

Final USDA figures on market arrivals for the week ending September 15 showed cattle and calves at 235,464, compared with 176,048 the week before and 231,658 for the like period a year earlier at terminal markets. For the twelve major markets, hogs tallied 284,586 against 183,955 the previous week and 311,314 during the week a year before. Even the grip on the interior hog market of Iowa and southern Minnesota appeared to have slipped during the second week of the holding action when hog receipts numbered 265,000 as opposed to 155,000 during the first week of the NFO drive.[51]

Price trends showed butcher hogs 25 cents to $1.25 lower (but mostly a dollar lower) on the terminal markets and about 50 cents lower on the interior markets. The Market News Service said the drop in prices at terminal markets was largely due to the 55 per cent increase in offerings.

The cattle market at the twelve major points dropped 50 cents to $1.50 on fed steers and heifers. Again, this was the result of a heavier volume of marketings.[52]

However, Staley claimed that livestock supplies had reached "the bottom of the barrel" and that "the opposition is trying hard for heavy livestock receipts the first part of next week. If they get the stock they seek, it will be their last big punch. It will clean out the feedlots and pastures of producers under contract to the processors and those who refuse to join our movement," he said. "Next week, the real core of the holding action will be reached."[53]

Staley's cheerful confidence in the holding action came in the face of several less promising factors. Receipts, as have been shown, were back to normal volume and several packinghouses in Iowa and Omaha announced they were rehiring the men they had laid off the week before because of light livestock supplies. In Iowa alone, some 500 slaughterhouse workers were being called back to work.[54]

In the wholesale meat trade, choice steer and heifer beef dropped $1.50 to $2.50 a hundredweight with clearance slow in some areas. Pork loins skidded four dollars to $4.50 and were as much as $6.50 below Monday's highs at the end of the second week of the holding action.[55]

This weakness in the dressed meat trade could have offered Staley an opportunity to declare that his protests against the earlier-announced hikes in meat prices had been effective since prices were now lower. However, this appeared to be one of the few instances where he did not seize an opportunity to claim credit on behalf of the NFO action. Perhaps he was too busy thinking about the big gain in market receipts which had a bearish influence throughout the livestock and meat markets.

In an embellishment of the NFO's less colorful attempt to hold grain off the market, Staley announced a new plan to centralize large holdings of corn and soybeans at central grain markets.[56] As a part of this effort, Staley said grain storage facilities with a capacity for 1.2 million bushels had been contracted under one roof at Chanute, Kansas, for three years. The movement against standing grain markets was generally ignored by grainmen at terminal points.

Additional opposition to the holding action was voiced during its second week. The Livestock Auction Markets Association denounced "all attempts by threat and violence which seek to close down livestock markets."[57]

With headquarters in Kansas City, the auction market group's statement was in protest against NFO demonstrations the week before at Palmyra and Lewistown, Missouri, and Fairview, Illinois. The general manager of the auction association said that NFO officers were blaming the demonstrations on their opposition. He added that NFO committeemen had contacted him in seeking to prevail on market owners to close down their operations in support of the holding action.[58]

Also coming out against the NFO movement was the American National Cattlemen's Association, which cited its members' "traditional stand in favor of supply and demand marketing and in opposition to deliberate 'withholding' or supply management of livestock." The association pointed out that the shortage of finished beef appeared only temporary and regional in character. At the close of its statement, the cattlemen's group, based in Denver, said it represented "thousands of breeders, ranchers and feeders through nearly 150 affiliated organizations, none of which are involved in the 'holding' action."⁵⁹

In St. Paul, Minnesota, the executive director of the St. Paul Retail Food Dealers Association said he thought the NFO was violating Minnesota law in its holding action.

"In fact, members of the NFO who have agreed to interfere with or restrict the marketing of food products are in direct violation of the Minnesota Constitution," he said, citing an anti-monopoly clause of the constitution. Additionally, he commented, "For someone to create a false market, to cause increased prices and to interfere with the volume of retail stores does not set well with our people."⁶⁰

The NFO was "just treating symptoms" instead of the "basic ills" of the farm problem, an officer of the Red Poll Cattle Club of America said in a letter to Oren Lee Staley. He urged Staley to "take a hard look at what it [the NFO] was doing and consider what the ultimate effect of the action might be."

"You could indeed get an industry in serious trouble, an industry which has long fought to keep itself free of outside price interference and which by and large as a result has been the most prosperous segment of agriculture for many, many years," the cattleman official said in reference to the holding action on beef animals.⁶¹ He also speculated that higher prices on beef might result in lower consumption of the product.

Staley fired back that the NFO marketplace principle was one "everyone else uses who wishes to stay in business. If consumers stop eating because prices are higher, what else besides food are they going to eat?"

"Major manufacturers have continued to raise prices for years, and in most instances, consumption has increased," the NFO chief argued. Besides, he claimed, the NFO was merely asking for the "bare minimum price a farmer needs to stay in business."⁶²

As the second week of the NFO holding action drew to a close, the farm organization found a new complaint to

lodge against the marketing system. A representative of the
NFO called on the head of the Animal Disease Eradication
Branch of the USDA to report he had seen evidence of a rat
infestation in the stockyards in Omaha.[63]

"It is not uncommon to see as many as 15 rats in cattle
pens and 20 to 30 rats in hog pens. Requests may be lodged
to close the public market until the situation is corrected,"
he said. Claiming that similar conditions existed at other
markets, he pointed out that the rodents were carriers of
the animal disease leptospirosis, a hazard to feeder cattle
which go back to farms and to feedlots from the stockyards.

The USDA man contacted said the matter was out of
his hands and that he saw no imminent threat of disease
being spread by the rats. The president of the stockyards
company in Omaha reported that the firm always employed a professional exterminator and "works at control
all the time, year in and year out. We hope to keep the
problem down to a minimum. I thought, frankly, that the
situation was a little better."[64]

While the "rat battle" carried over into the next week
of the holding action, perhaps it is well to finish its story
here. After the complaint had been made over the weekend, the head of the city-county health department in
Omaha reported, "I've personally visited six or seven major
stockyards in the last two or three years and I would rank
Omaha's number one in sanitation. We've never had complaints before from shippers or from members of our staff.
I can't conceive how anyone can suggest the stockyards
should be closed as a result of what we've seen."[65]

The president of the Omaha stockyards then observed,
"Apparently the NFO has abandoned its previously stated
objectives of increasing livestock prices and now is
launched on a program of harassing the stockyards company."[66] He added that fly and rodent control measures
were being continued.

As the holding action continued, the "rat front" petered
out, largely because of the lack of its validity. Certainly
rats were to be found. As long as the stockyards were used

for animals, there would be food and shelter for the rats. This is a problem in major cities whether there are stockyards present or not. At any rate, the NFO blew the issue out of proportion and once this was publicly known, the matter was dropped.

Despite the Livestock Auction Markets Association's announced opposition to the NFO drive—or, perhaps as a reaction to the auctioneers' statement—an estimated 300 to 400 farm women took over an auction barn sale at Colchester, Illinois, for 25 minutes. Six of the ladies moved down to the auction block and took the microphone from the auctioneer, who did not resist. After each delivered a short speech on the NFO holding action, the women led the assemblage in singing "God Bless America" and the sale was resumed.[67]

Elsewhere during the week, activities linked with the holding action were less jolly. The driver of a truck hauling dressed meat had a dozen slivers of glass removed from his eyes after someone had hurled a beer bottle through the windshield of his truck near Lancaster, Missouri.[68] The driver told police that his truck was met at night by a car driven by someone who refused to dim his lights. As the car went by, the trucker saw an arm reach out and throw the bottle. Shattering glass temporarily blinded the man driving the truck. A relief driver in the sleeper compartment of the truck grabbed the wheel and brought the lumbering vehicle to a safe stop. Later in the week, NFO officials announced they, too, were looking for the party responsible for the attack.

Numerous reports came in that trucks had been assailed by men shooting shotguns and rifles. One driver said a car pulled up beside his moving truck and shot out the windshield. At the end of the week, the Missouri highway patrol reported seventeen cases of firearms being used to disable livestock trucks. A barn burned on a farm near Mound City, Missouri; the owner had shipped livestock to the St. Joseph market the day before. Two other barns burned near Albany, Missouri. Bottles, rocks, tomatoes and paint were also tossed at trucks on the way to market. In Missouri, most of the trouble was occurring in the livestock marketing areas of St. Joseph and St. Louis.

To cope with the lawlessness, the Missouri highway patrol called out extra troopers and cancelled all vacations. A spokesman for the police agency said, "There have been many crimes of violence that have never been reported to the highway patrol."[69] More fence cutting was reported near Maryville, Missouri, and at Slayton, Minnesota, at least two dozen shots were fired at tires of three market-bound trucks headed for Sioux City, Iowa. All of these shootings occurred between one and three in the morning, and following the incidents, the trucks were conducted under police escort to the Minnesota-Iowa line.[70]

Also during the week, crowds of NFO members showed up at markets "to see what is going on." More than 500 gathered at Sioux City, Indianapolis, Indiana, and East St. Louis, Illinois; and some 200 each came to Omaha and Kansas City. At St. Paul, several members bunched up at the gates and spread through the stockyards. Some shouted "Scab!" and "Go home!" at truckers.[71]

In all, it was a busy week. NFO checkers stood their posts at country crossroads and at the marketplaces. Meanwhile, Staley called "strategy meetings" in 70 cities and towns to discuss progress of the first two weeks of the holding action. He predicted stockyards officials and processors "will throw one more big punch" in an effort to promote a big market run the third Monday of the holding action. He urged his followers to "outwork them during the next 72 hours" and keep their stock pens closed. The "big pinch" was near, he reiterated.

Despite Staley's exhortations for farmers to keep their lot gates shut, the big pinch never came. Market receipts of cattle at the twelve major terminal markets slipped again a little from the heavier run recorded during the second week of the holding action, but the decrease was not so significant that it could be called an abnormal fluctuation. Arrivals of hogs at the central markets started climbing

slowly and on the interior markets, hog receipts were notice-
ably higher as the holding action continued. With the
greater marketings, prices sagged further.

Fresh from the series of "strategy meetings" called over
the weekend throughout the Midwest, Staley commented:

"Area meetings were held Saturday night and all reports
are that our members are enthusiastic and determined.
We expect the packers will make every effort to get big
receipts in the next two days for the psychological effects
and because they need the cattle to continue operating.
Then they will be scraping the bottom of the barrel and
we will be in the driver's seat."[72]

He again charged that packers were already slaughter-
ing unfinished and poorer quality cattle and starting to buy
stockers and feeders because of the shortage. The packers
said this was not true.[73]

At the opening of the third week of the NFO drive, the
president of the Omaha stockyards company was prompted
to dispel rumors that the market had been closed because
it was "contaminated." He said several truckers had told
him they heard the rumor in outlying areas and that there
had been some long distance telephone calls asking whether
it was true.[74]

More opposition to the action came to light. The
Colorado Cattle Feeders Association said that "mob rule"
cannot substitute for efficient production and marketing in
achieving a stable, prosperous beef industry.[75]

"Despite their claims of having created higher cattle
prices, in reality the credit belongs to the feeders and
ranchers who efficiently have gone ahead to create a steady
supply of high-quality beef which is gaining in public
acceptance daily," an official of the Colorado organization
said.[76]

On the political front, a boner caused fiery reaction from
Republican congressmen when the Republican National
Committee, in its publication *Battle Line,* said that the NFO
was conducting a "useless and wasteful strike" and that

the President should intervene on behalf of consumers.[77] For obvious reasons, farm belt politicians were incensed by the statement and quickly made public that they had no part in making it since they had not been consulted and that the committee was misinformed. There was no comment from Corning. Secretary of Agriculture Freeman, a Democrat, labeled the Republican National Committee attack on the NFO as "vengeful."[78]

With another statement of opposition to the holding action, the National Livestock Feeders Association said, "It is emphatically evident that livestock feeders handling the bulk of the animals being finished for slaughter want no part of any movement that would disrupt the orderly flow of meat animals to the markets and processors and into the meat trade channels.

"Any deliberate effort to keep slaughter livestock from being sold was doomed to dismal failure before it started, but the last two weeks have served to drive this fact home," the organization said.[79]

And it was another week of trouble in outlying areas and in some marketplaces. Missouri Governor Dalton warned that no acts of violence would be tolerated. "I can guarantee you this, as long as I am governor, we are going to try to stop these law violations." He charged that the NFO had sent men in from outside the state and that neighbor was being pitted against neighbor in the holding campaign.[80] The chief executive said that 50 incidents had been reported to the Missouri highway patrol. Several rifle slugs hit a truck traveling the road between Maryville and St. Joseph. A Buchanan County, Missouri, farmer reported that he had been stopped along a road by two autos driven by men who told him his barn would be burned if he sold livestock. He said he was not an NFO member himself and had no livestock. Another farmer reported that his driveway had been covered with hundreds of roofing nails.[81] Near Norborne, Missouri, a farmer who took two loads of stock to market came home to find a stick of dynamite lying in his driveway.[82] At Osceola, Missouri, members of an NFO checkpoint told police that liquid in a toy balloon had splashed on them when thrown from a passing car. Members said the fluid in the balloon was "water with a little something in it."[83] Other NFO checkers later reported they were victims of similar ambushes.[84]

As illegal violence continued, the Federal Bureau of Investigation said in Kansas City that it was keeping an eye on developments. In a few places, individuals and pairs of assailants were arrested for assault and malicious mischief.

Missouri was not the only place where malicious mischief was being done. When the NFO scheduled its "strategy meetings" at the end of the second week of the holding action, a gathering in Humboldt, Iowa, was threatened by a mysterious telephone call made to the meeting hall:

"You've got just ten minutes to get out. We're going to repay you for those things in Missouri. If you don't get out, it will be nothing but blood and guts." The threat proved a hoax when the 200 persons present stayed on for the session and no bomb went off.[85]

In St. Paul, Minnesota, about 25 pickup trucks showed up with one or two pigs in each and backed up to unloading docks and refused to move so other trucks could unload. Five men were arrested for trespassing and failure to remove themselves from private property.[86] As a result of the tie-up at the chutes, large trucks were backed up for three blocks for about two hours before the interference was eliminated. Also, some 300 NFO'ers picketed the St. Paul stockyards while the blockade was going on. An official at the market said the stockyards were "almost in total disorder" until police dispersed the crowd.[87]

In Iowa, a county NFO chapter offered a $250 reward for information about the defacing of an NFO sign that had had a communistic symbol and two "X's" painted on it.[88] Of a more serious nature, more fence cuttings were reported in Poweshiek County, Iowa. Authorities said seven instances of the cutting were done to make ten to fifteen breaks in each fence.[89]

In other protest measures, 500 farmers descended on a fertilizer plant owned by a major packer in Madison, Wisconsin, and dumped cans, cartons and bags of the company's meat products in front of the plant's main office. Reason for this was believed to be the firm's rejection of contract talks with the NFO.[90] In East St. Louis and Kansas City, more pickup loads of one or two pigs showed up at the markets to tie up traffic, but had little effect. Two hundred and fifty persons milled around for three hours at the Peoria, Illinois, livestock pens, but there was no trouble.

In Sioux Falls, South Dakota, police were called to restore order when about 175 NFO members marched through the yards, occasionally locking gates as they came. The lockup tied up some transactions for a half-hour or so, authorities said. As the NFO'ers marched through the yards, they discovered one of their members from Luverne, Minnesota, with cattle on the market. A small crowd jeered "Traitor!" as they surrounded him.

A spokesman for the Sioux Falls stockyards said, "We are glad to have them tour the yard so long as they don't interfere with normal operations." After a conference between police and NFO leaders, the farmers agreed to make one more swing through the yards and end the demonstration.[91]

During the week, Staley announced that 25 meetings would be held by members to decide whether to add milk to the all-out holding action. The ultimate outcome of these meetings indicated a majority of the members in the dairy industry were willing to hold their milk off the market, but the national board of directors of the NFO rejected the additional holding the following week, saying that such a move would be postponed for at least a week more.[92]

In another move for sympathy for the holding action, NFO members in Kansas City threw up picket lines around two major packinghouses. About 25 men participated and the main placard read: "We the farmers in the Kansas City marketing area are conducting a holding action in this area and would appreciate any support given." In smaller

print was the notation that it was not a request to honor
the picket line by not crossing it. The picketing was
conducted without incident for about two hours.[93]

As the holding action went into its fourth week, much
of what occurred was becoming "old hat." Sporadic outbursts of gunfire aimed at livestock trucks were still being
reported, but the incidence of these attacks was lower.
Pickets hoping to influence packinghouse workers turned
up again at Kansas City, Omaha, and in the Iowa cities
of Dubuque and Waterloo.[94] These were peaceful demonstrations and an official of the NFO declared that "picketing
has not been advocated by the national office and no direc-
tives have come out of this [Omaha holding action headquarters] office."[95]

Rumors that Staley had resigned as president of the
NFO circulated at a Marshalltown, Iowa, packing plant and
among livestock trade interests in Kansas City.

"I wouldn't quit in the middle of a fight," Staley said in
reply to the hearsay. He pointed out a drop in cattle
receipts at the twelve major markets and said that this indicated his organization still had a firm grip on supplies.[96]

Back in Missouri, two men admitted they had dumped
sugar in the gas tank on a truck. A dummy bomb was found
in the stockyards at Puxico, Missouri. Equipped with a
clocklike device, it was harmless. And at Westphalia, four
farmers, unable to find local truckers to haul their hogs,
called on an Illinois man to take them to market. But the
trucker refused to load them after a crowd of NFO members showed up.[97]

"We're trying to prove a point here," one of the farmers
who intended to ship said. "We're trying to prove this is a
free country and that we can ship when we please. This
holding action isn't working. They have tried this four
times in the past and each time prices ended up lower than
they were before.

"When the NFO is strong enough to make this thing
stick, then I'll go along with them," he added.

Another of the farmers who could not find a trucker

asked, "What's a man going to do when he has bills to pay and his hogs are getting too fat to bring top prices?"

A dog-in-the-manger attitude transpired in South Dakota when NFO members bought a full-page advertisement in the Sioux Falls *Argus-Leader*. In massive black print, the page was headlined:

FARMERS FAVOR NFO

The main message of the advertisement was devoted to an argument for the NFO's collective bargaining program and telling what a plight the farmers were in. In the lower right corner, inside a border was this message:

NOTICE TO ALL HUNTERS: The National Farmers Organization maintains that we have as much investment in our wild game as any other farm commodity or product. The farmers in the past have been generous with their hospitality and courtesy in entertaining our city friends who enjoy hunting. *In the past few weeks*, the farmer, for some reason, has not been able to enjoy the same hospitality and courtesy in the city. *In some cases*, we have been ordered out of public places. *All farm land* is private property and we feel this would be a more effective way of notifying all hunters of how they stand rather than posting the grounds.

In recent weeks, the farmers have not been received very courteously in the city and in the future it is the general opinion of many rural people that we will not extend these same courtesies that we have in the past.[98]

Perhaps the writers of the advertisement felt they had been snubbed when they demonstrated at the Sioux Falls stockyards earlier and police were called to disperse them. At any rate, the ad did not meet with much sympathy. Eastern South Dakota prided itself as a pheasant hunting paradise and this was poor publicity to attract out-of-state hunters. It also offered a mighty poor hunting prospect for natives living away from farms. Besides, South Dakota's ringneck pheasant hunting reputation had suffered from a disease and winterkill scare a few years earlier and, as a state, it had been in a wrangle with Nebraska, where some officials claimed hunting was just as good, maybe better.

A member of the NFO's national board of directors, representing the eastern South Dakota members, explained that the ad had been placed after a meeting of NFO officers in the region. He added that the suggestion to keep hunters off farms was not binding on NFO members.[99]

In reaction, the director of the South Dakota Game, Fish and Parks Department said the move would backfire on the farmers. He maintained that if the harvest of birds were curtailed, "landowners would probably get quite a bit of damage from pheasants." However, he pointed out that the farmers had every right to keep hunters out of their privately owned land if they wanted to.[100]

The South Dakota Grange came out with a statement that it had no intention of barring hunters from its members' farms. "As one of the largest farm organizations in the state, we want to be on record as favoring the idea of entertaining the hunters on our lands as we always have done in the past.

"The members of the Grange have appreciated the friendly relationship enjoyed between the people living in the towns and cities of our state and the farmers. We therefore hope this relationship will continue," the organization said in a public statement.[101]

The president of the South Dakota Motel Association blasted the NFO-sponsored ad by saying that "irresponsible statements by men in public or quasi-public office are costing the state a considerable amount of money in tourist and hunting business."

The South Dakota NFO directors' ". . . subsequent softening of the statement to say 'only some individual members' are taking the action against city hunters is undoubtedly much closer to the truth. But the damage has already been done," the motel group official complained.[102] In time, the hunting ban was largely forgotten, but it had served no good purpose and probably lost a good deal of sympathy for NFO'ers in South Dakota.

An article in the Des Moines *Register* revealed that farmers opposing the NFO movement, especially the violence accompanying it, had started a vigilante organization in Clarke County, Iowa, in the south central part of the state, called the Clarke County Citizens Protective Association. The story said its members were patrolling their farms and adjacent roads at night after several fence cutting incidents and the mysterious burning of a barn. The association had placed an ad in the Osceola newspaper to offer a $1,450 reward for information leading to the arrest and conviction of those responsible for the vandalism.

The story pointed out that members of the group were careful not to blame the NFO or its holding action for the damages done. Members were quoted:

"We don't object to any farmer belonging to the organization of his choice, as long as they mind their business and let us run ours," one pointed out.

"We don't have any proof who is doing these things. We just want to start protecting ourselves," a farmer explained.

"This protective association is just a means to get a large number of people together and let the guilty ones know that we don't care for violence," another said.[103]

In a visit to Osceola, the seat of Clarke County, the author talked to a resident who said a number of people were ashamed of the fact that such ill will had developed in their community and that the story had appeared in the newspaper. The person, asking that anonymity be maintained, said local law officers patrolled the county's roads at night and made full investigations of the barn burning and incidents of fence cutting. Common feeling was that the newspaper account had been sensationalistic and made the situation seem much more explosive than it actually was. Nonetheless, tempers flared and many farm neighbors began suspecting one another of committing the vandalism. As far as court-admissible evidence was concerned, the vandals left no clues that could be used for making an arrest.

A similar organization took root in the area of Maryville, Missouri, where the Citizens of Nodaway County Organization For Free Enterprise raised $3,750 for rewards leading to the arrest and conviction of the parties responsible for four incidents of fence cutting. The money was solicited from farmers and businessmen who were bitterly opposed to the violence occurring at the same time as the NFO holding action.

As a leader of the group said, "If they call another holding action, we'll be ready for them this time." Even months after the all out holding action was over, opponents of the movement still had unconcealed wrath for the violence that had occurred and indicated they would not hesitate to take up arms to protect their property in the event of a return of like incidents.

The Nodaway County group distributed posters and cards that read:

THIS WE BELIEVE

- Worship as you please
- Vote as you please
- Sell hogs and cattle when you please

And should we lose one of these three
This country would fail
To exist as a Free Nation

Citizens of Nodaway County
Organization
For Free Enterprise

With zealous righteousness, the group felt that its God-given rights were being threatened and that if they should be taken away, the nation might as well be turned over to the communists, one man told the author. While it was apparent that there were hotheads who fervently believed in the NFO cause, it was evident that opposition organizations were leaning similarly on highly emotional principles, but in the opposite direction.

One observer told the author that he had heard there were nearly 100 opposition groups of the "vigilante" variety that worked clandestinely to protect themselves from violence accompanying the holding action. Like the Iowa and

Missouri groups cited above, most of these never mentioned the NFO by name, but it was clear that the NFO was considered cause for their ire. Too, an actual count of these opposition groups was never verified.

Meanwhile, during the fourth week of the holding action, NFO officials at Corning announced that they were putting off for another week a final decision on whether to include milk in the market moratorium.

"The board of directors will meet again next Thursday to announce our final decision on milk," Staley said. "We will spend next week explaining our program to all dairy handlers and processors and give them a chance to sign our contracts.

"Those that sign will be supplied milk to the best of our ability when the holding action on milk starts," he added.[104] A few days later, Staley made public that one milk processor had signed a master contract.[105]

"We'll keep up the battle until we win," the NFO president told newsmen, adding that the holding action thus far had "proved for the first time that farmers will stick together."[106] However, before the deadline arrived for the milk holding action to be added to the livestock and grain holding, Staley announced that the drive was being "recessed" as a result of a national board meeting the night of October 2.

"We do not intend to recess very long," Staley said. "This is merely a recess to enable some of our members to get rid of livestock they can no longer handle," he said, claiming that "we are not calling off the holding action."

"It depends on livestock prices and if processors agree to our contracts during the recess." Staley said the NFO was "near complete victory three times" in the livestock holding, "but we loosened up—perhaps from overconfidence—and our ultimate victory has been delayed."[107]

Six months later the all out holding action hadn't been called out of recess and the author asked Staley for his appraisal of the 1962 all out holding action:

"We showed tremendous strength and the success of the holding action, or the success of the organization, depends on how much progress you've made. Certainly, the all out holding action to date has shown a lot more strength than any previous actions and I think that the breakthrough, the starting to sign contracts with processors, is far more significant than most people realize because this is the first time that farmers have ever had contracts signed that would determine future price levels. This is a result of the strength; the publicity we received is due to the strength, so I think it's very evident that we have tremendous strength."[108]

When the acts of violence were committed during the holding action, the NFO and its opposers both were hasty to blame the other fellow for what happened. Some rumors were spread that the packers had hired professional gunmen to shoot at trucks and then lay the blame on the NFO. A few said, "No, the NFO is the one that hired hoodlums to do the shooting." With the exception of a few arrests where men were caught throwing rocks or other things at trucks and caused trouble at the marketplaces, few incidents were connected directly with NFO members. No fence cutters were apprehended. By some quirk of fate that some people jokingly said denied logic, the attacks on trucks and other mischief "just coincidentally occurred when the holding action was on and just as coincidentally ceased when the action was recessed."

Asked for his opinion as to who was responsible for the vandalism and trouble during the holding action, Staley said he had no idea, but, ". . . as far as violence was concerned, we never advocated it or recommended it. It is always hard to analyze something like that, just where things like that happen. It's a good time to settle grudges. It's always likely that some of your opposition is going to create incidents to try to smear your efforts. On the other hand, you're going to have people that get very energetic and they're working very hard to try to convince their neighbors that they should support the efforts—that it's for the welfare of everyone— and then have their neighbors promise that they're going to hold and not do it. It's bound to have an atmosphere of antagonism."

Asked what would be done to deter violence in the event of future holding actions, Staley predicted, "We, of course, will make every effort; those things are bound to subside because no one that gets involved is going to want it to happen again and the people that cause it aren't going to be anxious to cause it again."

As the holding action dragged on into the third and fourth weeks, Staley reiterated many times that victory was near and called for members to hold just a little longer. When asked if this was an indication that some of the members were shipping livestock to market despite the holding action rules against it, Staley explained that these urgings were "always a psychological effort to keep your people working hard and we felt we were getting close."

About the only incident reported by newspapers of an NFO member shipping despite the call to hold was in Sioux Falls where the owner was caught and scolded as a traitor. However, there were other leaks in the holding action. Market interests at major terminal points said they knew of many NFO'ers who sold during the holding action, especially after the first two weeks. However, in all instances they declined to identify these shippers for fear reprisals would be made. By the same token, they insisted that their own identities be withheld so that they might not be victims of possible revenge.

What had the holding action proved?

For one thing, it made well known the fact that some farmers were actually in dire financial straits, but it falsely implied all farmers were poverty stricken. At the same time, the violence and some of the demonstrations—such as the hunting ban in South Dakota—were deleterious to whatever good farm-city relations had been developed earlier.

If the violence were to have helped to win in the drive to bargain collectively, it would have had to be conducted as a reign of terror, a move for which most of the members

TABLE 6.1

CATTLE RECEIPTS AT THE TWELVE MAJOR TERMINAL MARKETS
AND AVERAGE PRICES OF CHOICE SLAUGHTER STEERS AT CHICAGO,
BY WEEKS*

| | | | Like Period, 1961 | |
Week Ending	No. Head Received	Average Price	No. Head Received	Average Price
September 1, 1962	236,608	$28.91	246,667	$24.18
September 8, 1962	176,048	28.19	208,133	24.13
September 15, 1962	235,464	29.91	231,658	24.12
September 22, 1962	220,472	29.86	249,652	24.45
September 29, 1962	212,972	29.75	248,846	24.60
October 6, 1962	229,325	29.08	257,364	24.45

* Source: U.S. Department of Agriculture.

would not have had the stomach and which the opposition, along with police and governmental agencies, would not have permitted.

As it was, the resort to violence bordered on sheer idiocy and, it should be emphasized, was not favored by the rank-and-file member. Marketmen reported that they had talked to members who said they were ashamed of being a part of the movement because of the incidents that occurred.

In the marketplace itself, the effect on prices and sup-

TABLE 6.2

HOG RECEIPTS AT THE TWELVE MAJOR TERMINAL MARKETS
WITH AVERAGE PRICES FOR NO. 1 AND 2 BUTCHER HOGS WEIGHING
200–220 POUNDS AT CHICAGO, BY WEEKS*

| | | | Like Period, 1961 | |
Week Ending	No. Head Received	Average Price	No. Head Received	Average Price
September 1, 1962	301,931	$18.71	279,697	$18.80
September 8, 1962	183,955	19.49	259,173	18.61
September 15, 1962	284,586	19.54	311,314	18.58
September 22, 1962	272,701	19.56	273,635	18.66
September 29, 1962	311,973	18.72	305,517	18.51
October 6, 1962	339,319	17.64	322,319	18.44

* Source: U.S. Department of Agriculture.

TABLE 6.3

Hog Receipts at Interior Markets in Iowa and
Southern Minnesota with Average Prices of No. 1 and 2
Butcher Hogs Weighing 200–220 Pounds, by Weeks*

| | | | Like Period, 1961 | |
Week Ending	No. Head Received	Average Price	No. Head Received	Average Price
September 1, 1962	297,000	$17.80	291,000	$18.04
September 8, 1962	155,000	18.46	284,000	17.88
September 15, 1962	265,000	18.20	336,000	17.88
September 22, 1962	319,000	18.31	324,000	17.87
September 29, 1962	344,000	17.60	353,000	17.64
October 6, 1962	312,000	16.40	366,000	17.15

* Source: U.S. Department of Agriculture.

plies will probably be long debated. Most persons on both sides of the controversy would admit that the interior hog market was definitely influenced by the holding action. And some auction barns had their sale volume nearly choked off in the early part of the drive. Tables 6.1, 6.2 and 6.3 show better than words the changes in market receipts and price levels for the period involved as compared with the year before.

For the critic who thought the holding action was a senseless and harmful demonstration, it is well to remember that it could have been worse. When members gathered in crowds at the markets, they generally conducted themselves agreeably; they could have rioted. When those responsible for throwing things and shooting at trucks did that, they might have taken it a step or two further and deliberately wounded or killed the drivers. But they didn't. For this forbearance, everyone involved could be thankful.

Despite claims that the market interests made efforts to thwart the holding action, there was no prima facie evidence to substantiate these charges. It was true some packers solicited livestock from points that were outside their usual buying areas. This was their privilege and most everyone recognized it whether he liked it or not.

More than ever before, the public heaved a sigh of relief

when the holding action was recessed. While market interests relaxed their watch over the NFO, the farm organization itself was not ready to rest. Later chapters will treat other developments in the movement's restless drive to win prosperity for its members.

AS A POSTSCRIPT to the 1962 holding action, a court case involving a charge of false arrest of a young farm boy was heard early in 1963 at Montezuma, Iowa. It was connected with a fence cutting incident. On October 26, 1962, a six-year-old son of a farmer filed to sue both the sheriff of Poweshiek County, Iowa, and the principal of the Guernsey, Iowa, public schools for $10,000 damages each resulting from an alleged false arrest. The petition said the defendants did "falsely arrest and imprison" the lad while he was attending first grade classes at the Guernsey elementary school on September 26, 1962.

At the time, the Poweshiek County sheriff was investigating "ten or fifteen" complaints of fence cutting and questioned the boy as to whether his father was involved.

As a result, through his father and with financial assistance of the NFO chapter of which his father was a member, the boy filed a petition claiming that he had been held in the school principal's office "wrongfully, maliciously, forcibly and against his will" and that the sheriff "harassed" him with "questions concerning certain acts of malicious mischief" and sought to cause the boy to "implicate his father."

The boy's father said, "The imprisonment was reckless, oppressive, insulting, wilful and malicious" and that his son had suffered severe mental pains, a loss of appetite and adopted to "desire to stay home from school."[109] He also claimed that the sheriff had no lawful warrant and was without cause in arresting the boy[110] after second-handedly hearing from a pair of schoolmates that the six-year-old had talked about fence cutting activities in the county.

Later, the boy said he had talked about fence cutting, but that he did not say his father participated in it.

After the non-jury case was heard in Montezuma on January 21, 1963, the presiding judge dismissed it on the grounds that the boy had not been actually arrested or imprisoned and that the sheriff "was acting in the performance of his duties." He added that the plaintiff "has wholly failed to establish any damages."[111]

AT THIS JUNCTURE, it may be well to point out that the incidents cited were largely those that were reported in newspapers. Doubtless the working press missed covering many developments, some of which may well have been concealed, in connection with the NFO holding action. Perhaps the most enduring effect of the drive was that it caused suspicion among neighbors and outright ill will between not only neighbors, but between brothers, between fathers and sons and even between men and wives. For many involved, hot arguments over such emotionally charged topics as religion and politics took a back seat to "talking NFO." As one observer told the author, "As with the earliest Christian converts, every new member was an apostle who went out to spread the word about NFO." But by the nature of the crusade, some wielded "a flaming sword of NFO" rather than more peaceful means of winning more "converts."

7

Background:

A GLANCE AT MARKETING

SINCE THE FARMER spends his working hours in three general kinds of endeavor—planning, producing and marketing—we need to know more about the various channels of trading farm products before we can appraise the National Farmers Organization program to boost farm prices.

When a farmer exchanges his livestock or grain for money, he can either handle the entire matter himself or utilize the services of middlemen. When a farmer talks about "the market," he can mean one of several things.

If he refers to the demand for a given product—hogs, for example—he will ask, "Is there a market for them?" Or if he says he is sending his hogs to market, he means he is taking them to a physical facility where products are assembled in a large supply that will fulfill buyers' needs, in terms of size, quality and number. Should the farmer ask, "How's today's market?" he is inquiring about price trends, levels and the behavior of the interplay between supply and demand.

The simplest means of selling that the farmer can employ is the use of private treaty on his own premises. To attract a buyer, he might advertise in a newspaper, put up a sign at his driveway gate to make known that he has something to sell, or "pass the word along" to his neighbors. Also, the product he has to offer may be one with which he has built up a reputation that would attract potential buyers whether he actively advertises or not. A good example of this kind of transaction is that practiced by purebred livestock breeders. Often purebred cattle, hogs or sheep are sold off the farm to another breeder simply on the grounds of the buyer coming to ask about and inspect the offerings and inquire about the price.

The seller has an advantage of setting the price asked or declining any amount offered by the buyer. Usually prices are determined by factors of quality or perhaps the "going" price at the established markets. This method of trade is not limited to livestock or any other particular farm commodity. Such items as grain, hay, timber or even a sack of potatoes might be sold to a buyer calling on a given farm.

Also, the enterprising farmer might set up a roadside stand for selling such items as fruit, vegetables or eggs direct to the consumer. Occasionally a farmer will contact customers off the farm to sell a portion of a meat animal or poultry which the farmer agrees to supply and butcher. Here again, prices paid are arbitrated between the farmer and his customer.

This isolated kind of selling is obviously limited to small-volume transactions because of the number of customers a farmer can take care of, along with the fact that in operating his own little "market," the average farmer would be able to offer only a limited supply in terms of selection and number. Besides, most of the farmer's products have to be processed before they are of much use to the consumer.

Before the advent of railroads, most farm marketing was limited to this kind of private treaty transaction. Other than awkward transportation over water—mainly on rivers or canals—a team and wagon was about the only way grain could be moved. Livestock could be trailed to towns for sale and subsequent slaughter, but this, too, was slow and inconvenient.

With the coming of railroads, a new kind of market system was born. In the 1860's, Chicago emerged as a new central market for both grains and livestock, largely because of its being a railroad center.[1]

Even though it was hundreds of miles from many farmers, the central market grew because it offered facilities to amass a large selection of a product that would attract a number of buyers. The basic essentials of a terminal market include that it be a logical assembling point on the cheapest or most convenient route between producing and consuming areas; that it be a convenient outlet for the farmers and dealers who use it; that it accurately value products, including quality differences; and that it offer a broad outlet for the products after being gathered for trading purposes.[2] In essence, the coming of railroads brought the growing central market within a few miles of many farmers. Also, with the development of refrigerator cars, slaughterhouses had a means of transporting meat to the East Coast outlets after it was processed nearer the producing area. So, as the terminal livestock market at Chicago expanded, it attracted more packers to set up plants in or near the stockyards facilities where trading was conducted. The pattern of growth was similar at other major points. Often the farmer or rancher patronizing the terminal market does not accompany his animals to market. The livestock is consigned to a commission agent who takes care of such tasks as finding pens to hold the animals until they are sold, seeing that they are properly fed, watered and bedded down and handling the transaction of selling them. A "commission" fee is deducted from the gross amount paid for the livestock before the agent remits the pay for the producer's shipment.

The stockyards itself serves as a huge hotel for animals and usually is owned by a private company which charges rental on livestock pens and sells feed and bedding to the commission companies receiving animals they sell. Also, they provide office facilities for commission firms and some packinghouses.

As compared with the individual farmer who might sell one or a dozen cattle from his farmyard to a visiting buyer, most stockyards can accommodate as many as 20,000 or more cattle and still find buyers for them all in one day's trading. The same is true of other kinds of livestock.

Although the coming of motor trucks, improved highways and immediate communication by radio and telephone served as an influence of decentralization of the terminal market system, these central markets are still an important part of trade.

A visit to any of the major terminal markets—Omaha, Sioux City, South St. Paul, Chicago, East St. Louis, Kansas City, St. Joseph and others—offers a number of interesting observations. In fair weather or foul, trading goes on as usual. The "commission men" are early risers, thinking nothing of being out of bed and off to work at four or five in the morning. Early-morning chores such as penning animals and making an accounting of what they have on hand, appraising and sorting the animals and seeing that they are properly cared for are duties to be taken care of before trading begins at an hour decided on by members of the local traders' exchange.

These businessmen look like perhaps "just another farmer" because of their need to dress for outdoor work. Most commission men wear pull-on boots with tops that reach above the ankle. Pantlegs are tucked into the boot tops and most of the men wear cowboy hats. They generally carry a whip or a cane for urging livestock into or out of pens. While trading of sheep and hogs is often done inside large sheds, the buying and selling of cattle is done out in the open. Cattle salesmen, and buyers too, are fully as weather-beaten as the average farmer.

When trading for a given day opens, the commission men are stationed at the livestock pens and buyers move through the alleys of the stockyards to inspect the offerings. If the buyer sees a pen of cattle or hogs that interest him, he will ask what the salesman wants for them. Or, he might make a bid, offering to pay so much without first asking what the commission man thinks the animals are worth. Generally, however, the buyer first finds the asked price and then counters with a lower bid. Some haggling may ensue. If both parties agree on a price, the buyer usually nods or gives the signal, "Weigh 'em!" to indicate he is buying at the agreed price. The sale is consummated upon the animals being weighed and the total amount to be paid is figured from the liveweight price dealt for. Livestock prices are paid by the hundredweight of the live animal. Scale houses are maintained by the stockyard companies and are inspected periodically by government officials.

If the buyer and commission agent do not agree on a price, the buyer moves on to another pen and the salesman waits for another buyer to make his bid. However, the salesman can call the buyer back at a later hour and agree to sell at the bid price if the buyer is still agreeable.

While the stockyards is a public market, the dealing between buyers and commission men is carried on privately so that one buyer does not know what another has bid on a given load of livestock until it is sold. Competition is keen not only between buyers but also between commission companies operating a given market.

Not all buyers in a terminal market represent packers. Order buyers fill requests for packers at distant points and dealers make purchases for livestock feeders who are not on hand to do their own trading. Farmer-feeders, too, come into the marketplace and make purchases by employing commission men or livestock traders who have to meet federal and local exchange regulations to deal in the stockyards. Payment for all animals bought is usually required the same day of trading.

The costs of marketing at terminal points include transportation to the central market, yardage and commission fees. Charges made for services at the marketplace are impressively low. In 1955, for example, marketing costs at the major terminal points posted under the Packers and Stockyards Act, were $2.33 per head of cattle arriving from the country for initial sale.[3] While this would seem high on a per-head basis, it was very low when compared with volume by weight. To pay $2.33 in commission and stockyards fees on, say, a 1,000-pound steer that sold at $25 per hundredweight would be sur- rendering less than one per cent of the gross in a $250 transaction.

The average marketing costs on hogs were 77 cents in 1955, which, on a 200-pound butcher selling at, say, $18 per hundredweight, would be less than three per cent of the gross returns. Although the commission and yardage charges quoted here were standard in 1955, it is interesting to note that they were still nearly the same at the close of 1963.

Transportation is another important expense in market- ing livestock. Although railroads were at one time the major carrier of animals moving to market, trucks, which are more versatile and maneuverable, have taken over as the most important means of moving livestock. Because every truck line has its own system of determining rates for hauling livestock, along with the fact that the methods of arriving at rates vary greatly, it was impossible at this writing to come up with a meaningful average figure on what it costs to truck, say, cattle to market. To be con- sidered were such divergent factors as distance, size of load, direction to be traveled and whether the driver of the truck would have a "payload" during the whole trip or whether he would "run empty" part of the time.

Examples of charges for trucking cattle in the Omaha area were given by a truck line official who said that if a farmer had cattle to haul to market from a point about 30 miles away, it would cost 10 cents per hundredweight to have them moved to Omaha. If, however, the farmer wanted to truck them from Omaha to Chicago, a distance of about 500 miles, it would cost 80 cents per hundred- weight for the whole trip. In other words, if a feeder had twenty head of 1,000-pound steers to be moved 30 miles to the Omaha market, it would cost him a dollar a head to get them to the market. But if he were trucking them the 500 miles from Omaha to Chicago, it would cost him $8 a head or $160 to get them all to the Windy City.

The terminal livestock system continued to play an important role in the over-all livestock market picture even though it has declined somewhat from earlier prominence. Among the factors that lessened trading volume at the central markets were better roads and motor trucks which enabled farmers to more conveniently patronize local markets. This trend gave rise to expansion of local auction barns that took some business away from the terminal markets. Another important factor was that many packers instituted programs of buying direct from farmers rather than satisfying all their needs by obtaining livestock at the central points. Besides having country buyers call on farms to offer bids there, many packinghouses built country buying stations where farmers could unload their animals—especially hogs and sheep—and sell them without having to pay the expenses of shipping them to a distant market. However, there are hitches to selling direct. The packer sometimes pays less, arguing that he has to make up the transportation costs through the lower price. Also, a "pencil shrink," the subtraction of a percentage of the actual weight of the animals to compensate for losses of weight in transit, might be levied against the price paid to the producer.

Selling direct to packers includes various methods of payment. For one, the farmer can accept a price based on the live weight of the animal. Or he can agree to accept pay on the actual meat of the animal under the system of "grade and yield." This hinges on the quality of carcass and the percentage of usable meat products from each animal. This system has long been in use in Canada's hog markets and as one observer commented, "It takes all the guess work out of buying for the packer." If the producer has animals of superior quality, he enjoys a price advantage.

However, the use of grade and yield buying in the early 1960's was far from perfection in the United States.

The advantages of shipping to a terminal livestock market or selling direct to packers are argumentative. In 1951, only about 40 per cent of the hogs went to terminal markets, while 60 per cent of calves, sheep and lambs and 75 per cent of the cattle in the United States were sold through the terminal marketing system.[4] In later years, these percentages decreased, especially on hogs and sheep. Those who believe that the central markets are the most competitive argue that direct buying removes "all the competition." And with the growth of decentralized marketing, they believe that prices and the whole market price structure are weakened by taking volume away from the terminal trade. These arguments imply that the terminal market trends are the basis for all prices on a given class of livestock.

Although the tendency of decentralization does take some volume away from the terminal markets, it does not necessarily follow that it takes away competition, too. Since prices are established mainly by the interplay of supply and demand, outside buying more or less leaves a balance since both buyers and sellers are taken out of the terminal trade.

However, there is a quality factor that could have a definite depressing influence on the whole price structure of livestock as a result of selling direct to packers. Some market men and some farmers maintain that the best quality animals are often sold direct to packers. This means, consequently, that animals of less quality set the highest prices at terminal markets. Since country buyers for packers often use terminal market price levels to establish the prices to be paid in the country, it is possible that top quality animals may be bought direct off the farm at a price below that paid at central markets for kinds of animals that are inferior to the ones sold direct. As a result, the whole price system would be weakened.

As far as competition in direct selling is concerned, it

is up to the farmer whether the transaction is competitive. Although only one buyer might be present at one time to make a bid on livestock, the farmer, if informed, knows what is being paid on the central markets and other points simply by listening to the radio market reports. Or he may telephone another buyer and seek an opposing bid. Because his animals are still on the farm or at a nearby country buying station, he can easily turn down the packer buyer's bid. This still leaves opportunities of selling at a local auction barn, shipping to a terminal market, or finding another packer buyer. On the other hand, when a packer buyer makes a bid, the farmer knows "here and now" what he would be paid for his animals as opposed to risking a decline in prices between the time he starts his animals on their way to the terminal market and the time they are actually sold. If prices enjoy an upturn, then the transit time lag is to the farmer's advantage.

While selling direct offers some convenience to the farmer, it is most unlikely that packers promote the practice for any other reason than that it is more economical for them.

An example of the importance of the terminal points in livestock marketing is the fact that in 1957 about 21 million cattle and calves changed hands in this system. Cattle and calf volume declined slightly in the early 1920's up to 1932, then generally increased. It stood at nearly 18 million in 1962. Sheep receipts slid in the period of 1943 to 1951. During this time, sheep and lamb arrivals on the terminal markets slumped from 30 million to 14 million per year in less than a decade.[5] Hog volume on the central markets has been erratic comparatively in the past half-century with noteworthy declines owing to direct selling. However, salable receipts of hogs at these points totaled nearly 22 million in 1962.

These trends might indicate a dim future for central markets. However, it should be noted that predictions that "they won't last another ten years" have been made since the 1920's. A considerable number of producers, especially cattlemen, believe that the terminal markets offer the most advantages. With this in mind, it is fairly safe to say that it will be a long time before central markets are eliminated, if they ever are.

UNTIL ABOUT 1900, livestock auctions were relatively scarce in the United States. Although this method had been used as early as 1676 in the area of New York City, it was not until the 1930's that auction barns started to play an important role in livestock marketing. Improved hard-surfaced highways and the adoption of using motor trucks to and from the market place were integral in the development of the auction system. Additionally, an increasing number of small packers located away from the central markets were able to buy livestock more efficiently at the auction barns. The development of uniform grading and classification systems for livestock and federal market news reporting also were factors in the rise of auctions. Auction facilities, drawing most of their business from within a 25-mile radius, offered a convenient means of disposing of small lots of livestock and at the same time enabled farmers to keep informed on local livestock market conditions and prices.

Low livestock prices in the early 1930's meant that a greater chunk of the paycheck for animals sold on the terminal market would go for transportation costs. Also, at that time, central market commission fees were based on a percentage of the gross amount of a sale rather than a flat per-head charge that came into practice later.

In view of these cost factors, the use of auctions was attractive because of the small marketing costs at local facilities. Drought conditions in 1934 and 1936 also caused abnormal distribution of feed and auctions offered a handy means for farmers to sell stocker and feeder and other unfinished livestock without sending them all the way to a terminal point. And in terms of farmer-feeder buying, an operator could simply get in his truck, go to the local auction on "sale day" and buy small lots of livestock.[6]

Currently, most auction barns hold a sale once a week. Facilities include stock pens with feed and water available. Many are located on rail spurs to accomodate large shipments coming in or leaving by train. Loading chutes for trucks, the major means of livestock transit in recent years, are provided too. Potential buyers are free to travel through the yarding area of an auction market to see if there is any livestock that they may want to buy.

The sale itself is usually conducted inside a barn that has arena-like seating around a pen or sale ring with gates at both ends for offerings to be driven in and out. A scale for weighing livestock is usually nearby, depending on whether the animals are selling on a per-head or per-hundredweight basis. One auctioneer conducts the process of selling. This does not mean that an auction barn employs only one auctioneer, but that only one can call sales in a sale ring at one time. The auctioneer calls for an opening bid on a pen or an individual animal driven into the ring. If no buyer in the barn makes an opening bid, the auctioneer might arbitrarily make the bid himself and start his melodic calling, a mixture of words and nonwords poured out in a rapid, rhythmic stream. If no buyer accepts the opening bid, the auctioneer continues working downward from the proposed opening until he gets a bid. Once bidding is actually opened, buyers know what price is being offered and they have their chance to enter the competition by signaling that they are willing to buy at that price. This signal usually consists of raising a hand, giving a shout or any other means of attracting the attention of the auctioneer or one of his assistants. After that, only a nod is needed to indicate he is bidding again. Some buyers, whether they are packer buyers, farmers or dealers, pride themselves in being able to bid without anyone else in the buyer audience knowing that they are bidding. A dip of a cigar in the buyer's mouth, a wink or a scratch of the nose may be his way of saying he will buy.

Because of a kind of "sporting" element of the competition at auction barns, prices are sometimes erratic.

Spirited bidding may show up on a low-quality offering while a desirable animal might meet with limited bids and sell for less. A full salebarn does not necessarily mean that the sale session will be active since many persons may simply be spectators. By the same token, an auction attended by a half-dozen buyers may be quite snappy because all are buying actively. Over the long haul, however, auction prices do reflect supply and demand and generally are in linc with prevailing prices in other branches of the livestock market system.

As a sidelight of color in the auction market, outsiders often ask why the presiding auctioneer rates the title of "colonel." After asking a number of livestock producers and market interests who admitted they did not know the origin of this practice, the author speculated that the title could be credited to two possibilities. For one, the auctioneer was in charge of the sale, which implied that he was the ranking man of the day; hence, he was in a position similar to that of a military colonel. Or the title could have been borrowed from the southern tradition of addressing a gentleman and landowner as "colonel."

Charges for livestock being sold at auctions are figured by four general methods. The most prevalent is a straight per-head charge with usual fees of $1.50 to $2.50 charged on cattle and 50 cents to a dollar on hogs. Auction fees for sheep on a per-head basis run about 25 cents to 50 cents per head. Another method is to charge a per-head fee plus a percentage of the gross returns on the sale offering involved. The third method is comprised of a flat percentage assessed on the gross amount from the sale, and the fourth means is to charge a percentage plus small per-head charges. Where percentages are deducted for services, three per cent is usually charged on cattle and hogs and a maximum of five per cent is assessed on sheep sales.[7]

Growth in auction markets went from a few at the turn of the century to 1,345 in 1937 and a high of about 2,500 in 1952. By 1955, however, this total had slipped off to 2,322, according to USDA sources.[8] While a majority of these outlets were located in the major livestock producing areas of the north central region of the United States, many were spotted in the East and along the West Coast too. Volume of business done at each auction varied between 100 and 200,000 head of animals during 1955. For the nation that year, auctions handled over 30 million cattle and calves compared with about 23 million being sold at 64 terminal markets. Auctions sold 15,481,000 hogs that year, while central market hog volume was at 24,579,-000 head. Sheep and lambs numbered about 8.5 million at the terminal points and about 6 million at auctions.[9]

Besides the privately owned facilities of surviving auction barns, this method of selling is commonly used for purebred livestock sales on the producer's farm. An auctioneer is hired to sell an offering advertised to attract buyers to the farm. Also, this method is often used to auction off machinery, household items and livestock when farmers sell out to leave the farm. Less frequently, land is sold by auction. In this particular kind of sale, the auctioneer charges a percentage of the gross returns. As in all auctions, the sale is made to the highest bidder.

Regardless of the market system, all are organized to work toward obtaining the highest price possible for the producer in the cause of furthering their own business. It would be untrue to say that prices are set in one place, such as the Chicago stockyards, since all facets of marketing outlets play a part in the over-all price structure and its trends. Economically, supplies at the marketplace, on the farm and in the feedlots influence pricing. Government reports of pig crops and cattle on feed serve as measures of these supplies and indirectly affect the markets. On the demand side of marketing, the financial aspects of buyers—whether they are farmers and feeders buying replacement livestock or whether they are consumers buying retail meat itself—play an important part in establishing demand. Obviously a packer will not buy many animals if he cannot sell meat. Additionally, seasonal and cyclical variations in production are reflected in price fluctuations. Because of these and other factors that make livestock marketing somewhat com-

plicated, there are many things for a producer to consider
when marketing.

THE ORGANIZATION of the grain markets is somewhat different from the avenues of trade that a farmer has available
for livestock. While a farmer can sell a load of grain to a
neighbor or some other buyer, the general practice is to
truck it to a local grain elevator for sale. The farmer may
store it for use on his own farm, which is usually the case
with corn. Or he may store it under a contract with the federal government and make use of a support price loan under
one of the government grain programs. The Commodity
Credit Corporation, an agency of the Department of Agriculture, plays a large role in the grain trade at this writing,
but for our purposes, we will examine the established open
trade system.

As touched on above, most grain that is sold off the farm
is taken to a local elevator. Consequently, the farmer is paid
off and out of the market picture early in the process of
grain going from farm to market, to processor and finally to
the consumer. The country elevators, located on rail lines,
are of three general classifications. The independent elevator is owned and operated by private individuals, usually
local businessmen. An important class of owners and operators of country elevators are farmers cooperatives. The
third kind of country elevator is the line elevator owned and
operated by the large grain companies which have a number
of facilities over a large area. Some of the farmers co-ops
have grown in size and carry on operations similar to the
large grain firms with line elevators, large storage facilities
at terminal points, and memberships in terminal market
grain exchanges.

When the farmer is paid for his load of grain, the price
is determined by the quality of similar offerings at levels prevailing at one of the terminal markets. Adjustments between the price paid to the farmer and the price paid for
comparable grain on the terminal market include subtract-
ing costs of grading, handling, transportation and storage

and a reasonable profit for the elevator operator. Consequently, the farmer may wonder why he is paid a lower price locally for his No. 2 yellow corn than the quotation of actual cash sales at Chicago, for example.

From the country elevator, the grain may travel one of two major routes. The first is that the elevator operator may have a local buyer such as another farmer, a feeder or a local processor such as a feed manufacturer or miller. Or he may consign the grain to a distant processor to dispose of it. The second major alternative is to send it to one of the terminal markets. Some major grain outlets are Chicago, Kansas City, Minneapolis, St. Louis, Omaha and Duluth.

Once grain arrives at the country elevator by the truckload it is generally handled in railroad carlot units of 2,000 bushels. One thousand-bushel units are sometimes used, however.

When a carlot of grain arrives at the terminal market, it is left on a special railroad siding so that licensed inspectors can open the car and take samples for grading. In most cases, these inspectors are licensed by the USDA under provisions of the U.S. Grain Standards Act and are employed by state agencies or possibly the local grain exchange. They are impartial judges of the commodities they inspect since they are not directly involved in the selling or buying of grain. Factors in grading grain include weight per bushel, moisture content, percentage of damaged kernels, foreign material or dockage. Odor is also considered. In wheat, the percentage of protein content is important.

The commission firm to which the country elevator operator consigns performs several services. First is checking the grade of the newly arrived carlot of grain. After evaluating the freight rates and conditions to dispose of the grain, the unloading weight is determined and the commission man can make immediate payment to the country elevator. If there are any claims against the railroad handling the shipment, the commission man takes care of the matter. Besides the actual handling and reselling of the shipment, the commission man supplies the elevator man with central market information.

The grainman at the terminal market who receives car-lot shipments is known as a trader in the "cash market" since he is dealing with a commodity that is available for immediate delivery. With the grain on hand, he has three main outlets for it—large processors such as flour millers, corn or soybean processors, feed manufacturers, distillers and maltsters; or terminal elevators which store and condition grain with intentions of merchandising it later; or exporters.[10]

A MUCH MORE COLORFUL and often misunderstood aspect of the terminal grain markets is the "futures" market. In short, this is the selling of a contract to deliver grain at a later date. The practice of buying and selling futures to protect cash grain dealings is referred to as "hedging." One source says:

Hedging is the primary and principal function of futures trading. This is simply insurance protection against possible loss from a change in the market price and is paramount in the activities of grainmen, processors, exporters and farmers. Others who trade in grain futures are not hedgers since they have nothing to protect or insure against loss, but they perform a necessary economic service of great value. They are called speculators.

Most unjustly and unfairly has speculation in grain for future delivery been charged as "gambling." Such charges can be justified only through ignorance or vicious propaganda on the part of those who would destroy the free-enterprise system of life enjoyed in these United States. . . .[11]

While anyone who has the money to invest can enter the futures market, most of the trading is done by hedgers in the grain trade. These generally include country, sub-terminal and terminal elevator interests; cash grain commission merchants; and processors such as flour millers, feed or cereal manufacturers and soybean crushers. Commodities on which futures are bought and sold at Chicago include wheat, corn, milo, oats, rye, cotton, soybeans, soybean oil and soybean meal. In the past, futures trading was done on drummed lard and some experimental trade was conducted on futures dealing on pork sides.

To illustrate how hedging is a means of minimizing the risk against price change on the cash commodity, examine the case of the grain hedger. First he buys a quantity of grain and immediately sells an equal quantity on a futures contract that will mature during one of the regular delivery months (March, May, July, September and December on most grains). As one authority says:

> The basic principle is that the level of prices in the cash and futures markets tend to move up and down together. Both markets respond to the same general factors of supply and demand, so if cash prices go down, futures prices usually will also. Conversely, if cash prices go up, futures prices will tend to rise. Since the hedger's position in each market is equal and opposite—a purchase in one market and a sale in the other—a loss in one market is approximately equalled by a gain in the other, no matter which way prices move.[12]

Although these changes in price levels do not usually match cent-for-cent, they do offer considerable protection to the holder of a futures contract.

Futures trading is done only by members of the exchanges who handle their own transactions or represent speculators and others making use of the system. Contracts are processed and recorded in clearing houses which operate independently of the boards of trade themselves.

Advantages of the futures system not only protect cash grain holdings, but serve to stabilize the market on a year-round plane. This does not mean that prices do not change, but it does help guard against erratic changes in prices. Because supply and demand are constantly changing, so are grain prices. Some of the influences on supply include injurious insects, frost, plant diseases, drought and floods. Any of these can seriously reduce the supply of a growing crop and then be reflected in the price of that grain. The amount of grain sold by farmers varies from week to week, also affecting the supply available at the terminal points. Situations that affect demand include changes in total export operations, government support programs, flour demand from bakers and seasonal buying activities of millers. In case of a shortage of one crop, a substitution of another might change demand on both. Weather, world news and many other factors influence price trends too.[13]

If a farmer wants to make use of the futures market, he can do so for the purposes of establishing a price ahead of the harvest or the sale of cash grain; or to earn a storage charge without assuming the full risk of price change; or to speculate by selling out his cash grain and buying futures contracts; or to establish the cost of purchased grain for livestock feeding or other purposes.[14]

To illustrate how futures marketing of grain helps the farmer obtain higher prices for his product, the following figures were calculated to show how farmers' prices would be figured if there were no futures market:

Chicago market price of cash wheat .... $2.00   per bushel

    Less freight (average) 12
    Less country elevator handling costs 04
    Less terminal market handling 015
    Less estimated reserve that would
        probably be deducted against
        possible price loss 25
    Total deductions 425
    Price to farmer .... $1.575 per bushel

However, since the futures market practice removes the need for deducting a "reserve" against price losses, total deductions actually run about 16.5 cents per bushel, thus returning $1.825 to the farmer.[15]

Transportation is an important marketing cost in the grain business, too. While most livestock is moved by truck and a small percentage goes by rail, the opposite is true in the movement of grain, most of which goes to market by rail. Of course, some moves by barge on rivers and some is shipped by seagoing freighter on the Great Lakes, as well as the high seas. Only a small fraction of the grain moving along marketing channels is transported by truck.

Establishing freight rates for moving grain by rail is just as complicated as setting up truck rates. Although railway rates are regulated by the federal government, variations between pre-established zones result in vast differences between charges for grain shipped a given distance, direction, etc. Here again it would be virtually impossible to arrive at an average cost that would be meaningful, according to railway rate specialists. However, to illustrate how expensive these costs are, one railway agent cited the charges that would be levied on a carload of wheat moving from Des Moines, Iowa, to Chicago and also the rate for sending the same car from Des Moines to Los Angeles. For a rail boxcar of wheat weighing a minimum of 60,000 pounds, a charge of 37 cents per hundredweight would be made to move it to Chicago. If the same car were going from Des Moines to Los Angeles, the cost would be $1.51 per hundredweight. This means it would cost about $223 to ship it the 350 miles to Chicago or about $906 to send it the 1,850 miles to Los Angeles, using Des Moines as the point of origin of the shipment.

Because of the costs involved, it is obviously important that grain commission men carefully study the various freight tariffs, as they are called, before setting a price on a shipment of grain to be delivered a great distance. Miscalculations could be quite expensive.

Terminal grain markets have a flavor of their own. Office facilities and trading floors are usually owned by the grain exchanges or boards of trade which consist of members representing firms operating in the given market. The boards of trade or exchanges have rules of operation, but do not function in buying and selling commodities other than in the formulating and enforcing of rules and regulations of trade practices.

In Chicago, for example, trading is done in a mammoth room five stories high, a block long and a quarter of a block wide. About two-thirds of the trading floor is taken up by "futures pits." These are octagonal platforms with steps descending on the inside. The shape of the pit allows all participating in trading on the commodity involved to see one another. While buyers and sellers mingle, the level on which a trader stands on the steps indicates the month of delivery he is trading in.

Trade is opened and closed at an appointed hour by the sounding of a gong that clangs like the bell used in boxing matches. At the opening signal, seeming pandemonium breaks out in the pits as traders begin shouting and flaying the air with their arms. By an intricate system of hand signals and vocalizing, futures trading is carried on efficiently despite the appearance of disorder.

In addition to various trading pits for futures markets, the floor of the board of trade is equipped with banks of telephones, commodity quotation boards, a stock market quotation board, a weather map, news service teletypes and, of course, an area where tables are reserved for cash grain trading. Cash trading is carried on by carlots or 1,000-bushel units in a method of private treaty quite similar to that used in terminal livestock markets. Samples—usually contained in a paper bag or a metal pan—are on hand for inspection by the buyers and sellers, along with official grading results. Cash trading outwardly appears much quieter and more casual than the futures market.

BECAUSE RAW MILK is so perishable, the predominant method of marketing it has to be considerably different from those of livestock, grains and other more stable farm products. Since milk is produced every day of the year and has to move steadily to market, it usually goes directly from the farm to a nearby processor who passes it on to the consumer in a relatively short period of time. A farmer might have an agreement with a local processor who picks up the milk daily, transports it to a plant for pasteurizing or homogenizing, packaging and distribution. Prices are negotiated before delivery of the milk and hinge on quality factors such as butterfat content.

Since the perishability of milk makes it relatively impossible to hold it for deliberate marketing or storage until market conditions improve, milk producers marketing associations, often in the form of cooperatives, have been organized. Purposes of the organizations are to bargain for prices, to guarantee supplies and to locate new buyers if needed.

For many years, milk was handled in ten-gallon cans which were kept in coolers for the short period of cooling and temporary storage before the milk was trucked to a local processor. Today, nearly all dairy farmers have adopted the refrigerated bulk storage tank. A tank truck pumps the milk from the farm storage tank and moves it to the processor in bulk form. The truck driver takes samples and measures the amount of milk to make a record of quantity and quality of the production picked up. The tank truck calls on each dairy farm every other day or twice a week and sometimes oftener.

Except in the cases of major metropolitan areas, milk is assembled from a surrounding "milkshed" and goes directly from farm to processor and on to consumer without traveling a great distance. In the cases of such cities as New York, Chicago, Boston and other major urban areas, milk is assembled at a given point, loaded into refrigerated railway bulk tank cars and shipped to the city for processing and distribution.

While early milk producers associations had negotiated for prices on their milk, there sometimes arose the problem of surplus production. The handler or processor of milk could dispose of some of the excess in milk delivered by selling it at a lower price to other fluid milk processors or to creameries, cheese plants or evaporating and powdering concerns. The initial handler of the milk would then pass the price reduction on to the farmer, paying him less for the "surplus" milk. Or, the handler could refuse to accept any milk in excess of his immediate needs. While cooperatives and other dairy producer associations had made good strides in dealing with their own problems of marketing, the federal government offered a program under the Agricultural Adjustment Act of 1933 under which producers would be licensed. Handlers or processors were required to pay producers on a classified price basis, to pool the returns to farmers either on a handler or market-wide basis. The original plan was replaced by an act in 1935 that established federal milk marketing orders. Many of these features were restated in another Marketing Agreement Act of 1937.

Federal milk orders are legal instruments which define the terms under which handlers who engage primarily in the handling of milk for fluid distribution in a regulated city market can purchase the milk from dairy farmers. The purpose of these orders is to make sure that ample supplies of wholesome milk are available to consumers at all times. This is done by promoting and maintaining orderly marketing of milk by farmers.

Orderly marketing is achieved in part under the program through the certainties produced by a marketing order which spells out in advance the terms of purchase of milk to both the producer and processor. These terms are drawn up from the results of public hearings which are held prior to the issuance of a marketing order. Interested groups supply basic information needed for the instituting of a marketing order. The program requires accurate and complete reporting for decisions on prices designed to reflect market supply and demand conditions.

The marketing orders do not guarantee a given price level, but do provide prices related to local and general economic conditions. They do not guarantee farmers a market for their milk nor control production. However, the program does establish sanitary and quality standards.

As one source says, "The responsibility of the federal government in the development of milk orders is to determine the fairness of the various proposals, to resolve the difference in the public interest, and to enforce the orders after they have been put into effect."[16]

Price scales are established on milk for various uses. Class One milk goes for fluid milk consumption and rates the best price, while other classes are scaled downward and are used in such manufacturing processes as evaporating or powdering milk. Cheese making is also an outlet for surplus milk. In some of these "manufactured" grades, sanitary requirements are not as stringent as are those on Class One milk. Under marketing orders, in 1955, Class One milk made up 64 per cent of the milk handled and other classes made up 36 per cent sold under the government-supervised program. At that time, Class One milk was valued at $4.82 per hundredweight and remaining "surplus" milk sold at $3.06 per hundredweight.[17]

IF YOU were a farmer who was selling eggs at 25 cents a dozen and one day stopped at a cafe for breakfast, ordered two scrambled eggs and ended up paying 50 cents for them, you would begin to wonder who was getting all the money. At that rate, eggs would be costing the consumer $3 a dozen. This is an extreme example of the spread in prices between the farmer's returns and what the consumer pays for agricultural products. Whether or not the costs of marketing, processing and distribution appear exhorbitant, they are necessary. Some examples of how marketing margins affect the final price of a farm product follow.

White bread—In 1961, the average price of a loaf of white bread was 20.9 cents. Of this total amount, the farmer received 2.9 cents for the wheat or grain products that went into it. Costs of transportation, handling and other processing charges amounted to another 1.5 cents. Milling the grain into flour cost 1.0 cent, and the baker and wholesaler added 11.7 cents for their part in converting the grain into a loaf of bread. The retailer added another 3.8 cents to the final price that the consumer paid. Even if the farmer had given away the grain for the bread, it would have cost about 18.5 cents per loaf.[18]

Pork—Using the costs of marketing a hog from a farm in Iowa to consumers in New York City, the consumer's dollar spent on pork in early 1955 was split four major ways. The producer received 40.1 cents for the live animal. The livestock handler (commission man or order buyer) received 0.4 cents of a dollar spent on pork and the

8

"SIGN ON THE DOTTED LINE . . ."

Putting muscle into the National Farmers Organization's program of collective bargaining depended largely on the use of two contracts. One was the NFO membership agreement which set forth the obligations of farmers supporting the movement. The second, drawn up some time later to outline the conditions processors would have to meet to satisfy NFO demands, was known as the "master contract." Both documents had points that were disfavored by some quarters and in some cases aroused the suspicions of non-members and outside observers.

Some critics said the NFO membership agreement took away the farmer's freedom to market as he pleased. Others felt that once a farmer signed a contract, it was extremely difficult to get out of the organization if one so wished. These allegations were in part true.

A study of the membership agreement revealed nothing ominous, suspicious or misleading. The contract was printed on a standard 8½ by 11½-inch sheet of paper containing two columns of small type. It was headed simply "MEMBERSHIP AGREEMENT" with an NFO insignia in the upper left corner. Beneath the heading were blanks for name, township, county and state in which the applicant lived and the date of joining. At the bottom of the page were lines for a witness to endorse, the member's legal signature and his mailing address. There were no blanks for NFO officials to sign.*

The body of the agreement consisted of twelve articles printed in tiny five-point type. For being a contract printed on one side of a standard sheet of paper, it was fairly lengthy—about 2,000 words. In typewritten pages this would have been about eight to ten pages of double-spaced material.

The first article of the agreement authorized the NFO to act as the member's exclusive representative in collective bargaining in respect to all commodities marketed from the member's farm. Commodities from the farm already being sold under marketing agreements were excepted. The agreement also authorized the NFO to serve as the member's exclusive agent in matters of presenting, prosecuting and adjusting any complaints the member might have against a processor of farm products.

The point that some potential members objected to was that the authorization clause of the agreement specified that it would be irrevocably in effect for three years from the date signed. The signer also agreed that the authorization would be automatically renewed every three years unless the NFO were notified by the member not more than twenty days before and not less than ten days before the expiration date. Written notification of termination had to be presented within the ten-day period for a member to legally get out of the NFO agreement. Often farmers are not too concerned with specific dates and deadlines. Consequently, this presentation of a deadline appeared to some to be a kind of trap to keep members in the organization. While this did have the semblance of a loss of choice, it in fact was not since the member could divorce himself at the end of the three years if he paid attention and got his notice into Corning at the right time. However, once members were "sold" on the NFO program, this clause was not very objectionable to those who joined. Nonetheless, others reportedly

_____
* For complete text of the NFO membership agreement, see Appendix A.

refused to sign a membership agreement even though they were otherwise sympathetic to the collective bargaining idea. This reflected their suspicion of the automatic renewal clause which obligated them to pay dues of $25 a year for another three years.

The next three articles of the membership agreement outlined the organization of commodity departments to be set up by the national office of the NFO. Departments were to be instituted on dairy, grain and meat, and heads of each were to be appointed by the NFO president. The departments were to designate geographical marketing areas each of which would have its own area bargaining committee. Area bargaining committees and county committees would deal with processors in their own territory and when contracts were signed with processors, agreements would be applicable to only those members within the bargaining area. Contracts obtained by local bargaining committees would not be binding until ratified by a two-thirds vote of NFO members in the given marketing area.

Among the requirements of marketing, the member would be free to market as he pleased until a contract was signed with a processor. However, once an area committee obtained an agreement with a processor of a given commodity, the members in that area would be bound to deliver to the named processor. If a member sold to a processor that had not signed a contract with the local NFO committee, the member would be assessed ten per cent of the gross amount of that unauthorized sale of the commodity "for liquidated damages." These marketing requirements could be waived in case of unforeseen developments and the national board of directors had final say on whether the waivers were valid.

If marketing quotas became necessary to satisfy the needs of processors under contract, the members in a given marketing area would vote to determine a fair price formula, to be ratified by a two-thirds vote of approval. Expenses of these price adjustments would be financed by a check-off at the processor level from commodities marketed.

A program of distributing surplus production to "needy worthwhile organizations" or forming welfare agencies was offered in the membership agreement to help keep production in balance with demand.

Until contracts were in effect, with processors buying the member's production, the member was to pay $25 a year in membership dues and fees. When marketing contracts were obtained, each member would be assessed one per cent of the gross amount of his marketings and that would be accepted by the NFO in place of the regular $25 a year. In addition, another two per cent of the member's marketing returns would be deducted. This deduction would go into a fund to finance NFO's proposed surplus production disposal program. In the end, the member would be paying out three per cent of the gross of his marketings handled by the NFO, a figure not far from that of current commission fees charged on hogs sold on the terminal markets.

Article Eleven of the agreement specified that the NFO could not become the legal owner of commodities and that it would function solely as a service organization bargaining for marketing contracts.

The member signing the contract agreed to abide by the other articles of the agreement and to process any complaints against the NFO in accordance with the organization's by-laws.

If modification of the contract was needed, a two-thirds majority vote of the members in a given marketing area committee would approve changes.

An agricultural journalist who wrote about the NFO membership agreement commented:

I have discussed the contract with bankers and lawyers to find out if there are any loopholes or objectionable features. Lawyers were of the opinion that the contract would be binding in the courts. One called attention to the fact that the contract is signed by the farmer but there is no place for a signature of an NFO official. Since the contract involves more than power of attorney, there might be some objection in the courts to such a contract signed by only one party to the agreement.

One man said that from a legal viewpoint the contract is harsh in spots, a bit vague in places and complicated administratively and except for the unilateral aspects of the single signature and one other questionable situation, the contract appears to be legal. . . .[1]

Another farm journalist wrote:

There is nothing in it *per se* which might be damaging to a signer. But the individual who signs it should realize that it is a legal document, drawn up by legal talent, and there is good reason why he should discuss it with his attorney before putting his name to it. It contains clauses which definitely affect his future rights and income.[2]

It is fairly obvious why the NFO would need a binding agreement with its members to conduct their program of collective bargaining. Without it, the NFO bargaining committees would have nothing to offer processors. It was possible to argue that the farmer who signed the agreement had nothing to lose—except perhaps his $25 a year in dues and fees—since if the NFO did not win in its drive for collective bargaining the farmer was free to market as he pleased. If the NFO did obtain contracts with processors, the farmer-member would be bound to abide by the agreements involved, but he would enjoy an advantage since the contracted prices paid by processors would show a premium above prevailing free market prices.

There were no sinister or misleading clauses in the agreement to cheat the member. Generally, NFO officials were willing to go over their contract point by point to satisfy any questions offered by members or potential signers of the contract.

The legislative basis of the NFO's program for collective bargaining lay in the Capper-Volstead Act of 1922.* A letter written by a Washington, D.C., attorney to Staley explained the connection between the Capper-Volstead Act and the NFO's policy:

You have requested that I give you an opinion regarding the legality of farmers bargaining collectively. In this connection I

---

* For complete text of the Capper-Volstead Act of 1922 and comments by the sponsors of the legislation, see Appendix B.

have studied your form of membership agreement. All of the plans, procedures, purposes and objectives of the Marketing Agreement are legal for an organization under the Capper-Volstead Act. The object of the Capper-Volstead Act is to authorize farmers to act collectively in organizations in the selling and marketing of their agricultural products with the same rights, force and effect as though all of the agricultural products of all the farmers who are members of the organization were being sold and marketed by one farmer.

Congress knew at the time that the Capper-Volstead Act was enacted that the bargaining power of individual farmers was weak or nonexistent; that farmers were many while the buyers of their products were few. Congress knew that farmers were the only producers (manufacturers) that were not in a position to name the prices of the commodities that they had to sell; but on the other hand, that farmers were compelled to ask buyers what they would pay for their agricultural products. In order to make it possible for farmers to have more bargaining power in the sale of their commodities, the Capper-Volstead Act was passed by Congress. Just as a labor union may legally bargain for all of the workers employed in a given plant or by all the employers in a given industry, an organization of farmers meeting the conditions of the Capper-Volstead Act may bargain collectively for all of its members for the sale of their products; and there are no restrictions on the number of farmers who may be members of such an organization.

All farmers could voluntarily join one organization and it could bargain collectively for the sale of their products; and all this would be legal. The Capper-Volstead Act is an exception to our Anti-Trust Laws. It was enacted to make it clear that farmers could act collectively without violating the Anti-Trust Laws.[3]

The conditions that had to be met by a farm organization to legally bargain collectively under the act, the lawyer said, included:

● The organization must be entirely composed of persons engaged in the production of agricultural products.

● The organization must be operated for the mutual benefit of the members thereof.

● No member of the organization shall be allowed more than one vote in stock, or membership capital of "dividends on stock or membership capital" shall be restricted to not exceed eight per cent per annum.

● The organization "shall not deal in the products of non-members to an amount greater in value than such as are handled by it for members; but it is not required to deal to any extent in the products of non-members."

Obviously the Capper-Volstead Act of 1922 was a piece of legislation that the NFO had nothing to do with in terms of drawing it up and having it enacted. In fact, it was not until about six months after the NFO decided on formulating a program for collective bargaining that the leadership learned—almost accidentally—of the act. One official of the NFO told the author that members got together and drafted a legislative bill to have presented in Congress to lay the legal groundwork for the NFO program. However, as research was done in drawing up the bill, a University of California faculty member informed NFO officials that the Capper-Volstead Act filled all the NFO's needs.

The Act itself came more than 30 years before the NFO was conceived, during the period when Farmers Union and Farm Bureau co-ops were struggling for success. Although the Farmers Union had long since given up its early ideas of collective bargaining, one of the purposes of the act was the protection of cooperatives. The NFO could thank earlier farm leadership for laying this legal foundation.

Assuming that NFO membership agreements were signed by enough producers of farm commodities to enforce their demands for higher prices by withholding their goods from markets, it followed that a contract to be offered to buyers and processors should be prepared for the "day when NFO started to win victories." With this eventuality in mind, NFO leadership drew up their "master contract." *

In September, 1961, a proposed draft of the contract to be offered to processors was presented to members to discuss in their county meetings. Eight pages of mimeographed material, including a foreword (which amounted to a pep talk) and explanations of the fourteen major articles of the document, comprised the master contract. Reading through it, one found that many of the points of agreement would be solved "at the bargaining table." In the foreword, NFO said it had in 1961 two-thirds of the "necessary strength to bring the processors to the bargaining table . . . we will continue to prepare for an all out holding action at the ear-

---

* For complete text of the master contract with explanations as distributed among NFO members, see Appendix C.

liest possible date, but in the meantime we will be offering the processors an opportunity to bargain in good faith."

Hogs were used as the sample commodity to explain the contract to NFO members. In the first article of the document, the NFO agreed to serve as a procurement agency to deliver hogs to the processor at its plant or at receiving stations that might be agreed upon. Next, the processor was to agree to pay a price for hogs demanded by the NFO and subject to adjustment "seasonally from time to time by NFO, based on production costs and approval by the members concerned." The proposed contract asked $22.75 per hundredweight for hogs weighing 190 to 200 pounds and grading No. 1 or No. 2. Prices for other classes of hogs would be scaled on relative merit. In no case would the contracted price be lower than prevailing market levels.

The fourth article of the contract specified the number of hogs that a processor would buy during a year, allowing a tolerance of 20 per cent more or less as the case might arise. The NFO argued that this clause assured the processor a steady source of supply and at the same time made known to NFO members the processor's needs.

The next two points of the contract dealt with processors and NFO working together to promote delivery of the animals as needed and keep NFO members informed on the kind of hogs that "best meet the needs of consumers and the demands of the market."

As with the membership agreement, the master contract had an automatic renewal clause. The packer—as would be the case in marketing hogs—would have a five-day period in which to notify the NFO that it would like to terminate the contract. Otherwise, the contract would be binding for another year. However, the agreement with processors would not be "in full force and effect" until an unspecified percentage of all packers had signed contracts with the NFO. This percentage was left open, the NFO said, because of "strategic reasons." However, NFO officials later indicated that about 60 per cent of all production of a given farm commodity would have to be covered by NFO master contracts before the agreements would be in effect. The percentage would be figured on three years of processing volume of the plants involved.

The processor was held responsible for keeping records of purchases of hogs under the NFO contract. Also, the processor was to agree to pay an additional percentage* to the NFO for services rendered by the farm organization. This was to be paid monthly.

The NFO was to agree to keep the processor informed in advance by two weeks on the volume of supply of hogs during the contract period and would deliver this information within three days of the beginning of each two-week period.

NFO and processors would have joint supervision of grading and weighing of hogs handled under the contract and would work together for the establishment of uniform grades.

In final analysis, the contract seemed to leave the processor on the short end of the stick. NFO would have higher prices, an assured market and possibly a means for leveling out production to meet demands, but the processor was stuck with paying higher prices plus extra fees. Also the processor was at the mercy of NFO members who might boost their prices whenever they thought they needed more money. About the only point in the packer's favor was that of being assured a steady supply of hogs for slaughter. At any rate, not many processors would be easily induced into signing such an agreement. While NFO's program would offer stabilized prices and supplies, the processor still had

---

* NFO president Staley told the author in early 1964 that this service charge would be 5 per cent of the gross amount of purchases made by packers dealing with the NFO. Of this 5 per cent fee, 0.5 per cent would be allocated to a farm product promotion fund and the remaining 4.5 per cent would be disposed of at the wishes of voting NFO members involved in the transactions from which the service charge came. Possibly this 4.5 per cent would be divided and returned to the members as a kind of dividend, Staley said. Since many packers reported that their average profits amounted to about 1 per cent of their total investment, this proposed service charge seemed extremely high and would run into vast sums of money quickly if brought into effect.

to deal with the economic realities of changing demand and prices paid to him for dressed meat. In the past, the risk and price fluctuations had always been more or less passed on to the farmer.

Except for a few small processors who felt a great deal of local pressure, virtually no one signed these contracts. Possibly those who did sign them did so as a compromise with the local farm folks who demanded a contract. But it was quite likely that those who did sign the NFO's master contract believed that the percentage-of-processing require-ment to bring it into full effect would never be attained, thus it did not matter whether a few small operators agreed and cooperated with the NFO.

Signing up processors was the goal of NFO's battle. To the members it promised more money in the farm larder, a stabilized market and certainty of price levels. It was utopian—or at least sounded nearly perfect.

But why shouldn't farmers bargain collectively? Using the examples of labor unions that had fought for better working conditions and better wages, NFO members felt that they had every right to economic equality, both on moral and legal grounds. Speeches by NFO leaders often emphasized that agriculture had more potential bargaining power than labor and industry combined. The trouble was, it just was not organized. The task of uniting farmers was one which NFO claimed to be doing rapidly.

Everyone else prices the products they sell, so why shouldn't farmers? Getting back to the emotional pitch that there "must be justice at the market place," NFO leaders again argued that farmers had a moral and legal right to price their own products and services. This was indeed true and even the severest critics of NFO policies assented to this fact. However, there was no mention by leaders of the farm group that those manufacturing and production inter-ests that allegedly set prices to assure their own margins of profit were the same interests that governed, to the best of their knowledge, their production in accordance with the potential market.

If the master contract offered by NFO could be brought

into effect, it was possible that eventually production would be brought in line with demand through the quotas outlined in the membership agreement. While this might mean a slight increase in consumer prices, it could mean a great deal to the economy of the states where agriculture is an important industry and, of course, it would mean victory for the NFO in its struggle to improve farm prices.

Although the holding actions on livestock attracted most of the attention that the NFO received in its first eight years of existence, similar actions were called on grain. Because of the difference in farmer-participation in the grain marketing system, coupled with the huge role the Commodity Credit Corporation played in marketing, the results of these actions were questionable. Some critics felt they were negligible. The NFO, naturally, claimed success, especially at the end of a test holding action on soybeans which started early in 1961. Here, however, was a commodity that was enjoying good prices and gains due to a market situation that was healthier than, say, wheat or corn.

Controversy sparked from NFO's efforts to boost milk prices. Since a great deal of milk was being sold under federal marketing orders, there were problems of contracts that might have conflicted. While the membership agreement specified that commodities already under marketing agreements would be exceptions to the NFO authorization clause, members were agitating in dairy production areas for processors to sign the master contract. In a later chapter this development, along with NFO activities in grain marketing, will be treated in more detail.

What kind of people belonged to the NFO? Oren Lee Staley rocketed to a paradoxical peak of being a hero and a "bad guy" at the same time, depending on the observer's point of view. What were he and his lieutenants like? Some people suspected the NFO of various kinds of suspicious activities. Was there anything to it? These and other questions will be examined in the next two chapters before taking up the arguments of NFO's so-called "big foe," its opposition.

9

STALEY'S KIND OF ORGANIZATION
Part I

IT WAS A BIG JOB. Anyone who had the courage and the spirit to tackle such an endeavor as leading a farm organization which in essence was setting out to revolutionize agricultural marketing had to be a person who would work tirelessly and with the tenacity of conviction to wage a "do-or-die" battle. Oren Lee Staley displayed these characteristics as president of the National Farmers Organization. Among some of those who followed him there was the opinion that Staley was almost infallible. Those who opposed him thought he was, at best, a refined rabble-rouser. But there was no doubt that he attracted thousands of farmers, some of whom traveled hundreds of miles to hear his emotion-charged—some said self-righteous—speeches. With indignant fervor, he attacked the marketing system, the buyers and processors of farm products and the chain food stores. Because of the price-cost squeeze, it was easy to blame these off-the-farm interests for the farmers' problems. Without much subtlety, it was not hard to convince farmers that they were being victimized by middlemen. "Justice at the marketplace" and "farmers are being farmed" were among the expressions he often shouted to arouse his following. A farm operator in financial trouble found it

easy to agree with Staley. Nearly all his speeches boiled
down to this:

*If farmers want higher prices, they will have to do it
themselves by organizing to bargain collectively. A hard
battle will have to be waged to do this, but it is the only way
of saving the family farm.*

With undaunted optimism, Staley reiterated his argument for farmers to back the NFO drive. Some newsmen
said the movement resembled a religious crusade. "Mostly
because the 39-year-old Staley has the public style and
some of the aversions of a tent-meeting revivalist, the organization he heads is often likened to a religious sect. Its
300 paid organizers [later this number reached 400] are
the 'missionaries' who scour the back roads in door-to-door
drives for new members. There are passages in Staley's
fervent addresses that call forth the secular equivalent of
Amen. At times, his mighty words lift a whole audience
from its seats to shout an affirmation of the vision," one account said.[1]

Away from the speaker's stand, Staley had anything but
the appearance of a vociferous farm leader. He was a large
man, standing six-feet-one and weighing about 225 pounds.
His weight was distributed on his large frame well enough
to compliment his easygoing, almost jolly manner in public.
Those who didn't like him or what he stood for often remarked, however, that he was fat. He seemed to know virtually everyone attending a national convention and was
always willing to shake another hand or take a minute or
two to chat with NFO members or outsiders. In dealing
with the press, he was friendly, but cagey. Regardless of
the question, he usually had a ready reply and sometimes
his explanations grew lengthy. To queries that were point-
edly barbed, he usually returned answers that were as casual as talking about the weather. By and large, he cooperated very well with newsmen.

On two of the occasions that the author interviewed the
NFO president at his headquarters office in Corning, the

sessions took place in his rather small cubicle at the back of the NFO building. The NFO headquarters was located in a high-ceilinged, old grocery store building, like many to be found along the main streets of Corn Belt towns. Worn wooden floors, oily from years of sweeping compounds, and patterned tin panels on the ceiling typified the building. At the front was a counter where a typist doubled as receptionist. Most of the floor space was taken up by the desks of some 35 office girls. There were many file cabinets. Hundreds of forms and papers were also seen filed in cardboard boxes placed on shelves along one wall. The office bustled with the chatter of typewriters and adding machines. The general appearance of the Corning operation was that of a makeshift office—but a busy one.

As the author waited to be admitted to see Staley, a stream of people entered and left the building. Many were members who casually dropped in to say hello; others came on specific business. On two occasions, the hour of appointment slipped by as the author waited for his interviews with the NFO head. Two-hour delays preceded both of these sessions with Staley and there was a four-hour wait before a third visit, this one nearly at midnight.

In Staley's office—a corner partitioned off from the main area inside the old brick building—stood a large, impressive walnut desk behind which Staley slouched comfortably in a big swivel chair. A couch and a pair of easy chairs were the only other furnishings. On one wall hung a pair of pictures, one a portrait of Staley and the other a photo taken of the 1962 meeting for action attended by 20,000 farmers. An advertising calendar adorned another wall. Stacks of papers cluttered the desk.

There was no carpet on the floor of Staley's office. This perhaps served to let visiting members know that their dues weren't being splurged on niceties for the national office and that this was in truth a farm organization of farmers only.

In slacks and a dress shirt, with collar open and sleeves rolled up, Staley lounged back and waited for questions. To

talk with him, there seemed little in his background to indicate that he would blossom into a dynamic leader.

He was born May 6, 1923, on a farm a half mile east
and a half mile south of Whitesville in northwestern Missouri. The only child of a farmer who also taught school,
Oren Lee shared his father's interest in purebred cattle. The
younger Staley made an outstanding record in 4-H Club
work. He was the first boy from the St. Joseph area to win
an interstate award that included an expense-free trip to
Chicago. The Staley farm was twelve miles from King City,
Missouri, where Oren Lee attended high school, and this
limited his participation in extra-curricular activities. However, he was once elected president of his high school class
and served as president of the student council. He was
graduated as salutatorian of his class of about 50 students.

In the two years that he attended Northwest Missouri
State College at Maryville, he majored in agriculture and
carried a minor in mathematics. Here again, he did not
take part in extra-curricular activities. His father's declining health forced him to quit college in 1946 to go back to
the farm. The last semester he was in college, his grades
were straight "E's," the top grade given. Other than two
years before college when he served as a land-locked phar-
macist's mate in the Navy and his college days, Oren Lee
spent all of his life on the farm.

When the NFO came into being, he was farming a 400-
acre operation adjoining his father's farm. He had a herd of
about 60 purebred Shorthorn cattle, which he pampered,
and also raised between 500 and 600 hogs a year. Married
to a pretty, dark-haired farm girl, he was the father of two
girls and a boy. He was also a member of the Farm Bureau
at that time.

Able to claim that he had never had an alcoholic drink
in his life, Staley said he starting smoking cigarettes only
after he became president of the NFO. A religious man, he
occasionally taught Sunday School at his local Baptist
church and served many years as clerk of the church.

Asked if he thought he had any especially strong personality traits, Staley said in an easy Missouri drawl, "Well, I guess other people would have to be the judge of that; I don't know." Given a similar question on his personal weaknesses, he said, "No, no, no, I don't know as I have any. I'm not perfect; I know I make mistakes, but I'm always willing to admit them." How about situations or things that he found pleasing? "I just enjoy life, period. I make the best of the situation whatever and wherever it is. I take things as they come."

Regarding his attitude toward the job of president of the NFO, Staley said:

"I feel as president of the NFO, you just have to do the best job you can, realizing the tremendous responsibility that the NFO has because I feel that the very future of the family type farm hangs on the success of the NFO." Adding a comment on what he enjoyed most as head of the movement, he said, "I like to surround myself with hard-working people."

An active local league baseball player in his youth, Oren Lee said he was still a fan of all kinds of sports. Also for relaxation, he said he liked to work with his purebred cattle.

As president of the farm organization, Staley maintained a punishing pace. He said he averaged three or four speeches a week, but didn't have any idea how many miles he traveled in the average year in office. Usually flying by light airplane to meetings where he made appearances, it would be safe to say that he traveled nearly a quarter of a million miles a year. Besides traveling thousands of miles for speaking engagements, he presided over national board of directors meetings, supervised all activities of the national office, had final control of some 400 paid organizers in the field and was reported to have done most of the writing for the organization's newspaper, *The NFO Reporter.* For this kind of performance, he was paid $175 a week, plus expenses. By late 1963, his salary was reported at $200 a week.

According to the NFO's bylaws, the president's duties

included having authority to appoint all personnel hired by the organization, subject to the approval of the national board of directors. As principal executive officer of the group, the president presided over all conventions and meetings of the board of directors. He also was empowered to appoint—with the board's approval—all committees of the board of directors to which would be delegated any executive or administrative functions. The national president also signed, with the national secretary, any deeds, mortgages, deeds of trust, notes, bonds, contracts, or other documents authorized by the board of directors under the bylaws. He was also to "perform all the duties incident to the office of president and such other duties as may be prescribed by the board of directors from time to time."

In the original bylaws also appeared a section authorizing the president to appoint an executive committee from among members of the national board. This committee could act in lieu of the entire board. The number of members of the executive committee was to be decided by the board itself. Obviously this offered an opportunity for the president to appoint hand-picked members of the board who might agree with any proposal he should offer. Simply by convening such an executive committee, it was possible for the president to have complete control of the NFO. Although there was no public information to indicate that this ever happened, a change in the bylaws was proposed at the 1962 national NFO convention to wrest this power from the chief executive of the organization. Replacing the practice of appointment to the executive committee by the president was a plan to have all of the members of the board elect members of the committee. After long and labored debate, spiced with confused bickering over parliamentary procedure, the proposal was enacted into the bylaws by the 1962 convention delegates. This, however, was just part of the unrest that followed the recessing of the 1962 all out holding action.

THERE WERE four general levels of organization in the NFO. The highest, of course, was that of the national officers and the national board of directors. Under the national organization were state, district and county units:

State Organizations—"It shall be the duty and responsibility of state organizations to work for the enactment of laws that are more responsible to the needs of the membership of the organization, and to repeal laws which may be reactionary in nature and which do not represent the viewpoint of the majority of the members of the organization." According to the NFO's bylaws, this was the purpose of state-level NFO bodies. The state group also was charged with the duty of keeping members informed on legislative developments and to make recommendations of support of or opposition to pending legislation. Officers of the state organization included a state executive committee made up of the chairman of each congressional district NFO organization (if organized at that level in a given state) plus the national board members from that state.

Congressional District Organizations—The usual officers showed up in the organization at the district level. There was a president, a vice president, secretary, treasurer and a board member from each county organization within the congressional district, plus three trustees. Except for the trustees, elected for three-year periods, the officers served terms of a year. Officers were to be elected at district meetings held in August or September. District board members representing county groups were to be elected in county meetings. Purpose of the district organization was nearly all political, as outlined in the NFO's bylaws.

County Organizations—The county organizations had the same slate of officers as the district counterpart. The president, vice president, secretary and treasurer served one-year terms and three county trustees were in office for three years each. At both district and county levels, a new trustee was elected each year so that all three would not come into office at the same time. County meetings were to be held monthly.

To finance the four levels of NFO organization, of the $25 each member was assessed annually ($5 dues, $20 service fee), $23.25 was forwarded to the national office and the remaining $1.75 stayed with the county organization. Of the sum received by the national office, 50 cents, according to the bylaws, went for a member's subscription to the organization publication, *The NFO Reporter*. The national treasurer then was to disburse 60 cents per member to the district treasurer and 15 cents to the state treasurer. This meant in the end that $22 of the $25 a member paid in dues and fees per year went into the national treasury. In the event of marketing contracts (where a likely 3 per cent checkoff would be deducted), 75 per cent of these receipts would go to the national coffers while county organizations would get 20 per cent and district and state organizations would each get 2.5 per cent of the checkoff from each member's sales under NFO contracts.

In terms of financial equality, it appeared to the casual observer that the national office was taking a big rake-off of the member's dues. However, it is well to note that most of the expenses of the NFO were at the national level where officers often put in full time and also had considerable travel costs and expenses. Work at the intervening levels was largely done on a voluntary basis. Noting that all of the NFO's income was coming from membership dues and fees and that most of the spending was at the national level, this system of distribution was not really out of line.

IF AN ORGANIZATION has a purpose, it has a message. The NFO's message was that of collective bargaining for agriculture. Several avenues were used to spread the gospel that Staley and his cohorts were preaching. The most stirring was the personal delivery of speeches. Television and radio appearances offered a diluted counterpart of the personal appearance. Besides pamphlets and mimeographed handouts, the NFO's message came printed in *The NFO Reporter*, a monthly newspaper of tabloid format that offered news of organizational activity and gave arguments why the movement's program was desirable and necessary.

Usually consisting of six or eight pages per issue, the *Reporter* was published on a lackadaisical schedule. For example, the issue for June might reach a subscriber during the first or second week of July. This was about the only unpredictable feature about it.

A regular front-page feature was the "President's Message. . ." column written by Oren Lee Staley. It read as his speeches did.

The "lead" or main story on page one usually touted accomplishments of the organization. For example, beginning with the July 1962 issue through the December 1962 issue (there was no September 1962 issue), the main stories in the *Reporter* carried huge, black headlines that read:

Ultimatum to Processors; "Meeting for Action" Set

More Than 20,000 Vote All-Out Holding Action

Foot in Door

First Big Breakthrough As NFO Signs Contract

5,000 Voting Delegates
To Attend Convention

Staley Re-elected to
8th Presidency of NFO

The headlines outline how the NFO reported its progress through the month preceding 1962's all out holding action up through the time Staley was re-elected president in December of that year.

On the inside of the monthly newspaper were editorials reminding members that their personal financial position, compared with other segments of the national economy, was anything but good. Other articles were more cheery, with stories of farmer neighborliness and ideas that would be useful or profitable to farmers.

Letters and occasional poetry written by NFO farmwives sometimes showed up in the *Reporter*. A verse titled "An NFO Widow's Lament" appeared in the November 1961 issue, telling how one farmwife hardly ever saw her mate after he became enthusiastic over the NFO program. The poem closed:

> I think I know how Martha would feel
> When George wouldn't come home for his evening
>   meal,
> But Washington won his Revolution,
> So I'm going to make this resolution.
> Loyal and true to the cause I will stay
> And hope NFO brings a happier day.

The editorial philosophy of *The NFO Reporter* resembled that of most "house organs." Its contents were written in a fashion to best plead the NFO case. Only news that was favorable to the organization appeared. For example, there was never any mention of violence connected with the holding actions or was the "opposition's" case presented in detail. This was only logical, since it was the NFO paper.

There was one unusual aspect. In the masthead—the inside portion usually found on the editorial page of a newspaper that lists editor, publisher, etc.—the officers of the national organization appeared, along with names of the board members. However, no editor was named in the *Reporter*'s masthead. One inside source said that Staley himself wrote or edited every word printed in *The NFO Reporter*, even though the organization had an editor on the payrolls for that purpose.

As the official organ of the NFO, the *Reporter* doubled as a purveyor of news and as an educational tool. Since the basic program of the organization was explained fairly simply, much of the material carried in the newspaper consisted of argumentation for support of the collective bargaining movement. Additionally, Staley said the organization had an "education department" set up to prepare material to help members and non-members alike to understand the farmer's plight.

Analyses of holding actions, reports of cost-of-production, a history of the NFO and a rather lengthy report on the current livestock marketing system were among the educational projects turned out by the organization. Although some of the speeches and other propaganda put out by the organization was accusatory, it is interesting to note that a report issued by the NFO in 1961 opened mildly:

The NFO does not charge that chain stores, meat packers, commission men, etc., are plotting against the American farmer, nor do we believe that corruption is any more prevalent in these industries than in any other. We do maintain that failure to administer laws governing the packing industry, the natural economic pressures involved in the concentration of consumer buying power through a comparative handful of chain stores, and the lack of vigilant farm organization in the Midwest to protect producer interests, have resulted in a livestock marketing system that is as carefully controlled as any slot machine at Las Vegas.[2]

The study proceeded to examine trading practices of the dressed meat market, direct livestock marketing, the role of chain stores in the livestock and meat industry and the part played by commission firms. NFO's recommendations were prefaced:

The NFO doubts that laws can be passed or present laws enforced that will fully correct our marketing system. The only really satisfactory answer is probably through organization of farmers or use of federal marketing orders. We do believe that enforcement of existing laws would greatly benefit agriculture. Our specific recommendations follow:

● That packers and chain stores be forbidden to operate feedlots.

● That packers and chain stores be forbidden to enter into contracts with individual farmers in which delivery date is determined by packer and chain stores.

We believe that the Secretary of Agriculture possesses adequate legal authority under the Packers and Stockyards Act, 1921, as amended, to stop these practices. . . .

● The dissemination of pre-market information to packers by the USDA market reporting service should be stopped immediately (by order of the Secretary). While this has been denied by some officials of the department, we quote from a letter from Assistant Secretary of Agriculture Miller to an Iowa congressman:

"In contacting the buying stations and packing plants for the purpose of collecting information, the Federal Market News Service also disseminates some price and receipt information. The first round of calls is generally paid for by the packer and buying station operators, and for this reason it is feasible to provide estimated receipts from other markets, early price trends, etc., that are available. Our Livestock Market News Branch furnishes receipt and price data to everyone calling any of its offices regardless of whether they are buyers, sellers or traders."

● The use of the "yellow" sheet put out by the American Meat Institute, official organization of the meat packers, should be stopped under authority of both subdivisions E and F of Section 202 of the Packers and Stockyards Act [which outlawed manipulation of or controlling prices].

● That packers and chain stores be forbidden to ship livestock purchased direct into terminal market areas under authority of Section 202.

● That commission firms or their employees be forbidden to feed or handle their own livestock. The possibilities of corruption where market agencies are allowed to handle their own livestock in addition to selling other livestock on commission is obvious."

● Reports on foreign imports are inadequate and should be kept current. Today there is a 60-day lag. We suggest daily imports be carried as part of our regular market reports.[3]

In the end, the study called for a congressional investigation of the marketing system and urged the Secretary of Agriculture to enforce more stringently marketing laws already in effect. It was interesting to note that NFO had shifted its blaming packers for low livestock prices to a viewpoint that chain food stores were controlling the market. Although some market interests would debate the validity of the NFO's market studies, these educational efforts did serve a constructive purpose. Many farmers were made more aware of the importance of studying the market, how it works and planning production in relation to market trends.

Of course, NFO's purpose in presenting the material was to show why the organization's program was necessary to "straighten out" the market in such a way that the farmer would make more money.

The NFO also developed its own means of mass communication, "the minuteman system." Reminiscent of tales of Paul Revere and the minutemen of the American Revolution, the NFO's setup was really only a twentieth century version of the earlier form of passing the word. While the organization might have had at its disposal most news media for distributing an announcement, there was the problem of not all members getting the message. Also, there was the likelihood that everyone, including "the opposition," could learn of NFO's plans for action before all of the organization's members were informed.

As a result, the NFO organized a system under which all members could get "the word from Corning" within a matter of hours. This was done by a system of relayed telephone calls. If, for example, a surprise move was decided on in Corning, a telephone call would be made to a key man in each state where the NFO was organized. The chief minuteman in each state would in turn call each of the political districts where a subordinate minuteman would be stationed. The top minuteman at the district level would call one minuteman in each county. From there, the message would be spread by more subordinate minutemen. At the county level, there was one minuteman for every 30 farmers in his area. The system was organized so that no one had to make more than four telephone calls as the message branched out in a series of three major relays. The minuteman system was used for communications in connection with holding actions and also was put into use whenever local NFO'ers decided to pitch in on a service project, such as helping farmers in distress after tornadic storms, floods and other emergencies.

While all these relays of calls obviously could have provided an opportunity for error—as is the case with a story passing from mouth to mouth—Staley said that the system had been perfected to the point that messages could reach every member efficiently and accurately in a matter of five or six hours.

BRINGING NEW MEMBERS into the flock required hard work on the part of national staff organizers and local membership recruiting teams that went out "selling" the NFO to non-member farmers. In areas where there was no NFO organization, a national organizer would travel unobtrusively about the countryside and arrange to hold a series of small meetings, perhaps one per night for a week or ten days in a given county. A handful of up to about ten farmers would be invited to hear the NFO story and encouraged to join in the campaign for higher prices. The initial efforts to organize in a new area were usually done with little or no publicity, a practice that avoided any adverse public comment from NFO's opposition. A county organization was chartered as soon as there were 25 NFO members in the county. Once the county unit grew to about 100 members, officers were elected.[4]

The organizers themselves were farmers who had been "sold" on NFO's program and were so enthusiastic about it that they in turn were ardent salesmen of the movement. About the only qualifications needed for the job were that they hold the conviction that NFO was the answer to the farmers' problems, that organizers be NFO members in good standing and that they meet the approval of Staley and his lieutenants in Corning. All organizers were under the direction of Lloyd Fairbanks, the movement's organizational director. He was paid $135 a week. Under Fairbanks were assistants who were paid $100 a week plus expenses. These assistants directed the efforts of some 400 staff organizers in the field. Full-time employees, the staff organizers made a steady $100 per week. They were paid from the money they gathered by getting new memberships. Out of each $25 paid by a new member for a year's fees, $7.50 was set aside for paying organizers. Even if an individual staff organizer did not sell enough memberships to make $100 a week out of the allotments set aside, he was paid his full salary. And if he sold more than enough memberships to fulfill a week's pay, he still got his regular $100. The lowest level of paid organizers were part-time workers who made $15 a day providing they sold two memberships per day.

Remarkable is the fact that a great portion of the organizing of NFO was done by volunteers rather than paid organizers. This was particularly important to the growth of the organization in its early days since there usually was little money in the treasury to finance organizational efforts. In 1962, some 60 per cent of the whole NFO's expenses was devoted to organizing.

After a county unit of the NFO had a foothold, local members would call on their neighbors and other farmers throughout the county to sign them up as NFO members. Membership teams of two men often called on non-members in the evenings during the planting season or in the fall when farmers normally had to be in the field during daylight hours. "Rainy-day" calls were also made when wet weather kept farmers from outside work.[5] By sitting down with a farmer at the end of the day, the organizers and the potential new members both had time to discuss the points of the membership agreement and policies of the organization. Besides, it gave an opportunity for farm wives to hear the NFO's arguments too.

Although it was never mentioned, the advantages of sending a two-man team to talk to a non-member were fairly obvious. For one thing, some farmers who were not sympathetic to the NFO movement reacted unpleasantly. From various sources, the author heard accounts of disagreeable farm operators who forced NFO organizers off their property at gunpoint. In any case, two men would have been better than one when organizers encountered opposition among the farm populace. Another point was that two men could "work on" a farmer better than one organizer alone. If the non-member argued that the NFO program would not work, two men could take turns firing back rebuttals and, if need be, take turns badgering and cajoling until the farmer gave in. A number of farmers said they were tired of arguing with the persistent organizers and finally signed the NFO membership agreement just to be left alone. Others said that when the NFO became strong in their neighborhood, they had to go along with the movement or fall victims to abuse by neighbors who had joined and felt strongly that everyone with good sense should join up.

Ill will between NFO members and farmers who did not belong to the organization became newsworthy during the all out holding action of 1962, but it had been potentially boiling as long as there were supporters and opposers of the movement living side by side in any area. And while the holding action posed a kind of crisis situation for NFO members who were determined to prove that their program would work, the undercurrent of opposition became more acutely felt as members stepped up their efforts to win in their campaign. Numerous market interests at the major points told the author that in their dealings with folks out in the country, they heard of cases where men and wives became bitterly separated because they did not share the same view of the NFO policies. Other splits were reported among otherwise close families that operated farms together or on a work-sharing basis. Neighbors who had long been friends suddenly became enemies because one had joined the NFO and the other refused to go along with the movement.

It would have been most fortunate if the NFO organizers had adopted a practice of arbitrating the differences between some of the NFO members and farmers who did not like the organization's plan for action. Doubtless some of the proponents of the program worked tirelessly to recruit and sign up a larger following without stirring up ill feelings. In some cases, members went out of their way to help patch up disagreements and minor feuds that were started because of differences over the farm organization. Although many members were getting their backs up over low farm prices, they still highly valued the blessing of friendly, cooperative neighbors and a general atmosphere of peacefulness in their communities.

What kind of farmer did the NFO organizers sign up? It would be impossible to quickly generalize that the average NFO member was an operator of so many acres, raised so many hogs, etc. While it is easy to say a man is a typical farmer, it is important to remember that no two farms are alike, any more than two farmers are identical. The common denominator of NFO members was that all shared the discouragement of low farm prices in the face of high costs. If a farmer was not making much money, it did not matter whether he had a large acreage with vast herds of livestock or whether he had less than 100 acres of marginal, worn-out farmland and no livestock. In either case, he would favor a movement that gave hope for more personal prosperity. Oren Lee Staley told the author in an interview that the average NFO member was a large producer of livestock. The NFO president explained that since his organization's dues were higher than any other farm organization at the time, only bigger farmers were willing to put $25 a year into an NFO membership. While there were a goodly number of older farmers—considering the fact that the average age of farm operators was increasing—a large percentage of the NFO following consisted of men in their 40's and younger. These had been farm boys who fought in World War II and the Korean Conflict and returned to the farm with hopes of some day owning their own profitable operation. Having left country living for several years, they were keenly aware of what labor unions had done for urban workers. When they returned to the farm and were caught up in the price-cost squeeze that tightened up after the Korean Conflict, they had cause for complaint.

Purely at random, the author obtained interviews with four members of the NFO, three of whom were attending the August 1962 meeting for action in Des Moines. It is well to stress at this point that the "case histories" of these farmers should not be construed to serve as examples of the "average" NFO member. But they do represent some of the feelings and some of the problems that Staley's followers talked about.

FARMER A, FROM SOUTHWEST IOWA

At age 49, Alfred, as we'll call him here, was the third generation of his family to run a 300-acre crop and livestock operation in southwest Iowa. He had been born on that farm and reared there through his high school days. He attended Colorado State University and was graduated with a degree in geological engineering. He spent five years in the Army during World War II and afterwards went to work for a major petroleum company. Fifteen years with the oil firm, plus the years he spent in military service gave him a record of having lived in Iowa, Texas, Louisiana, New Mexico, Florida, Massachusetts, Kansas, Arkansas, Colorado and Oklahoma. Despite the good earnings of his engineering job, a gnawing desire to return to rural living brought him back to his father's Iowa farm.

When the NFO started up in 1955, Alfred put a dollar into the "dollar days" protest movement. But it was not until 1960 that he rejoined the movement, after it had adopted a program for collective bargaining. When he was interviewed during the fall of 1962, he was president of his county NFO chapter.

"Only a farmer can be really acquainted with a farmer's problems—outsiders might have a fair understanding of what the farmer faces, but he couldn't know the full impact of the farm problem unless he is directly involved in it," Alfred said. Commenting on what he liked about the NFO, he said, "It's an organization striving for farmers, run by farmers. When I see the sincerity, earnestness and fairness shown by the leadership, I can't help but think we're on the right track. Another thing, the control of the organization is written into the membership agreement, at the member's level. Any important decisions require a two-thirds vote of the membership. As long as people in the organization are active, it will be a democratic operation."

Asked what he disliked about the NFO's program, he replied, "I'd really have to do some thinking about that—I can't think of anything I object to. That may sound pretty biased, but it's the truth."

As a county leader, Alfred said the three main reasons farmers gave for not joining NFO were that they didn't want to lose their individual freedom because the membership agreement seemed restrictive; they felt that if the NFO contracted higher prices, everyone would raise twice as many hogs and flood the market; and they feared the organization would eventually be dominated by labor unions. Alfred's answers to these objections were that the first one simply wasn't true; the second argument was only a guess about what would happen and Alfred said that this situation most likely wouldn't develop because of the NFO's quota clause in the membership agreement; the last was impossible since it was illegal for organized labor to be affiliated with the NFO.

"I wish you'd tell me the answer to that," Alfred count-
ered when asked how local townspeople were reacting to the
NFO movement in his county. "From what little I've been
able to find out, some businessmen in town are afraid that
the NFO will go into business for itself as a cooperative and
end up in competition with them. This can't happen under
the provisions of the Capper-Volstead Act. Others are non-
committal, saying they don't want to take sides and offend
other farm groups. But the bankers and some of the others
who understand the program pretty much go along with
it."

Although he would not say how many members his
county organization had, Alfred said that it was still less
than 25 per cent of the county's total of 1,075 farms. He
added that once a member or two was obtained in an area,
a community colony of NFO members would often spring
up. In other areas, some members were isolated and had no
neighbors who would join.

"After having lived in several states and met a lot of
different people and understood their varied viewpoints,
I've come to the conclusion that people in this part of Iowa
are—if you want to put it in a nice way—very conservative.
Or just plain backwards. They went along with new developments such as fertilizer, weed sprays and insecticides,
but unless they can see that something new will add to their
pocketbooks, farmers in this part of the state are likely to
stay away from something new like the NFO's program. My
dad tells about the early organizing of the Farm Bureau
many years ago. Ours was one of the slowest and last
counties in the state to 'go Farm Bureau' and now it's one
of the real strongholds of that organization," the Iowa
farmer said.

On the 300 acres owned by his father and operated in
an informal partnership, Alfred said row crop production
on the farm was usually kept to around 115 acres. Since he
and his father both disagreed with the idea of raising crops
that would eventually be turned over to the government for

price support loans, they had generally kept their production down to a level where their corn and other grains would be consumed by livestock fed on the farm. For a while, Alfred farrowed his own sows and fed out the pigs to be sold as finished butchers. However, his farrowing sheds fell into disrepair and the profit margin became so narrow that upkeep was impractical. Consequently, he turned to the practice of buying feeder pigs to finish on the farm.

In addition, he generally fed out about 100 head of cattle a year. By buying calves, feeding them a growing ration through the winter, pasturing them the following summer and putting them on a fattening ration the following fall, he was able to make some money on them, Alfred said. He generally did his marketing of livestock at Omaha or St. Joseph.

Pointing out that the buildings on his farm were not in very good condition, Alfred commented that in the previous three years (1959-1961), farmers in his neighborhood had been very fortunate in having crops that were above average. "But I say that we're just one crop failure from going broke," he added.

With a daughter in nurses' training and a son in the eighth grade, Alfred said he'd like to see his boy stay on the farm if that was what the boy wanted. "But with the farm situation as it is now, I can't say that I'd encourage him to stay. He'd be better off to go to town and find a good-paying job."

Alfred pointed out that his county's organization had a good number of younger farmers filled with energy and enthusiasm to get out and work as a good team for the NFO. At the same time, it had some of the older farmers in the county, whose years of experience and older judgment helped lend maturity to the organization, he said.

"We've been called a radical organization. I don't think we are, unless you want to say that pricing your own products is something radical," the Iowan concluded.

FARMER B, FROM EAST CENTRAL MINNESOTA

On a 160-acre dairy and hog farm not far from Minneapolis, Ben (as we shall call him) lived with the personal ambition of rebuilding the barn on his place. The old basement barn, built in 1901, had become tumble-down and Ben said he some day wanted to "get it up to as nice a barn as any in the country" by remodeling it.

"We aren't getting cost of production plus a reasonable profit; the stuff we buy in town is just too high, interest is too high and it's hard to keep everything up in working order," he pointed out. The breadwinners—not counting Ben's labors—on the farm basically consisted of 25 milk cows in a manufactured milk operation and 100 hogs a year. With six children, ranging in age from one and one-half to nine years, Ben had plenty of responsibility. Having bought his own farm only about three years earlier, he had been fighting a very real battle with the price-cost squeeze that was hurting many long-time owner-operators.

"As prices are and the help [farm labor] situation as it is, you have to do all your work yourself—and you just don't get around to everything," he said. His oldest son was only nine, and Ben didn't believe in putting a boy of that age on a tractor.

Ben joined the NFO in hopes of working to improve his and other farmers' incomes. He said that his county unit was "real strong." About 250 members had been signed up from the 447 farms in the county. Those who had not joined had held back because "it's got to be proved to them that it will work," Ben explained.

Born on a farm in the county where he settled, Ben had spent all of his life in agriculture. He attended parochial grade school and was graduated from high school in 1943. Physically unfit for military service, he stayed home during World War II and helped run the family farm while his five brothers all served in one branch or another of the military service. Active in his church and a member of the Knights of Columbus, he once served as Grand Knight to his regional council. He married a city girl from St. Paul, Minnesota, and took her back to the farm.

Faced with the challenge of continued low farm prices and rising operation costs, both Ben and his wife agreed, "We hope to hang on and be able to leave something behind for our children. But the way things have been going, it makes you wonder if we will ever get ahead."

Asked whether it was hard to keep up with the technological developments in agricultural production and methods, Ben replied, "A guy can keep up with them in his mind, but financially you can't keep up with them. You can't come out on them. The little bit that you gain in one year isn't going to pay for it. You're going to have a machine worn out before it's paid for."

Ben was an ardent follower in the NFO, although he didn't hold any office in his county chapter. He said that those who understood the program, whether they were farmers or townspeople, believed in it. He also belonged to the Farm Bureau ("I belong in order to get the group insurance they offer—it's as cheap as you can get, but you have to be a member to get it."), but appeared to be much more strongly impressed with the NFO's program. Only five months after signing a membership agreement, he and his wife were in Des Moines for the loud meeting for action that preceded the 1962 all out holding action. As Ben's wife commented:

"Oh, we were a bit skeptical at first whether it [the NFO concept of collective bargaining] would work. But when you come to a meeting like this one and see all the people here and learn that they all have the same problems and will work together, you just know it's got to work."

FARMER C, FROM WEST CENTRAL OHIO

Carl had a son 16 years old who wanted to be a farmer, but the father was trying to discourage his boy from taking up agriculture as a vocation. "He could do better in a city

job with a lot less investment," the 41-year-old Ohio farmer
said. Born on a farm within 100 miles of Columbus, Ohio,
Carl (which wasn't his real name) spent his youth on the
farm and upon graduation from high school, he considered
going into farming on his own. He told his own story:

"About that time, I saw I was getting close to being in-
ducted into the Army. So I went to work in Columbus for
a couple of years until World War II broke out and then I
went into the Navy. I was married while in the service and
had a first daughter by the time I was out.

"At that time I couldn't quite start farming because I
just didn't have enough capital. So I worked in town for a
couple of years to get enough money to start farming. We
moved to the farm in 1946 and farmed on shares for five
or six years to get a little accumulation of equipment and
so on. Then we bought a 100-acre farm, made a little down
payment on it and had to sell myself short to buy the farm.
I knew I had made a mistake—I had to sell so much livestock and stuff that I didn't have too much to make a living
with.

"I had to go back to work in town to supplement my income to get enough money to get breeding stock and equipment to start farming again. I worked at it [farming] for
three years full time and saw that I wasn't making much
money. Luckily, I live in an area where there's a lot of industry and it's fairly easy to get a job off the farm. So I
worked in industry and on the farm too. When another
100-acre farm came up for sale, I mortgaged what I had
and bought that second one with a lot of help from the Federal Land Bank and some of my friends.

"By that time, times were getting pretty hard on the
farm. Some of my buddies started leaving the country because they couldn't make a living farming. In the winter
of 1958 and 1959 there wasn't a day that within twenty
miles of my farm I couldn't go to a public farm sale where
one of my buddies was selling out. By five of my friends
leaving the farm, I was able to buy and rent enough land to

have a profitable operation. Since 1958 I've been a full time farmer, but I'm only getting a four to five per cent return per year on my investment."

With 500 acres of Ohio farmland to raise grain—mostly corn and some soybeans—Carl had a hog feeding operation in which he turned out about 700 finished butchers per year. He said that unless the price situation improved, he would have to increase his hog production to about 1,500 a year in order to make any money.

When asked if it were hard for him to keep up with changing technology that applied to farming, he said, "In my particular case, keeping up with the latest developments poses only one problem. The thing that bothers me is the financial adjustments of trying to keep up. Technical knowledge isn't too hard because I had a pretty good education in science. Our main problem is marketing because we have so little bargaining power." He said that he usually sold his hogs direct to the packer so he would immediately know what price he was getting for them.

Although he had been in the NFO for only five months when interviewed, Carl was vice president of his county chapter. He said the organization was very strong in his locality and that he was working very hard to make it effective. Considering that he personally was about $100,000 in debt on his farm operation, the business of obtaining higher farm prices was indeed important to him.

"Frankly," he said, "next to my religion, this is probably one of the things dearest to my heart." At the same time, being a member of a farm organization was nothing new to Carl. "I was practically brought up on the Grange," he said, adding that until about five years before, he had also been a member of the Farm Bureau. But he quit the Farm Bureau because "it got to the place where I didn't believe in the policy of the organization, so I'm no longer supporting it."

When NFO organizers came to Carl, he liked their plan for the farmer. "It's a plan for action, a way of going about securing a price comparable with the earnings of our city cousins and it looked pretty good to me," Carl said later. "Besides, if the thing works, my boy may have a chance to stay on the farm yet."

FARMER D, FROM NORTH CENTRAL KENTUCKY

"I just love to fish," the Kentucky gentleman drawled. But I haven't had one pole out this summer. I've been too busy organizing for the NFO. I feel that this is more important than spending a few days down at Kentucky Lake."

Daniel (a fitting pseudonym for a Kentuckian) didn't come from the farm originally. Although he was a native of the county where he settled, he was a city lad who went to work for a chain grocery store, learned about the food business and eventually opened a country grocery and general store in a partnership with his father. On the side, they operated a small farm nearby. With a 200-acre farm used for raising a small amount of corn and some hogs, along with a patch of tobacco, Daniel and his father sold the country store in the late 1950's because competition of chain stores undercut them and eventually forced them out of business. Using his 2.52 acres of tobacco as an example of costs of farm production, Daniel said that an acre of Burley should gross about $1,400 a year on the average. But the man-hours spent, along with costs of machinery, interest on loans and upkeep of a tobacco storage barn— which is used only about two months out of the year—cut the net profit to 40 or 50 per cent of the gross income. In the end, the tobacco farmer wasn't getting rich either, he said. Recounting his becoming attached to the NFO, Daniel said:

"I've dealt with farmers nearly all my life in a general store in the country . . . and I have spoken for the last twenty years as to why there weren't someone strong enough to organize the farmer so he would have a voice in pricing his production. And when this [NFO] came along, I grabbed at it. Now, I wasn't too sure at the time that it was going to work, but when I saw a group of farmers that were willing to stand up and be counted, I was willing to pay the small fee of $25 a year to go along with them. And that's all I gave up; I didn't give up any rights or privileges. I just gave up a $25 fee."

Describing what many of his farmer-neighbors faced in north central Kentucky, Daniel said that many were supplementing their farm income with off-the-farm jobs. "We have men up here today [at the 1962 NFO meeting for action] who have taken time off from their city jobs. Many of them are carrying union cards in carpentry. They have to carpenter to keep their farming operation going. They don't like it. And a lot have quit farming for the lack of funds. Others are deeply in debt."

At 45 years of age, Daniel also supplemented his farm income by working for a tobacco firm during the winter months. His wife also had a full-time job in town. The parents of two adopted children, a girl twelve and a boy seven, the family was operating 400 acres of farm land in 1962.

Daniel, like many of his fellow NFO members, was a veteran of World War II. He spent three and a half years in the Air Force. He served in New Guinea during four campaigns by flying 43 missions as nose gunner in a B-24 bomber. While he joked that he didn't think his nerves could take flying those missions anymore, it was quite evident that he was piling up a record "flying missions" for the NFO. Besides being president of his county chapter, he also served as a national NFO staff organizer.

Summing up his personal ambition, Daniel said, "I'd just love to see agriculture on a paying basis with the rest of the economy, that's all. I don't think we should ever be selfish in our desires because we have one commodity for market that people must have. But I do think that we should be able to say, 'It costs us this much to produce, counting our interest on investment and depreciation. Now, we want a fair return for our labors, a benefit which every other business enjoys today.' "

To SOME casual observers it might have appeared that NFO members were a group of disgruntled farmers that met monthly to grumble about low prices of farm products. This was a narrow view of their activities. While NFO meetings did involve making plans to improve the farm income situation, this was not the whole story. Often picnics or potluck suppers would be held in conjunction with the meetings. *The NFO Reporter* carried frequent accounts of NFO members gathering to perform a neighborly deed such as weeding a field of soybeans for a farm wife who had been widowed at a time when the crop needed cultivating. In another instance, fellow members pitched in to help an NFO organizer get his baled hay out of the field. The work had been delayed because the organizer-farmer was too busy with duties connected with the all out holding action in the fall of 1962. In Illinois, one NFO group sponsored its own fair which included contests, livestock showing and plenty of eats for everyone.

Wives of the members weren't to be left out, and in some areas organized NFO Ladies Auxiliaries.

When June floods hit in eastern Nebraska in 1963, NFO leaders put out a call for members to help farmers in distress. A similar call had gone out when farmers were in trouble with flooding in the Sioux City, Iowa, area a year earlier.

Besides serving to bring farmers together to discuss their problems, the NFO offered a social outlet. Many members gained new friends through organizational activities. Although the basic aims and goals of the NFO members were dead serious, it was quite evident that these people knew how to have fun.

An interesting facet of NFO meetings was pointed out to the author while attending the 1962 meeting for action in Des Moines. No one was drunk. Although there was the bustling atmosphere of a convention, there was no evidence of delegates trying to outdo themselves and others with liquor. If there was drinking, it was done in a respectable manner.

10

STALEY'S KIND OF ORGANIZATION
Part II

A T THIS POINT, it would appear that Oren Lee Staley was a good guy leading other good guys in a nice, tight organization to attain a worthy goal. The fact that Staley was re-elected president of the National Farmers Organization seven years running without being challenged indicated that he was very popular with the general membership. However, those who had personally worked with Staley said that he did not always enjoy this kind of hero-worship from within the circle of top leaders. One such leader, who asked not to be identified, said that when Staley was opposed in the presidential election at the 1962 national convention in Des Moines, a good 75 per cent of the leadership of the NFO wanted him out of office. Why?

To find out why some of the top officials of the NFO were against Staley, the author interviewed a group of men who had served on the national board of directors or who had been national officers of the organization. Most of them had helped to pioneer the NFO and had seen it grow from little more than the murmurings of discontent into a swelling farm movement. These leaders knew Staley personally and in a manner of speaking, "had seen him grow up with the NFO." However, because of their differences with Staley on policy and administrative practices, they eventually found themselves out of office. Although most of these men still felt that the NFO could help the farmer in his plight of low farm prices, they felt Staley's approach was wrong. When asked to explain why they had fallen out with Staley and his camp of leaders, these men usually had to be assured that they would not be identified by name or quoted directly on their views before they would talk freely. There seemed to be two main reasons for this wish for anonymity. One was that these sources of information did not want to invite retaliation from Staley or from his ardent supporters and the other was that they felt that some of their knowledge of internal affairs of the organization would be harmful to the NFO if made public. However, on the stipulation that their identities not be revealed, these men told what—from their point of view—was really going on inside the NFO up through the time of the 1962 national convention. In composite, here is what they had to say:

STALEY WAS a terrific organizer, but as an executive trying to administrate an organization as large as the NFO had grown, he was more awkward than Newt Gresham in the early days of the Farmers Union. Without practical experience as an executive, he refused to delegate authority, tried to do all of the office work at national headquarters himself, and in general, was always behind on getting work done. As an example of the manner in which Staley directed clerical duties in the Corning office, those who had served closely with him said that rather than parcelling out portions of work to be done by individual office personnel, he would give a certain task to one girl and then have another girl check on it. After that, a third girl would check on the second, a fourth on the third and so on until paper work had been channeled in a circle rather than being branched out and disposed of. When complications would arise—for example, a check from a county organization might be written for a few more cents than it should be—they would be tossed into a "problem file" rather than being straightened out immediately.

Staley's record for keeping appointments was generally frightful. It was the author's experience to wait a total of eight hours for three interviews that lasted about three hours altogether. NFO officials who had accompanied him on trips to call on important persons in distant cities related that often Staley would delay showing up for an appointment for several hours or might suddenly decide not to appear for the appointment at all. Sometimes on a whim he might call an important personage in the middle of the night, not necessarily on pressing business, but just to visit, those who had worked with him said.

"Oren Lee is the kind of person that might have all the money in the world but still he wouldn't have any at all— he just doesn't have any concept of money," one of his former lieutenants commented. When Staley went on trips, to Washington, D.C., for example, he wouldn't think about money enough to have cash in his pocket. A travel companion would have to pick up the tab for meals or any other expenses. Or Staley would have to write a check.

Staley's attitude toward money seemed to be reflected in the NFO's financial standing. Public financial reports of the national organization were always avoided, theoretically to keep outsiders from knowing how much money or how many members the NFO had. Even the national board of directors never knew the exact financial state of the organization. However, persons who had been on the board for several terms said that the NFO was forever in a financial crisis. Often staff organizers would have to wait a month or two or more before getting paid. Board members themselves sometimes sat out long periods of time for expense account checks to arrive. Money was spent as fast as it was collected and in the years prior to 1962, the national treasury would often be empty at mid-year and board members had to rack their brains to find ways to meet expenses of the national convention at the end of the year. Following the "catalog campaign" waged against the Committee for Economic Development and the all out holding action, both in the late summer of 1962, the organization picked up additional members and was in the best financial condition it had ever been in except during the initial spurt of progress back in its "dollar days."

Officials who had spent much time working at the national headquarters in Corning said the NFO chief executive did all of the labor of preparing *The NFO Reporter* for press, writing nearly all of the copy or doing the final editing of it. This took time he should have devoted to other administrative duties, his well-informed critics felt.

In the eyes of some board members, Staley was "bullheaded." As the 1962 all out holding action went into its second week and dragged on and on, members of the national directorate begged him to call it off while it appeared the holding action still had some real effect on the livestock market. However, it was 32 days after it started that the campaign was finally "recessed."

Men well acquainted with the situation said that Staley jealously guarded his position as head of the NFO. Whenever new leadership talent made itself apparent, unless it were fully in agreement with Staley's views, the new leader would be weeded out.

In 1962, the president of the Nebraska NFO faced the problem of planning action to take against a bill introduced into the Nebraska legislature, a proposal aimed at outlawing certain kinds of picketing and demonstrations. The bill was tacitly anti-NFO. The Nebraska NFO official had clashed with Staley a number of times in national board meetings, but still respected the national president's authority. In a consultation with Staley, the Nebraska leader asked what should be done in the Nebraska legislative lobby. Staley gave the order to do nothing at the time. Eventually the bill became law and the Nebraska official suddenly found himself the victim of rumors that he had sold out the Nebraska NFO to the Farm Bureau (sponsor of the bill), that he had helped draft the bill and that, worst of all, "he didn't do anything to stop its passage." More out of disgust than anything else, the Nebraskan declined to run for office again.

Few men got far enough "up" in the organization to pose any real political threat to Staley, who was in an advantageous position to watch over his presidency. *The NFO Reporter*, over which he had absolute control, was at his disposal. There were upwards of 400 national staff organizers out in the country telling members and non-members alike what a good job Staley was doing. On top of that, Staley was in a position to know all that was going on out in the country while the average member had little or no idea what was happening in national headquarters in Corning.

So, when members of the board of directors differed with Staley and tried to criticize him publicly, who was going to believe them? Particularly who would believe them after rumors started to fly? This kind of climate made it difficult to ascertain "the truth about the NFO." And because of the eventual consequences, those who were informed were usually reluctant to make the facts known, particularly when they were bits of unpleasant information.

After the 1962 all out holding action was "recessed," many members who had worked hard for success that did not come were disappointed; many were plainly disillusioned. It was indeed a time of discontent within the movement. However, before that time, the organization had its troubles too. After the protest movement in its early years, the NFO had to offer a new program to regain the membership it had lost. For all practical purposes, the NFO was out of business when the Iowa chapter moved to merge with the Farmers Union in the early months of 1958. Membership had soared to around 180,000 during the "dollar days" and then skidded to about one-sixth of that when the merger debacle was over. At that time, some county NFO chapters had more money in their treasuries than did the national office. The adoption of a program for collective bargaining for agriculture gave the NFO a new leg to stand on. Nonetheless, some former national board members told the author that the NFO national directorate never took action until unrest was so evident among the membership that the organization had to move or lose its members. The first test holding actions were demanded by the membership. When the Master Contract to be offered to processors was finally presented to the membership, it was done only after a great clamor for action was heard from the rank-and-file member.

At the 1961 national convention, Staley told delegates that an all out holding action would be called during the following year. It was held in September and early October, 1962.

As was seen in Chapter Six, the all out holding action did not make the NFO very popular with market interests. Another aspect of the holding action was that it ended up making the NFO unpopular with some of its own members. Members who had joined the movement mostly to "keep peace" in their neighborhoods and those who had been cajoled into signing a membership agreement were especially critical of the violence that accompanied the all out action. Commission men and other market interests at six of the twelve major terminal livestock markets[1] reported that they all had stockmen-clients who said they belonged to the NFO, but that they were ashamed of the fact. Others said they had been strongly in favor of collective bargaining, but the violence was more than they bargained for when they signed up. Parallel to the example of the farmer who increases his production when all farmers are advised to reduce their output, some NFO members thought the all out holding action was a good idea—as long as they could sneak some of their own livestock onto the market while the holding action was pressuring prices higher. Many commission men related that they had received for trade livestock that belonged to NFO members while the 1962 all out holding action was in effect. In many instances, the animals were sold under the name of a friendly neighbor who did not belong to the NFO or they were sold under a fictitious name. It was impossible to estimate how many NFO'ers broke the rules of the holding action and marketed livestock when they were supposed to be keeping it at home. The upturn in prices during the first and second weeks of the holding action made selling out while prices were still improved a tempting thought. At any rate, it is safe to say that more than a few NFO members did market animals during the holding action, and the percentage probably increased as the holding action dragged on and its apparent effect diminished.

While the holding was in effect, a rumor popped up in

Iowa and in the Kansas City livestock marketing area that
Staley resigned his presidency. Immediately and indignantly, the NFO chief executive denied the rumors, saying
that he would not quit in the heat of the battle. Prior to
the 1962 national convention, reports were that Staley did
not intend to run for office again. There was still some
doubt about the rumors of his earlier resignation. Former
board members told the author that Staley and Lloyd Fairbanks, also from Missouri and the national organizational
director in charge of staff organizers, had prepared and
signed resignations before the all out holding action was
called. These resignations were sealed in an envelope and
were not to be opened unless the NFO ran amuck of the
law. In the event of legal implications, Staley and his
friend could easily wash their hands of the whole mess
simply by producing the documents.

However, the resignations were not revealed until after
the holding action was over and most board members were
not very upset by the prospect of Staley and Fairbanks
quitting. In fact, some were relieved to hear that Staley was
going to retire; this offered the prospect of making progress
in areas where they had not been able to agree with the
national president. Besides, there were sound reasons for
Staley's retirement. Some of those that were working with
him at the time felt that Staley had pushed himself too
hard and that he was nearly exhausted by the energetic
pace he maintained. Besides, there had been some illness
in his family and he was needed back home on the farm.

Reportedly, the resignations were presented to the
board, then filed with the president's personal secretary.
Later on, these documents disappeared.

Although the resignations appeared to be a move that
could have left the other NFO officials holding the bag if
the organization had gotten into trouble over the all out
holding action, several board members interpreted the
entire performance as a political move to lure Staley's opposition out into the open, which it did. They said it was a
grandstand play that would end with drafting Staley to re-

main in office. In reality, they said, the chief executive from Missouri never really had any intention of relinquishing the position.

When questioned about this matter, Staley curtly told the author that he had never resigned but that he had "considered not running for re-election."

Upon hearing rumors that Staley was quitting, an energetic staff organizer who had helped formulate the NFO's program for collective bargaining decided to announce his candidacy for Staley's position. The man was Harold Woodward, a 39-year-old farmer from Bethany, Missouri, who operated a 320-acre farm.

Woodward campaigned actively before the election and was assured support of Nebraska's delegates. Shortly after Woodward's announcement in mid-November, 1962, that he was a candidate, national NFO vice president Robert Casper, of Winterset, Iowa, threw his hat into the political ring. In early December, Staley announced that he had considered retiring from the presidency, but members had urged him to stay on as the movement's top leader. Neither Staley nor Casper campaigned overtly before the national convention and election in Des Moines.

The 1962 convention seemed to be overshadowed by concern over the outcome of the election scheduled for the second and last day of the gathering. A business session was reconvened late the first night of the convention for delegates to consider proposals and bylaw changes that were being pushed by various groups. The bylaw changes that were offered included some that would reduce the power delegated to the president. Presidential candidate Casper played a large role in seeing to it that these measures were presented and eventually passed. At any rate, the delegates labored until one A.M. the first night of the meeting, trying to get measures prepared for approval. The next morning's sessions were just as hectic. The election was delayed several hours by the bickering that preceded passage of bylaw changes that limited to some extent the president's powers. Possibly some of the confusion was a direct result of tension over the election. After all, it was the first time that Staley had been opposed for re-election.

The three candidates' platforms were:

STALEY—The veteran president of the organization stood on his record as an advocate of all out holding actions and bargaining with processors to attain higher farm prices. By and large, he offered nothing new.

WOODWARD—This candidate was the most outspoken in his criticism of Staley's record. Woodward started his platform with a proposal that the president delegate "authority and responsibility to competent personnel and allow them to use their ability, intelligence and initiative to perform their duties." This implied that Staley had been running a one-man show. Next Woodward said that the all out holding action idea had served its purpose. In place of it, he suggested that the NFO hold "specific holding actions" on a commodity-by-commodity basis. Also, he recommended that the organization should hold farm products from one processor at a time and thus slowly divide and conquer all processors systematically. He assured a complete audit and public report of the organization's finances. More of the membership fees should stay with the county organization, he said, proposing that the $1.75 currently earmarked for county use be increased to $2.75 per member.

Woodward also suggested that the NFO set up an office in Washington, D.C. to lobby on behalf of the movement and to assure that no legislation be passed that would interfere with laws under which the NFO could bargain. However, he said that the home office should remain in the Midwest. He advocated expanding state NFO organizations for a stronger state lobby and better public relations.

Thorough and complete accounts of the proceedings of board of directors meetings should be made available to members, Woodward said. He added that board members should be elected from the areas they represented. Slapping at the sloppy schedule on which *The NFO Reporter* was issued, he said that the paper should be "an interesting and informative publication which would reach the membership promptly each month." He urged in another section of the platform that candidates in national NFO elections should have the opportunity to make use of the organization's publication to present all candidates' views and also that lists of all leaders should be made available to the candidates. He suggested that a limiting of national officers' terms was in order.

"Policies of the NFO have never been original with one individual. Ideas advanced by the membership have not been properly considered. Within, or incorporated among, the ideas of our members lies the answer to many of our problems. Personnel should be assigned to consider all ideas received by the national office," one of Woodward's planks read. He also said that adequate assistance from experts in such matters as legal advice, marketing and exportation should be hired by the organization.

CASPER—With six years of being national vice president of the NFO under his belt, Bob Casper knew what was going on in Corning. He advised three proposals to limit the powers of the president. Introducing his measures regarding the presidency, Casper wrote, "Delegation of power in an organization is determined by the bylaws. We profess to be a grass-roots organization, yet our bylaws give the president of the NFO almost dictatorial powers. The power of the president must be limited:

". . . The president must not be permitted to make major appointments from the board of directors unless the directors resign their positions from the board.

". . . He should neither be permitted to appoint directors from new areas nor fill vacancies by appointment. All directors should be elected.

". . . On the present size of our national board and expense involved in calling board meetings, there should be an executive board that can meet with the president on matters with which the president feels he needs consultation. The present bylaws already provide for such a board appointed by the president. Since their function is to represent the national board of directors, they should be elected by members of the national board of directors." [This bylaw change was enacted at the 1962 NFO convention.]

Casper also struck out at the idea that Staley was running a one-man organization: "No one man can build or operate this or any other major organization. The president must be the administrative officer of the organization. The president should be willing to delegate authority to other officers and push young leadership to the fore, challenging them with the jobs and responsibilities that should rightfully be theirs and give them the public recognition they deserve for jobs well done."

In offering new programs, the 48-year-old NFO vice president proposed better public relations, the establishment of offices in each county to build a better structure for the bargaining program, to wage a "no buy" program, "as we have talked about for several years," against individual processors and to develop and use plans to bring pressure upon individual processors. Casper also advocated "short holding actions for limited objectives and strategic purposes."

WHENEVER the NFO used Des Moines' vast Veterans Memorial Auditorium for their mass meetings they arranged to have a series of microphones, connected with the hall's public address system, spotted around the convention floor. At the 1962 meeting for action, one observer indicated he was amazed by the smoothness with which everyone had an opportunity to get up and make known his views by going to a nearby microphone on the floor. Eight microphones were installed for the 1962 national convention in December. However, this basically good technique whereby theoretically any delegate could make use of the public address system to support or oppose proposals and give his views on candidates in the election became the object of a great deal of bickering.

Once nominations were under way in the 1962 election, it became evident that a group of men had commandeered all but one of the eight microphones on the convention floor. These were backers of candidate Woodward and they carried small, portable two-way radios. These "walkie-talkies" were supposedly used to prompt hand-picked speakers and to keep the Woodward schism informed on what was going on. After the election, the author learned that many of these radios were inoperative and were simply used as a ruse to worry Woodward's opposition.

"In past years, the Staley camp had men posted on the microphones when it came time for the election. One would get up and nominate Staley, then another would second it and then another would get up and make a pitch for Staley and arouse the convention body on his behalf. Pretty soon someone else would get up and propose that Staley be re-elected unanimously. That way, no one had a chance to run against him," a Woodward supporter told the author after the election.

"So, maybe what we did wasn't very democratic, but we were going to make sure the Staley camp didn't take over the election again. When Staley called for the sergeant at arms to remove us from the microphones, we had our wives supervise the mikes and the sergeant at arms would not throw a woman out. Consequently, the election speeches were made from the stand up front rather than from the floor as they had been before," the Woodward ally explained. In addition, a national television network was filming proceedings at the speaker's stand at the front of the auditorium.

Several rounds of "seconding speeches" were made on behalf of the three candidates. When Woodward was nominated, a small brass band came booming onto the convention floor and snaked up and down the aisles for several minutes, followed by a placard-carrying group of members who supported Woodward.

Although Woodward's following made the most noise at the convention, many observers felt that Casper was the favorite. But when the final vote was in, Staley was the winner with 2,651 ballots compared with Casper's 1,606 and Woodward's mere 362 votes. The convention delegation roared its approval of Staley's victory. As the president was sought out and conducted to the stage, the defeated candidates moved forward to congratulate Staley, but were snubbed as he went to the rostrum. When Staley finished his fiery 30-minute acceptance speech, neither Woodward nor Casper was about to offer him congratulations. The speech had not treated them lightly:

What I have to say here this afternoon will center around what I know is very necessary for this organization. And that is to move ahead . . . I'm proud to be able to say one thing: I can go to bed tonight and sleep, knowing that I've not said anything about anyone. I was determined from the beginning that I would not use the office of president to perpetuate myself and that I would try to be as fair as I hope I have been. I wanted you to elect the one that you thought would get you there the quickest. I hope that those who opposed me will join in and help. I hope [for] that as we move forward together.

But there's some things that I want to point out here, that for the first time, we have had bitterness and strife in the organization, smear campaigns and such. But I think we all have to realize this is a part of a growing organization and out of it you find out who thinks big, who thinks little, and who acts big and who acts little. And that I think you will find out.

Now, I want to get down to what I feel is the real serious part of what we do and where we go from here. I feel that because—however, I think it's been very good for the organization—some things I think that with walkie-talkie radios and such that were going on here that the delegates were seeing democracy not really at work and those that have been charging me with these things are the very ones that were using tactics that they were charging me with which I was not [sic]. I wanted to say this as a matter of defense. . . .

For the first time there has been indication that there might have been compromise in this organization, *but I have never believed that*

there was going to end up in any way any compromise and that the processors just as well make up their minds, as Dr. Schlebecker [a speaker on the convention program] *said, "We'll hit harder and hit 'em again when necessary!"*
Then comes down to the policy, the real heart of the issues that must be at this convention. I say that anyone that can bring forth any plans that will be able to help us forward in bargaining, we will, I'm sure, as officers and new members of the board of directors, that they will examine them. But let me for just a little bit. . . . Now, there's something that I have not done before that I wanted; I wanted everyone to present their ideas, but now, let me state to you, here, that we have got to get away from any possible confusion as far as policy is concerned at this point. We must jell our opinion here towards a common objective. Let me analyze this so that when you consider the resolutions, you will consider these points. . . .[2]

At that juncture, Staley proceeded to tear apart, one by one, the proposals of the candidates who had run against him by giving points of argumentation to show why they would not work. The ideas of dividing and conquering processors by limited holding actions would not work because they would either be illegal or hopeless since the current marketing system would make it almost impossible to single out one processor and effectively put pressure on one at a time, Staley argued. Both Casper and Woodward had opposed repeating the all out holding action and at this point in his acceptance speech, Staley attempted to show why the all out holding action was the only way of attaining the NFO's goals. He closed his address with:

I do not believe my severest critics can say that I have not been willing in the past to sit down and discuss problems with them. I have tried to be fair; this I will try even harder to do than even in the past. And I want to surround myself with the most dynamic leadership we can have in this organization so that we can have teamwork at the top and solidarity of the ranks that we can move forward to victory just as soon as possible and with your help and Divine guidance, we will make it. And we are assured of victory. All we have to do is to move together. I pledge to you that I'll give all I have, all I have in the way of leadership to do the best that I can. . . thank you.[3]

Staley received a standing ovation and members nearly mobbed him to offer their congratulations after he left the stand. In listening to and examining his speech, it was obvious that the man was emotionally shaken by the ordeal of the election. At several points, he seemed to have difficulty organizing his thoughts.

Several months later, the author interviewed Staley in Corning. When asked about the significance of his being opposed in the election, the NFO president replied:

"It showed real democracy in the organization, that anyone could run for president that wanted to. I think that's a good, healthy sign." He denied rumors that there was continued dissension in the organization after the election and added, "I would say that you had a few disappointed people that had tried for office and this you can expect. A lot of it is the result of the fact that several of these people involved had seen people progressing faster in the organization than they were and the reason of people progressing faster is that as you grow, you have more, better leadership come on. This means that if your organization grows, you've got to have growth in the leadership; so, consequently, what you had happening was that some of the people who had been leaders were seeing people in their area that were making faster strides than they were because of more ability. Consequently, they were fighting to maintain a position or to get higher."

Once the election was over, what happened to the men who had opposed Staley? One former director who opposed the Staley camp said that 75 per cent of the leadership that was in office in 1962 was purged after the election. Some simply resigned or declined to run for office again. In a sense, they had become "enemies of the NFO," even though they remained faithful to what the organization was trying to accomplish.

Was Staley's ruthless kind of politics justifiable? Many of his critics said that more good, young leadership was chopped down in the NFO than some farm movements could ever have found. But, in attaining a definite goal where members of the movement had to be of one mind, it did make sense that such an organization might need to be ruled with an iron hand to keep it unified. No doubt if Staley were removed from office, his opposition would bring about policy changes that would most likely soften Staley's policy of a militant drive for collective bargaining. Even if it damaged his popularity with some of the leaders, Staley had preserved the original policy of the organization during his first eight years as leader of the movement.

And when Staley said others would have to be the judge of his strong characteristics and his personal weaknesses, it was inevitable that as a public figure, he would have enemies who strongly opposed him, both within the organization and outside it. But at the same time, he had many admirers whose fidelity to him was impregnable.

ANOTHER ASPECT of the NFO's activities that caused a great deal of suspicion was the organization's relationship with organized labor unions. When Jay Loghry started the NFO, he said he was going to unionize farmers. A couple of weeks later he was made to eat his words or lose the organization. After the NFO had enjoyed the rocketing membership gains of the "dollar days" and the ensuing decline when protest trips to Washington netted little more than discouragement, the movement was almost broke. The encounter between the NFO and the United Auto Workers ended in a scandal in which two national officers of the farm organization resigned in a huff. Staley described what happened:

"Our history [with the United Auto Workers] is very brief. Really what happened was that in 1956, our organization in Rea County, Missouri, invited a speaker to a county meeting one night. Now this was [during] the low ebb of our organization in 1956-1957. You made your initial push and went to 180,000 members paying in a dollar each, 75¢ to the national and 25¢ staying with the county organization. Now this invitation came in the fall of 1956, I'm sure. They invited a speaker who had grown up in their county. The fellows there knew the man, but didn't know what he did in the labor union, but they did know that he had gone to Kansas City to become a labor official in the Ford plant there. They invited him to their meeting and he proceeded to tell them he didn't know the farmers' problems. But he did know that the farmers needed to organize, and if they [the union] could help in any way, they would be glad to do it. But the organization had to be run by farmers.

"Now, this was his statement. Well, some additional counties were there and they wanted him to come and speak in their counties and it wasn't long before labor speakers were receiving invitations from almost all of our counties because one went to one county, the meeting was advertised and NFO people went to these meetings and then they wanted the speakers to come to their counties, too. Well, it wasn't long before this first labor speaker couldn't handle all of these meetings and two other fellows joined in making speeches.

"You can just imagine about what happened to us financially as far as 75¢ coming into the national and 25¢ [per member] to the county. We just didn't have any funds. And we had some people that just couldn't go any more or take any more money out of their pockets. They'd been taking it out and there were a couple of fellows here in Iowa, particularly, they were leaders, but they had traveled a lot and couldn't take any more money out of their pockets and from their families. So, from these statements, we decided to contact the UAW and we contacted Pat Greathouse, who was vice president of the UAW and was in charge of farm implement workers, which we felt were fairly close as far as problems were concerned because they certainly weren't going to work in the farm implement industry unless farmers bought.

"So, we went to them and asked them if they'd make a contribution, we were a liberal organization, and if they'd make a contribution such as they made to charitable groups and others, with no strings attached, then we would accept it. If there were any strings attached, then we'd just say we'd put up a good fight and couldn't make it rather than to accept any contributions with strings attached. So they contributed $3,000, a thousand dollars for three months for a total of $3,000. Now, at the time we accepted that and put it in our treasury, we made a statement to the press, giving the details on it because we didn't want any skeletons in our closet. We made it public at the time so that nobody could draw it up and say, 'We found something you hadn't been telling us about.'

"This was before our collective bargaining program. Now, when we started organizing on collective bargaining, we could not and did not and have not accepted any contributions from anybody. Legally, we couldn't do it even if we wanted to. We cannot be tied to any other group in any manner, any way that the courts would look upon as collusion or connection between the groups. Consequently, from a legal standpoint, we had to be made up only of farmers, producer members with no outside connections."

His account of this development overlooked the fact that the incumbent national secretary and national treasurer resigned after protesting that the matter had been handled without their knowledge of it and that the bonds that they had posted as officials of the organization had been jeopardized by the move. Also, they were vexed by the fact that the matter had been handled by other officers when such transactions should have been in their domain of authority.

After that, the allegation of being tied to labor unions was ignored or occasionally refuted by NFO representatives. Nonetheless, some farmers feared that there was a connection and that the movement would someday be taken over by labor people. Non-farmers in industry and among the agricultural marketing system also suspected that there was hanky-panky going on behind the scenes between the NFO and organized labor. Staley had admitted that the UAW affair had been embarrassing for the NFO, but he pointed out that the $3,000 contribution was the only

220 Chapter 10

instance of the organization's taking assistance from another group, especially labor. When asked if NFO organizers were recruited from labor unions or whether the NFO ever consulted unions for advice on organizing farmers, the farm leader said no. He pointed out that all NFO organizers were farmers. In spite of the resemblance to "union tactics," the NFO's methods of organizing and its policies for acquiring better prices for farm goods, there was no tangible evidence that there were any ties at the organization level.

One situation that formed a tenuous link between the NFO and labor unions was the fact that some of the NFO members who supplemented their farm income by off-the-farm employment had to belong to labor unions to find a good job. Recalling the case history of "Farmer D" in the previous chapter, it is noteworthy that the subject of the interview made reference to members of the farm organization who had taken time off their union carpentry jobs to attend the national meeting for action. Other sources told the author that NFO members in the Detroit, Michigan, area were members of the United Auto Workers while they worked at automotive plants in that industrial city. Similar cases were noted in the Kansas City area. By and large, the percentage of NFO members who carried union cards was most likely inconsequential. This "tie" with labor unions, if it could be called that, was more of a coincidence than a scheme to connect the two kinds of organizations. However, some NFO members extended their public relations program to include labor union audiences in a few instances.

When local NFO groups promoted farm-labor conferences in Kansas City and Omaha in early 1963, the farm movement's opposition again felt that there must be some clandestine connection between the NFO and organized labor. In both instances, NFO'ers held meetings with members of the United Packing House Workers of America, AFL-CIO. The Kansas City meeting had representatives from the Kansas City and St. Joseph labor locals and NFO members from these areas. In Omaha, NFO'ers from western Iowa and eastern Nebraska met with local union workers. They discussed their "common problems" and described their specific problems. "Big Business" was inevitably the common foe of both the farmer and the laborer. After dividing into workshops, the gatherings reconvened and passed resolutions that pledged cooperation and understanding between the two groups. Both labor and NFO members agreed that they should attend the meetings of one another, read the other's propaganda and work together on legislative matters that would benefit both. Other meetings in other cities were recommended by both delegations. Similar meetings were held in Fort Dodge, Iowa; Lincoln, Nebraska, and other points.

When the farm-labor conference in Kansas City was held, it had been announced that NFO president Staley would be on the program. He did not attend. It was then announced that Staley would appear at the meeting that was held a few weeks later in Omaha. Again Staley was not present. When asked about this, the NFO president told the author that he did not know of this and that he had not been scheduled to appear at either conference. It was interesting to note that neither of the meetings with labor unions was reported on in the NFO's publication. It appeared that Staley had had his go with labor unions and was not about to stir up new criticism by being involved in sessions that had been promoted locally by NFO and labor personnel.

It seemed dubious that farmers and laborers had many common problems. About the only thing they shared was the desire for greater returns on their goods and services. But since the laborers' role was one of consumer-buyer of farmers' products, it was not reasonable that they should want to increase the price of food; neither did labor need farmers to help them get better wages. At the same time, some union workers were quoted as saying that they didn't give a hang for the farmers because some of them had come in as "scab" workers when the union workers had been striking against the packing house where they were employed. On the other hand, it made sense that the farmer was losing some money because of the high costs of processing and marketing his products. After all, high labor costs figured in the growing difference between farm prices and retail prices.

In final analysis, these conferences may have been constructive. Basically, they were educational in function and served as public relations activities. The NFO was admittedly happy to meet with any group to tell their story and to win whatever sympathy they could from outsiders. Several national directors told the author that similar conferences had been suggested with business and industry representatives attending, but these never materialized. One pointed out that there was always the paradox of calling a processor or retailer an enemy and at the same time trying to be friends with him. This was particularly difficult when some of the national leaders were constantly attacking the "foe" while local NFO personnel were trying to negotiate in a friendly manner with the so-called opposition.

How POWERFUL was Staley's organization? Membership figures were among the "strategic facts" that the NFO guardedly kept secret. Considering that 4,619 delegates voted in the 1962 NFO presidential election and the fact that each delegate represented 25 members—although "chartered counties" could send five delegates at large—these figures would indicate that the NFO had a maximum of 115,475 members, according to the vote turned in. However, the NFO had estimated that about 5,000 delegates would attend the convention. Allowing 25 members per delegate, this would mean that the organization had around 125,000 members at the close of 1962.[4]

Considering that the National Grange reported a membership of 750,000, while the Farmers Union listed 300,000 farm family memberships and that the Farm Bureau claimed 1,607,505 dues-paid members, the NFO wasn't very big, comparatively, at the close of 1962. Also the fact that the total rural-farm population in 1960 was at 13.5 million, it was apparent that no farm organization had a lion's share of farmers advocating its policies. In addition, the total number of farms in 1959 was 3.7 million, according to the *1963 Fact Book on Agriculture*. So the NFO, as well as the other farm organizations, still had plenty of potential members to seek out.

Even the former board members and other high officials of the NFO whom the author interviewed for "inside information" on the organization declined to reveal the movement's membership. However, it was pointed out that a fairly accurate estimate was not hard to determine through the number of delegates to the 1962 convention.

Interestingly enough, when NFO officials were questioned on membership totals, they immediately informed reporters that they would not release this information. Then they proceeded to circumvent the question by saying that membership totals were not important to the organization, but that the amount of production signed up under the membership agreement was.

11

THE NFO'S "BIG FOE"

WHILE the National Farmers Organization was waging its "great battle," it was sometimes questionable whom the group was fighting. By and large no one fought back, although the NFO's officials often accused market interests, packers and chain food stores of spending large sums of money to thwart the farm group's efforts.

Noteworthy was a prevalent attitude observed among NFO leaders and members alike. From remarks heard by the author, it appeared that rather than being a range of support, opposition and indifference among parties involved in the NFO conflict, NFO'ers felt that there were definitely only two sides in the so-called battle. One was that of the whole-hearted supporter of the movement. The other was the element that did not support it. To be indifferent was to oppose it, many members felt. Newsmen told the author that in many instances they had been accused by NFO members, even after giving the farm movement much coverage, of opposing the campaign. Objective news reporting did not seem to be what NFO members wanted— they would have preferred to have the popular press carry the type of article that appeared in *The NFO Reporter*.

Then, too, many members felt that if a person was not in favor of the NFO, he was against all farmers. Because of the personal enthusiasm for the farm movement's program, some members felt they were being affronted individually whenever they encountered a lack of sympathy for the movement.

Beginning at the farmer level and on through to the consumer, there were several elements of opposition to the movement. Reasons for these feelings were varied.

The farmer who opposed the NFO felt its program would not work. Reasons for thinking this included his experience with other farm organizations that had failed to win sweeping reforms. Because of the wide variety of interests of such groups, it was understandable. Besides, the individual farmer cherished his independence and did not care to be "tied up" with such a movement. Others said that the idea of collective bargaining could never be effective because farmers would not stick together—at least not long enough to attain such a goal as that of the NFO.

Not all farmers cared for the evangelism that Staley showed. Rather than be stirred by roaring speeches, many felt that a solid legislative lobby in Washington could accomplish much more than farmers ganging up and trying to bring about changes for the entire agricultural industry.

The violence that accompanied the holding actions—especially the campaign at the end of the summer of 1962 —turned many farmers against the NFO. While some farmers had been fence-sitters and would go along with a holding action to see what would happen at the marketplace, the spattered outbursts of violence were more than they cared to be identified with.

The suspicions of secret labor union ties kept some farmers from becoming NFO members. They feared that even if the organization were not connected with organized labor, it would fall into the hands of "bossism" because of the NFO's organizational structure and its strategy.

On an individual basis, some farmers found themselves in trouble with their pro-NFO neighbors because they did not go along with the movement. Instances of the bitterness that arose from this kind of situation have been cited in earlier chapters.

Some farmers, as well as the market interests, felt that

the NFO's way of doing things was degrading to the individual person. To back up this idea, one farm leader who opposed the NFO termed its policy "impossible, assinine, unrealistic and in the long run a holding action hurts the market system more than the brief upturn it would cause."

As an example of how he felt NFO activity degraded people, he referred to the case of NFO members, their wives and their children standing on the board walks at the St. Paul, Minnesota, livestock market and jeering "Scab, scab, scab" at farmers who were patronizing that terminal market during the 1962 holding action. "Does that sound like people getting something constructive done?" he asked.

"This is a damn good way to destroy lasting good friendships and break up a neighborhood," one observer in South Dakota remarked when asked to evaluate the NFO's program.

Another person, connected with a major farm organization, said, "I think it is ridiculous for NFO to believe that they can force the major meat and grain concerns to sign contracts to pay a guaranteed price. Such ideas fit neither the present economic structure of the country nor the long-run best interest of farmers—you can't control production at the market place; it can only be done on the farm. Let's face it, farmers will never become organized sufficiently (unless their numbers are reduced to a small number of concerns) to deal effectively with the organized moneybags. Hell, if we [referring to his organization] could get the militant support from the percentage of farmers that NFO says it needs to get the job done, we could write our own ticket in the Congress. . . . But it just isn't going to happen, so it's stupid for the NFO to even talk about such pie-in-the-sky, utopian goals.

"Frankly, I think NFO is just a phase in a farm revolt— something like panty raids were in the liberalization of the thought pattern toward sex in the younger generation."

It's important to point out that as a few rotten potatoes spoil the whole load, a few radical NFO members served as extremely poor examples of the NFO membership. The same was true of the small local groups that sprang up in active and admitted opposition to the NFO. Groups such as the Citizens of Nodaway County (Missouri) Organization for Free Enterprise and the Clarke County (Iowa) Citizens Protective Association probably were justified in banding together to guard against having their fences cut and other vandalism that did occur in their vicinities. But the manner in which they operated and the pitch of their feeling against the NFO was unfortunate. With a little egging on, it was apparent that their bitterness would touch off the same kind of action as that of the hottest hotheads in the NFO. In this case, at least, it would seem better to fight fire with water rather than fighting fire with fire.

Although Staley often said that the NFO was aloof from other farm organizations and had no bones to pick with any of the others, there was evidence to the contrary. The Farm Bureau was the target of considerable NFO abuse. At the bottom of this was the wide difference in policy of the two organizations. The Farm Bureau was conservative and in ways did not feel that farmers were as badly off as the NFO would have had everyone believe. A strong legislative lobby was an important function of the older and larger farm organization. Besides, the Farm Bureau had cooperative business interests in farm supplies and insurance. One of the features of the Farm Bureau that irked a good many NFO'ers was the fact that the Farm Bureau had a considerable number of members who were not farmers, but businessmen from Corn Belt towns.

On the other hand, the NFO was a liberal "do-it-yourself" organization. It was only natural that they should clash.

In some counties of Iowa, at least, county Farm Bureau chapters circulated an inflammatory Washington newsletter called *The Lowdown*, which in several issues attacked the NFO and linked it with organized labor. As one farm editor said, most of what *The Lowdown* alleged was "hogwash."

At the same time, some NFO county chapters promoted

the circulation of a booklet called *The Truth About the Farm Bureau* which portrayed the Farm Bureau as a power-hungry organization that had for 33 years continued to betray the farmer and his causes. In the author's opinion, it was hogwash, too.

In Nebraska, where there was noteworthy disagreement between the state's NFO leadership and that of the national organization after Staley's re-election to an eighth term, there was a piece of legislation passed in the 1963 state legislature that aimed at curbing NFO demonstrations. This law, LB 452, was the handiwork of the Nebraska Farm Bureau. In essence, the law prohibited attempts by individuals or groups to interfere with a person's right to work by using "profane, insulting, indecent, offensive, annoying, abusive or threatening language toward such person or any member of his or her immediate family." It also outlawed picketing that would interfere with highway or street traffic about a place of work or a residence. Under the law, signs carried by pickets had to have the name of the protesting organization printed in letters at least two and one-half inches high. Violation of the law would constitute a misdemeanor and was punishable by a minimum fine of $25 (maximum fine: $100) or imprisonment up to three months in a county jail.

While the NFO was never named in connection with the legislative bill, it was clear that it was aimed at the farm movement's demonstrations, such as the "catalog campaign" that the NFO had waged against the Committee for Economic Development farm plan in August of 1962. It also could be applied to the violence that accompanied the 1962 all out holding action. Nebraska was the only state to pass such action. A similar anti-NFO resolution, sponsored by the Farm Bureau, was introduced in the Wisconsin legislature in August 1963, but it was defeated overwhelmingly after some 250 NFO members appeared at the state house in protest.

At the national level, however, the Farm Bureau gradually stayed aloof of the NFO. A letter from the national Farm Bureau office gave the organization's stand:

In checking our files, I find that we have no official policy statements regarding the NFO, and Mr. Shuman [president of the American Farm Bureau Federation] has made only a few remarks either in news releases or press conferences in which he has pointed out the difference between NFO and Farm Bureau methods of improving farmers' bargaining power. Mr. Shuman has said that while NFO objectives are generally similar to Farm Bureau—improvement of marketing and bargaining power—the methods are not similar. . . .

I'm sorry we don't have more material on this subject, but the American Farm Bureau Federation has not taken public issue with NFO even though the press and radio asked us repeatedly for statements during periods of withholding action by the NFO. This is in keeping with our position of promoting our own policies rather than criticizing those of other farm organizations.[1]

When asked about the Grange's policy toward the NFO, the director of public relations for the Grange wrote in a letter that he had informally and unofficially discussed the NFO and its activities with numerous Grange leaders. He said:

As we understand it, NFO is seeking increased "bargaining power" for agricultural producers. The Grange has no quarrel with that objective; sound programs providing equitable bargaining power for farmers has long been an objective of the Grange.

However, we simply cannot agree that "holding actions" such as engaged in, or advocated, by the NFO will lead to this objective. On the contrary, Grange leaders feel that such action may do serious damage to certain cooperatives which have already been successful in developing—and operating—programs substantially increasing the bargaining power of producers.

Equally significant, we fear that the militant treatment given certain of the "holding actions" by NFO may create public resentment which will make it far more difficult to gain acceptance of equitable producer-managed marketing programs such as those advocated by the Grange.

In other words, Grange leaders I have heard express themselves do not question the objectives of NFO—as they understand them. Neither do they question NFO's right to seek those objectives in an expeditious manner. They simply do not feel that methods advocated by NFO are sound or wise.[2]

However, publicly, the Grange made little or no comment on NFO activities and certainly did not become involved in a conflict with the newer farm movement. By the same token, the NFO did not battle the Grange. One reason for this is that the two organizations did not have a large share of their respective memberships in the same geographical regions.

The remaining major farm organization, the National Farmers Union, released a policy statement regarding the NFO which, in sum, said, "We have seen it tried and it won't work."

Released during the 1962 all out holding action, the statement said:

The proposal of the National Farmers Organization to withhold farm production from the market in order to raise prices has caught the imagination of thousands of midwest farmers. No one can argue with the NFO objective although some may entertain doubts about the method. Nevertheless, if the NFO activities recently announced at Des Moines, Iowa achieve nothing else, they will have dramatized the economic trouble and mounting unrest in rural America.

The failure of the Congress to again this year authorize programs permitting the producers of agricultural products to bring their production in line with genuine demand has created widespread disappointment and frustration among farm people. This has caused some of them to try the NFO type of solution. Both last year and this, the Congress has had all the support it could ask from the Department of Agriculture and the White House for effective legislation. Hence, the Congress must now accept its share of the responsibility for the present economic squeeze.

But the leadership of the American Farm Bureau Federation, the Meat Institute, the chain stores, and other like-minded groups must accept a great portion of the responsibility for the farmer's frustration and economic distress. It has been their large and well-heeled lobbies which have prevented the Congress from adopting anything other than make-shift and temporary patchwork legislation.

These groups callously continue their opposition to any form of supply management programs for American farmers.

The Farmers Union was first to point out the importance of equipping the American producer of farm products with bargaining power in the market place. At the same time, the Farmers Union has pointed out that there can be no effective bargaining power for farmers as long as their production continues to exceed genuine needs. Thus, the Farmers Union has persistently recommended to the Congress that farmers be provided with orderly and equitable legislative devices for bringing their production in line with genuine demand. This is the cardinal element of effective bargaining power. Supply management and bargaining power cannot be achieved without Congressional implementation and guide lines.

It was Abraham Lincoln who pointed out that it is a proper function of government to do for its people what they cannot otherwise do for themselves.

The Farm Bureau and its cohorts have to date induced the Congress to reject this Lincoln concept of the functions of democratic government. As a result, the NFO is undertaking to prove that farm people can achieve effective bargaining power all by themselves.

But Farmers Union remembers several previous attempts, such as the Farmers Holiday Association of the 1930's, and the futile cotton withholding operation in 1910. For these reasons, Farmers Union will continue to dedicate every resource at its command to secure a Federal legislative program for achieving a sound and effective bargaining position for the American farmers in the market place by and through the use of legislation which will permit farmers to bring their supply in line with real demand at just prices.

Farmers Union members are acutely aware that this struggle begins at home with the kind of people we send to Congress.[3]

While the majority of farm organizations had little or nothing to say about the NFO's program and its activities, there were at least two groups—made up largely of cattlemen—who voiced opposition to it. These were the National Livestock Feeders Association and the American National Cattlemen's Association. Both pointed out that disrupting the flow of livestock would create a stoppage of animals moving into the market place and would cause a price-depressing glut when turned loose for market. This attitude presumed the holding action would fail and that an inevitable glut would follow any attempted holding action.

AT THE MARKET PLACE, the opposition was largely silent. Except for a few comments from stockyards officials at the major terminal points and news releases by the Livestock Auction Markets Association, market interests kept their comments private. One point that caused central market officials to comment was the charge that market receipts were being shuttled from market to market and that the figures were being juggled. The first was a misinterpretation of normal traffic among the livestock markets and the latter was untrue. The "rat war" waged at Omaha was a maneuver by the NFO to attract attention when it charged that the stockyards were overrun by rodents. When these accusations and criticisms were made by the NFO, market interests refuted them and let it go at that.

A look at the terminal livestock markets reveals one common economic reason why stockyards firms and livestock commission companies would oppose the NFO. Basically, the NFO program was one of selling farm products direct to processors, with the stipulation that the transaction be done under a coercive contract to give the NFO the price it wanted. If such a program were implemented, it would eliminate the commission men almost completely and would chop down the size of stockyards operations to that of being only receiving stations for the packing plants. While Staley said there would be a need for qualified appraisers of livestock—which indicated the commission men could find a place within the NFO program once it was in effect—it was clear that the commission men did not care to have their businesses eliminated and then have to go to the power that eliminated them for a job.

At the same time, stockyards companies provided the facilities for commission firms to operate. If the latter were eliminated from the marketing picture, stockyards operations would cease to have a real purpose unless they were changed into feedlots.

"We feel that our open, free market is the democratic way of doing things . . .," a representative of one of the major terminal markets said.

What did the terminal markets do to fight back against the NFO? Virtually nothing. In the first place, to admit that the NFO was giving them concern would have provided the NFO with more ammunition to fire back at the market interests. Besides, most of the terminal livestock market men did not feel that the NFO was enough of an influence to worry about. Although Staley had described the average NFO member as a medium to large scale producer of livestock and crops, many persons in the livestock markets sized up the average NFO'er as a small, marginal farmer with no more than a handful of livestock in most cases. The market interests admitted that there were farmers with all sizes of operations that belonged to the movement, but from their observations, the NFO did not have a fraction of the marketing power that it claimed to have. At the same time, central market people did not feel that they wanted to become involved in a serious conflict. They felt whether the NFO won or lost its battle, they would have to deal with farmers for a good while anyway. So, why fight with them?

General feeling among livestock market men was that they themselves were trying to do the same thing the NFO was—to obtain the highest possible price for livestock. However, the market people felt that the law of supply and demand was the overriding factor and that unless production were curbed, little could be done about changing prices.

Asked what could be done if the NFO grew to the point where it would pose an unquestionable threat to the existence of the terminal markets, one official said that a tremendous propaganda program could be waged. He felt that compared with the NFO, market interests could raise vast sums of money to wage such an advertising campaign, if need be. He was confident that such a move would suffice in turning away any such threat. By and large, the threat did not exist and the situation was not expected to ever reach that point.

Perhaps the loudest objection that market interests had to the NFO program was that against the interference that took place at the market place and the violence that was waged against trucks of livestock moving to market. Although there were minor demonstrations at the stockyards at major points, the seriousness of these never exceeded cases of scuffling, of gates being left open, thus letting some animals loose, and the sometimes annoying gathering of crowds which slightly interfered with market activity. Most of the market people agreed that NFO'ers were well behaved whenever they encountered them.

As was seen in Chapter Six, the Livestock Auction Markets Association objected to the interference with their business operations. In several instances, farm wives and some farmers packed sales barns and delayed auction sales by making speeches, singing and being in the way. These took place only during the 1962 all out holding action and ceased when the action was called off.

In the grain trade, there was interest in the NFO's activities, but no concern and no public comment. NFO officials said grainmen were being stuffy and complacent about the farm movement's program, but grainmen themselves dismissed the NFO's efforts as futile. The same was nearly true in the milk and dairy products marketing system. Here, perhaps, the NFO had a little better opportunity to have an effect, but milk producers' association officials felt that if need be, they could fend off NFO efforts largely by court action.

AT ONE TIME in NFO's battle, livestock packers, as well as other processors, were among the so-called big foe. However, as with the stockyards and commission companies, the packers weren't talking about the NFO—at least not publicly. How many packers the NFO contacted to explain the collective bargaining program was not publicly known. NFO would have had everyone believe they'd talked to them all. Some packers denied meeting with the NFO even when it was known that the two had held sessions.

"We were pretty coy about the NFO," one representative of a major packing firm told the author. He agreed that the packing industry in general did not care to have most of its business made public and generally shied from the press when questioned about any of its dealings. This, he said, was not because packers had anything to hide, but was more a case of keeping their affairs private so that their competition would not be at an advantage. Also, since the packers had been the target of numerous federal investigations, most firms did not care to become involved in a conflict that might arouse more attention, he added.

At the same time, the packers that the NFO met with generally welcomed the farm organization's representatives and showed them the courtesies extended to any other business firms they dealt with. However, most packers felt that they could never be forced into signing the NFO's master contract. The two major reasons for this were that the price that NFO demanded was too high and could conceivably ruin any packer who tried to pay it. Additionally, there were grave doubts that such an agreement as offered by the NFO would in the end be legal. Packers felt that the contract would be in violation of fair trade laws and would be dissolved by the government if it were brought into effect by the NFO and packing firms.

In short, the packers felt the NFO's program was unreasonable and probably illegal.

ANOTHER "ENEMY" of the NFO was the food chain stores. NFO accused the large chains of monopolistic operations and thereby keeping food prices down. The chains denied this and said that they were doing everything possible to help the farmer. They pointed to the vast sums of money that chains spent on grocery advertisements and promotions to help popularize certain meats and other foods. If food prices were lower than what the NFO thought they should be to return the farmer a fair income, it was partly because the food stores were so highly competitive. The chain store officials contacted by the author felt that they should not be considered foes of the NFO or any other set of farmers since the chains were trying to get the highest prices possible, which in turn would profit the whole system of food production, processing and distribution.

The food consumer could hardly be considered an opposer of the NFO program, but it was conceivable that he would be if the farm group won its battle. If the NFO could force farm prices up, in the end, the consumer would have to foot the bill. The increased price to producers would essentially become another cost in getting food to the consumer. Many market interests and some processors felt that there would be a consumer rebellion if food prices were increased.

When asked how the NFO felt consumers would react to higher food prices if and when the farm group attained its goals, NFO president Staley said:

"We feel that it would be about the same reaction as when the price of cigarettes goes up. People would grumble a little, but they'd go along with it. Such an increase in prices would probably come at an inopportune time and wouldn't serve as very good public relations for the farmer, but we feel we're going to have to make them [consumers] realize that American farmers are entitled to a profit for their production. What has made our nation great is the fact that American people have been able to understand the problems of the other fellow when correctly presented. If the prices we're asking were unfair or unjust, you couldn't expect a suitable climate to attain our goals. But the prices we're asking are not as high as they have been at times in the past. It's not an abnormal price that we're after. We'll have to tell the story to the people correctly, factually and fairly. Then I believe consumer reaction will be one of sympathy with the farmer."

Others already in various fields of the food business were not so optimistic.

While the market interests, the processors and the retailers were sincerely concerned about the farm problem and were willing to work with farmers to seek ways of helping agriculture, it was not hard for the NFO to blame the ever-suspected "middleman" for low farm prices. Hence, these, along with unsympathetic farmers and farm organizations, were deemed enemies of the organization.

12

THE NFO SINCE 1962

DURING THE MONTHS that followed Staley's re-election to his eighth consecutive term as president of the NFO, the organization was fairly quiet. Membership drives continued and the organization held a series of over 500 "whole-hog sausage feeds" in which the farm populace and public in general were invited to hear the NFO story told by officials of the organization. These events were held throughout the region in which the NFO had organizations. One member said that it was a curious fact that these meetings attracted farmers who would pay a dollar or so for a meal and speeches when he would not come to a meeting that was free but offered a fare of speeches only. The crowds attracted to these events ranged from 500 to 2,500 persons. Staley termed the project a "tremendous success."

FORTY THOUSAND POUNDS of skim milk splashed into a ditch in Minnesota and the story of why it happened splashed across the front pages of newspapers across the nation on March 7, 1963. The NFO had turned its attention more strongly in the direction of collective bargaining on dairy products. Some reports indicated that the farm group had signed contracts with a dozen of Minnesota's 400-odd creameries.[1] A creamery at Annandale, Minnesota, had

signed a contract with the NFO. However, the dairy processor that the creamery delivered its skim milk to refused
to accept any more milk from the creamery unless it legally
broke its contract with the NFO. The creamery refused.
With more milk coming in from producers, the creamery had to dispose of the skim milk to accommodate the in-
coming production. It was decided that since there was no
immediate market for the skim milk, it would be dumped
out. It was, and the NFO made sure everyone heard about
it.

About 2,000 farmers gathered for a kind of rally that
preceded the milk-dumping ceremony in a field two miles
from Annandale. Staley was on hand to shout from the
back of a truck, "The eyes of the entire agricultural area are
on you here today. This should serve notice to everyone
they're not going to fight an individual co-op, that they're
not going to pick them off one by one. They're taking on
the whole National Farmers Organization!"[2]

In 25-degree, windy March weather, farmers surrounded
the tank truck and a signal was given to pour the 4,600
gallons of milk on the ground. Farmers splashed their
boots in the foaming milk and joked about the "sacrifice."
Others leaned toward the end of the gushing hose and
drank from the stream of milk as it sloshed on the ground.
Although the value of the milk dumped out amounted to
between $300 and $400, the publicity stunt attracted thousands of dollars worth of time and space in the news media.
After the incident was over—and after the Annandale
creamery had found a new buyer for its skim milk—*The
NFO Reporter* commented in an editorial:

> Milk was not made to be poured on the ground. It was made to
> help calves, kittens and babies grow, to put strong bones in school
> children and roses in the cheeks of old people.
> The 40,000 pounds of milk that was dumped in Minnesota
> splashed across the front pages of newspapers as America sat at
> breakfast.
> Many failed to understand. Their newspapers presented it as an
> act of senseless destruction by farmers "on strike."
> There has lately been a furor in the press about "news manage-

ment" by our government. The management of news has been, not the exception, but the rule for many years. The public is given news which is slanted and selected in the interest of the publishing giants and their Big Business friends, including the processors and packers of food.

There was no violence involved in the milk dumping. The men who turned the valve were the owners of the milk.

Why did they turn the valve? Because they had no place to put the milk, and the tank truck was needed the next day for more milk.

The processor had ordered the producers' cooperative to tear up their NFO agreement, or he would refuse to accept their skim milk. The farmers refused to be bullied. Another day passed before they could find a new outlet for their milk.

History demonstrates that farmers are devoted to production, not destruction. Their decent instincts have permitted the rest of society to abuse them. Decade after decade, farmers have pushed themselves to maximum production of cheap food while their wives wore old dresses and their children went without college educations!

Under the NFO plan, production beyond what the market will absorb is not to be wasted. A surplus disposal program is being developed to distribute surplus food in areas of human need.

Let that twenty tons of milk that went back to the earth be thought of as the "wasted" bottle of champagne that christens a mighty new battleship.

The farmer stands ready to deliver; all he asks is a reasonable payment for his labors. If the valve must be opened again, do not let your friends in town forget who really wasted that milk![13]

And thus the NFO milk-dumping came and went.

When compared with the livestock marketing system, the NFO had a slight advantage when it came to collective bargaining for milk prices. For one thing, most of the dairymen were already organized in a market system of cooperative creameries or milk producers' associations. In order to get control of these bodies, the NFO needed only a voting majority of the producers of a given co-op or producers' marketing group. At the same time, the co-ops and other milkshed organizations at the producer level were bound by contracts to deliver to processors under the provisions of federal milk marketing orders. Some of the major processors said they would not hesitate to prosecute if NFO members violated their contracts with the processors. At the same time, the NFO membership agreement said that commodities already under marketing agreements would not be included in the provisions of the marketing section of the membership agreement.

The NFO was seeking to get $5 per hundredweight for manufactured (Class II) milk, while in Minnesota this quality milk was selling at about $3.30 per hundredweight. Processors argued that if the NFO forced milk prices to the level the organization specified, the prices to the consumer of milk and butter would be enough higher to cause buyer resistance that could result in permanent damage to the milk marketing structure.

"For example, who would be willing to buy butter at over a dollar a pound?" a milk producers' association official asked in Kansas City. He told the author that his organization was having enough troubles of its own without having "amateurs" come in and disrupt the market further.

Nonetheless, local NFO members and bargaining committees in dairying areas pursued their goal of getting milk processors to sign contracts. A number of smaller operations were forced to sign the NFO agreement, but larger ones resisted. An example of a large milk producers' group balking at the NFO's demands developed when nearly 3,000 NFO members showed up at a meeting in August, 1963, of the Pure Milk Association in Chicago, a producers' group representing some 12,000 dairymen.

"Our members are ready to start dumping milk if they have to," the president of the Wisconsin NFO told the meeting in Chicago. "We want to know where they [PMA] stand before going into a holding action," he added.[4]

In reply, the manager of PMA told the NFO members, "We're squabbling about details," adding that the matter could not be resolved that afternoon because the board of the dairy group needed more time to study NFO's demands. For the time being, the matter was dropped.

Although there had been rumors in June, 1963, that the NFO was about to spring another all out holding action, Staley denied such a move was underway.[5] However, in August, several "wildcat holding actions" were called on livestock. Plans were announced for picketing to be held

in Kansas City and St. Joseph in Missouri and in East St.
Louis, Illinois, along with demonstrations at St. Paul, Minnesota, and Waterloo, Iowa. Similar activity was planned in
some points of Wisconsin. A small number of men turned
up in the Omaha stockyards for a few hours one morning
but left without talking to anyone or causing any interference with the market.

At the same time, Staley said he was heartened by these
"spontaneous demonstrations" and although the national
board of directors of NFO had not sanctioned any holding
actions, he would not stop NFO members from demonstrat-
ing or holding their livestock if they wanted to.

Within a week, the rumors of a new holding action were
gone. In most areas where signs had been posted announc-
ing the beginning of a withholding on August 19, nothing
happened. Some NFO leaders, including Staley, said that
these "wildcat actions" had thrown the processors off guard
and kept them wondering whether the NFO was actually
going into action or not. At East St. Louis, an NFO official
said that the effort had accomplished its purpose, but he
did not explain what that was.

In general appearance, these wildcat holding actions reflected some growing discontent within the organization
and eagerness for another all out holding action on livestock. Although Staley said these moves were being made
to "confuse" processors, they probably were more indicative
of confusion within the NFO itself. No one seemed to know
what was going on, a few local people tried to get another
holding action underway, and in general, nothing came of
any of their efforts. This all passed while the national board
took no action on the matter.

Another spark of controversy flared up in mid-September of 1963 when Staley made an unexpected appearance
at a meeting of the Farmers for Freedom Committee in
Baldwin, Wisconsin. The Farmers for Freedom were obvious opponents of the NFO and speakers at the meeting had
begun to lambast the larger farm movement when Staley
walked into the meeting of about 4,000 and challenged the

chairman to give him (Staley) the floor. Upon the NFO chief's appearance, NFO members in the meeting started chanting, "We want Staley!" At the same time, policemen blocked the big farm boss's path to the stage.

Within a few minutes, the Farmers for Freedom meeting was adjourned and Staley and his followers went outside the auditorium and held an NFO rally in an adjoining parking lot. The whole incident was only a part of NFO activity to sign up dairy processors in Wisconsin.

RECALLING THE INTERNAL UNREST and limited criticism by some members of the NFO following the 1962 holding action, it was not surprising that similar agitation should return in the fall of 1963. In view of the charges levied privately by some of Staley's critics, who said the chief executive ruthlessly purged persons who posed any political threat or disagreed with the big Missourian in national board meetings, these critics weren't surprised when they heard that the board had discussed a list of 28 men who "had to be disposed of." Presumably the list included the names of Robert Casper and Harold Woodward, who had been presidential candidates against Staley in the 1962 election, along with a number of NFO leaders who had supported these two candidates.

Another incident that occurred during the summer of 1963 involved a threatening letter Staley received in the mail. The letter referred to "another holding action" and warned that Staley had better find a place farther away than a foreign country to hide in if another attempted holding action should fail. The reference to the foreign country hailed back to a rumor that Staley had arranged for hideouts in Canada and in Mexico during the 1962 holding action, supposedly as a refuge, should NFO activities get too hot.

The letter was handed over to the Federal Bureau of Investigation. Among the persons the FBI questioned about it was a former president of the Illinois chapter of the NFO, Lawrence Walton of Clayton. Walton and others later opined that the letter had been faked by someone in the national NFO headquarters and that it was being used in a "witch hunt" against Staley's critics.

When asked about them by the author, Staley said he never heard about any hideouts and denied ever receiving any threatening letters.

In the fall of 1963, Walton and Casper took action to have a hearing before the national board to air grievances on behalf of themselves and others who did not favor Staley's administration. Claiming that they were the victims of "character assassination" through the spreading of rumors, the critics of Staley had been fairly well organized among themselves and had held sessions comparing notes. They were ready to present what they believed to be a strong case against Staley.

Walton tentatively arranged a meeting between the disgruntled faction and the national board, but the appointment fell through. Another such meeting was scheduled for October 21, but the NFO board canceled it. Nonetheless, about 250 NFO members showed up in Corning and a protest gathering was held in the Knights of Columbus hall across the street from NFO national headquarters.[6] For five hours, unhappy members complained about the alleged misdeeds of Staley and the incumbent board of directors. At this meeting, Robert Casper emerged as the general leader of the group.

Although virtually no specific charges were made at the meeting, there were claims of irresponsible leadership and that irregular methods were being used in handling business matters in the Corning home of NFO. There were no allegations that these methods were crooked, but simply the opinion that they left the road open to temptation. This referred to the fact that some officers had signed blank checks that were filled in later by office personnel.

Several former employees and officers of the organization said that they had been fired for little or no reason other than the fact that they did not see eye-to-eye with Staley's way of doing things. Although they were unprepared to cite specific examples, some of the members implied that Staley had been responsible for directing some of the incidents of violence that occurred during the 1962 all out holding action on livestock.

Another incident that was cited as a reason for holding the protest session involved a meeting of the national board on September 23–25, 1963. From what they had heard, Staley's critics fitted together the story that there had been a "leak" of information among board members. Information that was supposed to be confidential and "strategic"—in this case, some part of a financial report—had gotten back to a board member's home town in another state before he was even able to return home from a board meeting.

In an attempt to ferret out the person or persons giving out the confidential information, Staley was said to have called the board in, locked them in their meeting room, and told them they'd stay there until the leak was found. In an added effort to find the informants, four light airplanes were dispatched in the middle of the night with orders not to return until they each had a man from the group of known protestors against Staley and the board. Four men were rousted out of bed between one and three A.M. and flown back to Corning for questioning separately before the board. But the leak was never found, according to members of Casper's camp.

Another allegation made against the Staley regime was that of sending out paid organizers to campaign for or against contenders in state and regional NFO elections, which amounted to tampering with local politics.

Although some local NFO bodies had made what they felt was constructive progress in public relations by holding farm-labor conferences with packing-house workers, spokesmen for these NFO groups said that the Corning regime under Staley belittled and condemned these efforts.

Casper's speech at the Corning protest meeting reached its climax with:

This is the cancer that is going to kill your organization: This politicking all the time, this knifing people in the back, this having a group from the board spying on other board members, going all over the country, "What did this board member say? What did that board member say?" Do you think you can build an organization on that kind of principle?

What board member dares speak his mind in that [any] board meeting? And I've sat in one board meeting that was pretty rough. I had hoped that some of the board members would be here that would not hesitate to speak up and say what some of the things were that had been going on. It's asking quite a little. I think that if any of them decide that they do want to stand up in that board meeting, and they take the kind of a licking that I saw a man take one time, I hope they go to a phone and call some of us and I think we can get a crowd that'll ride them [the national board] out of town on a rail. And we should.

All we're asking these people to do is to conduct the organization like it should be conducted, sit down there and act like gentlemen. This brow-beating, this organization meeting where they were in session 36 or 38 hours, whatever it was, it doesn't make any difference.

You ought to recognize this, you read about it in the papers when we watched Hitler take over Germany. Do you think for a minute anybody was worrying about that leak on the board? There wasn't anything to leak of any major consequence. It was just the excuse to take over the organization. And it is in the hands of a small group of people today.[7]

In the days that followed, Casper and his group demanded that the board meet with them before October 26 or the dissenters would consider the board no longer in office. The board rejected the meeting. However, a few days later, Staley invited the group to chose 28 men from its ranks to meet with the 28-man board on November 14. Casper and his group said they would air their differences before the board, but stipulated that either of two officials of the National Catholic Rural Life Conference or a Hartington, Nebraska, banker chair the meeting in order that a fair hearing be made. All indications were that these terms were also agreeable to Staley and the board.

However, when Casper and his group arrived for the gripe session, they learned that there would be no objective arbiter to chair the meeting. Staley was going to preside. It was explained that an unauthorized committee had agreed to an outside arbiter chairing the meeting. However, the board decided that letting an outsider run the meeting would be against the bylaws of the organization which required meetings of the board to be chaired by the president (Staley) or another authorized high official of the NFO.

After an hour of haggling over who should chair the proposed grievance session, Casper and his party walked out.

In a news conference afterwards, Staley commented that this had been another attempt of the dissenters to violate the bylaws of the organization. He added:

"This was only a further effort of a few beaten politicians to get a fizzling campaign off the ground. This is the second time in less than three weeks that this group has tried to dominate the organization. But we won't close the door. We will meet with any group, even the one that was here today, if it wants to meet under conditions prescribed by the bylaws."[8]

Holding their own news conference in a motel room in Corning, the protest group said, "We've tried to keep this mess a secret, but it's gone too far for that now."

Members of the group said that they had hoped to "clean up the organization" without their charges being made public. However, since it was impossible to work with the board, they announced another protest meeting in Mexico, Missouri, the following Monday, November 18. They said they would then make public their grievances against the incumbant board and against Staley.

At the same time, Staley made public his availability as a candidate for re-election to the presidency. Dale Cochran, Eagle Grove, Iowa, who was also a spokesman for the dissident group and was one-time national publicity director for the NFO, promised that the group would put up a candidate to run against Staley in the election at the national convention in Des Moines in December.

The meeting in Mexico drew nearly 700 persons who heard many of the same grievances again, this time with claims that the protesters had court-admissable evidence to back up their complaints. This meeting, however, drew less attention in the popular press and probably made less of a publicity splash than the splinter group had hoped.

Even though the group was made up largely of former board members and other castaway officials of the organization, apparently not too many rank-and-file members stopped to listen. The climate for credibility was not in their favor since so many rumors had circulated that many NFO members probably did not know whom to believe. And in some of the older regions where the NFO had once boasted enthusiastic followings, many members apparently did not even care.

In this early round of clashes between Staley and his critics, it appeared that Staley was the winner. Without any doubt, the splinter group was aimed at ousting Staley and revising policies of the organization. For one thing, they believed the tactic of using holding actions as Staley advocated had served its purpose. Besides, these critics of Staley honestly feared that if another all out holding action were called, it would turn into a reign of terror. Pointing out that the incidents during the 1962 holding action included rocks being heaved and guns being fired at moving livestock trucks, these people, among others, felt that it was plain fool's luck that no one had been killed. They feared that next time the violence might be much worse.

Why had Staley won again? In appearance, the disgruntled group had demanded a showdown. Staley and the board refused. Then Staley invited the group to come in and talk, but they turned down the opportunity because Staley would not meet their terms. In the end, it made the insurgents look more uncooperative than Staley and his camp. Thus the exchanges between the two groups were at a stalemate with a final showdown expected at the national convention in December.

Later in November, 1963, Staley confirmed a news story that the crash of a light airplane carrying some NFO officials might have been caused by sabotage and that the case had been turned over to the FBI. Among officials injured in the mishap was the national vice president, who suffered a broken jaw.

"The plane I fly in had two or three similar cases of

sabotage," Staley added. "Once over Michigan the engine sputtered out. We landed safely and found out that sugar had been put in the gas."[9] Staley never mentioned who might have been responsible for any of this suspected sabotage. Nonetheless, publicity given to the investigation seemed to work in favor of Staley's election campaign.

Then there was a pause. To the public eye, all was quiet on the NFO front until the national convention opened in Des Moines on December 4.

The first day of the two-day convention was largely devoted to clearing the air between the splinter group led by Casper and the incumbent administration. During the day, Staley spent more than three hours defending his administration's policies and his own personal reputation. In his 70-minute state of affairs address before the 7,000 delegates, he challenged his opposition to "put up or shut up." It was not until about ten o'clock on the first night of the convention that the showdown between the insurgents and Staley began in earnest.

Casper took the platform and criticized the NFO as a one-man organization being run by Staley. He argued that the holding action principle was outmoded. He denounced violence in connection with holding actions. For four hours he made charges and answered questions about his statements. Some of his party had been seen at the convention earlier in the day, but as Casper went into the vicious debate that ensued, he stood alone against Staley and a delegate body that was nearly completely behind the president.

Casper said he did not want to indulge in a liar's contest and suggested that the truth might be reached through the courts of law or by using a lie detector.

At one point, Staley lost his temper and shouted, "I want to prove once and for all that these guys are the biggest bunch of liars ever to hit the face of the earth!"

As the debate continued, heckling came from the convention floor, where delegates shouted such jeers at Casper as:

"It's a damn lie!"

"Put up or shut up!"

"You're not worth the leather in the shoes you're standing on!"[10]

At nearly two A.M., reportedly near tears, Casper gave up and recanted all of his charges. He shook hands with Staley and the delegation let out a roar of approval. Casper was beaten for good this time, most observers felt.

During the debate, five uniformed policemen and two plainclothesmen roamed the huge auditorium, watching for trouble. At one point earlier in the day, a scuffle had taken place when one delegate booed at the national vice president as he was making his annual address. A policeman removed the protesting delegate "for his own protection."

Even after the debate between Casper and the pro-Staley multitude was over, some delegates hotly argued the issues that Casper had brought up.

The second day of the convention seemed anti-climatic. Forest Nave, Jr., from Lexington, Missouri, was a last-minute candidate opposing Staley for re-election. Although Nave was a critic of Staley and was supported by Casper's group, Nave's campaign speech was generally a half-hearted call for unity within the organization. As a parting shot at the close of his address, he threw one barb:

"Now, about these airplanes . . . if I'm elected president of NFO, I'll use commercial airlines in the performance of my duties—they're a lot cheaper and safer!"

As expected, Staley won the election over Nave by an overwhelming 4,774 to 581 votes.

Compared with his 1962 address after re-election, Staley's acceptance speech was short and sweet. After winning over Casper and Woodward in 1962, Staley had delivered a somewhat bitter 30-minute lambast at his opponents for stirring up dissension. Then he had called for unity.

However, after his easy win over Nave, Staley offered a 12-minute speech wherein he claimed the organization had reached manhood at this convention and was near victory in its collective bargaining program. He reported that the

NFO had continued to sign contracts with processors in 1963, progress which he termed very important. It was perhaps one of the shortest speeches in his career as president of the organization.

In a session with reporters after the election, Staley announced that an all out holding action on livestock, soybeans and dairy products (milk) would be called before spring, 1964. "It'll be an interesting winter with lots of activity," he predicted.

Perhaps the most significant development that came out of routine convention business was the approval of a bylaws revision that would speed hearings on charges made by members against NFO officials and in essence could hasten the process of expelling members from the organization.

Dale Cochran, one of the leaders of the protest group that had been defeated, commented that this bylaws change was "the ultimate weapon Staley had been looking for to keep the organization under his thumb."

When queried, various members of the protest group said after convention that they would "let sleeping dogs lie" by giving up their criticisms of Staley and hopes of changing the organization's policies. Many of these critics expected to be expelled from the organization under the new bylaws or at least be plagued by rumors. Others disgustedly said they were through with the NFO.

ANOTHER DEVELOPMENT in NFO activities that had not reached fruition or enough progress for full evaluation at this writing was the farm movement's 1963 campaign to bolster prices on soybeans. In early September, Staley called on NFO members to "shut the granary door. Nail it shut. If the market wants the grain, it can bring the crowbar—a fair price to farmers."

In a letter to the author, Staley explained this campaign:

> The NFO grain program is basically the same as any other NFO program. We feel that the only way to effectively sell anything is

to control enough of the total supply so that you can put a cost of production price on your product and hold until someone is willing to pay the price.

We have been recommending to our members that they build farm storage so that they can retain control of their grain crops. To supplement our bargaining efforts on soybeans, we are offering our members an opportunity to sign a voluntary grain sales agreement, authorizing the NFO to sell soybeans for a price that will not be less than $2.75 per bushel. [This was about 35¢ a bushel higher than the prevailing price paid to farmers in Iowa in the fall of 1963.] This is a supplemental bargaining effort. It does not take precedence over the membership agreement, but should assist in getting master contracts signed for marketing of both this year's [1963's] crop and future crops.

We are, at the moment, concentrating on getting as many soybeans as possible signed under the voluntary grain sales agreement. We are also planning to use a similar sales agreement for edible beans and perhaps some other grain commodities.[11]

As in the NFO membership agreement, the member was the only one that signed the voluntary sales agreement on soybeans. There was no provision made for an NFO official to sign it. If the signing member failed to comply with the terms of the agreement, he was subject to paying the NFO 10 per cent of the value of the listed amount of soybeans for "liquidated damages." Also, if court action should be necessary to collect liquidated damages, the member had to pay the court costs and attorney fees involved. The member signing the agreement retained title to the soybeans involved, but agreed to deliver them, when sold, to the buyer at a shipping point not more than 30 miles away from the member's farm.

The NFO assumed no ownership and no liability in making the sales, "other than performing the services in making the sales to the best of its ability." NFO also took the option of canceling the agreement "should unforeseen circumstances arise." The one-way contract was to automatically expire on July 31, 1964.

Staley said his organization's goal in the 1963 soybean campaign was to sign up 200 million bushels of soybeans from the record crop of 701 million bushels. To the NFO's advantage was the fact that most of the nation's soybeans were raised in the region where NFO was organized. This was not the case with most other grains and livestock. At any rate, if the NFO did obtain control of the marketing of 200 million bushels of soybeans, Staley said it would corner the supply for the last few months before the new 1964 crop would be ready for harvest and marketing. This would put NFO in a position to set the price virtually wherever it might want to. Some NFO officials optimistically predicted they'd end up selling their soybeans for as high as $3 a bushel. The prices mentioned here and earlier would be on No. 1 yellow soybeans, the top grade. Values on beans of less quality would be scaled according to merit.

Although the 1963 soybean crop was the largest in history, prices held up substantially and even gained at times because of active exporting and strong demand for soybean oil and meal on the domestic market. The soybean market outlook was still bright at the close of 1963. Persons in the grain trade agreed that if the NFO could corner 200 million bushels, or even considerably less of the supply of soybeans, the organization might put a grip on pushing prices up. However, most grain dealers seriously doubted that the NFO had strength enough to win.

In earlier attempts at holding grain off the market— attempts that received little publicity and showed no real success—the usual advised practice was for NFO members to "seal" their grain under the federal support price program and thus acquire a loan from the government. By keeping the grain on the farm, it was believed that supplies could be diminished at the terminal markets and eventually prices would rise to the point where they would be above government supports. By keeping the grain out of market channels, the NFO expected eventually to force processors to the bargaining table and to make them sign contracts with the NFO.

When asked their opinions of the NFO program on grain, officials at several of the major terminal grain markets said they weren't fully acquainted with the NFO plan, but from what they had observed, the farm organization's attempts to "corner the market" would be futile. Besides, they said NFO was attempting to compete with the Commodity Credit Corporation, the USDA agency that held vast amounts of grain in storage. If the market improved, the CCC would certainly take advantage of it and unload the grain taken over under its price support and loan program to farmers.

The NFO also studied the grain export business and in 1963 offered a contract for its members to consign grain for storage and eventual exportation—at a premium above prevailing prices—once the NFO found a favorable market abroad. Again, the central grain market officials consulted by the author scoffed that exporting was no field for amateurs in the grain marketing business.

13

SOME ALTERNATIVE APPROACHES
TO THE FARM PROBLEM

ONCE WE HAVE ACCEPTED the fact that the problems faced by those making a living in agriculture are extremely diverse and complex, it would be safe to say that there is not and probably never will be one easy solution to the farm problem. For example, when the cooperative movement was new in farm organizations, a few persons thought that their co-ops would be a panacea for the farmer's financial troubles. Co-ops were unable to provide a utopia, but they have proved helpful and today represent an impressive element in the field of agribusiness.

The legislative approach to putting farmers on their feet permanently has been far from satisfactory. Some critics say laws providing for crop controls and price supports have been a complete loss of vast amounts of time and federal money, and to draft farm bills to satisfy every facet of agriculture would require nearly a separate program for every farmer. However, advocates of this kind of farm policy would say that they have never been able to obtain exactly the kind of legislation they set out for, so who knows whether the legislative approach is the answer to the farm problem?

Many farmers have demonstrated their discontent with federal farm programs. The wheat referendum of 1963—

when a "no" vote won out—was one of the greatest displays of this unfavorable feeling. Some farmers said that if the government got out of agriculture and stayed out of it, adjustments would be made so that the farm industry would eventually stand on its own feet. Admittedly, the adjustment would be turbulent. Many farmers would go broke and have to find a way of making a living in other fields. The bottom might fall out of prices of nearly all farm products until production was brought in line with demand. This, of course, is the extreme possibility. However, considering the example of the livestock industry, and its history of getting along without farm programs of controls and supports, or shedding them as soon as possible—as was the case of hogmen—it seemed reasonable that this approach might be worth a try. In essence, this was the Committee for Economic Development farm proposal. It meant, of course, that some farmers would be squeezed out of business. Just the announcement of such a proposal caused a furor among NFO members, so it was clear that such an abandonment of federal farm program would not be too welcome.

In connection with government farm policy, the farmer was in an awkward position. Many of them did not like having to abide by regulations of the programs, but at the same time they realized that without the income that price support loan programs offered, their economic status would indeed be desperate. But, rejection of the 1963 wheat referendum seemed to indicate that some farmers were willing to try "going it alone."

A field that offered some new opportunity to farmers was that of farm product utilization research sponsored by some state departments of agriculture. In short, this meant seeking out new uses for old products such as corn. Chemically, the possibilities were seemingly boundless. Plastics of many forms could be made from the corn itself. Alcohol could be distilled from a corn preparation for such uses as fuel for internal combustion engines. However, this automatically posed problems of the synthetic products from

corn entering into competition with other fiber and petroleum products. Such possibilities were conceivable for
nearly all crops and seemed to offer a partial means of disposing of surplus crop production. Were they unreasonable? Not in the author's opinion. Such research, even
when the results were applied, would not offer a complete
solution to problems of overproduction from farms. But it
might well be helpful.

Another avenue for disposing of farm surpluses was
that of exportation. In terms of ideals, as long as there was
famine in the world, it was nearly impossible to say that
that there was overproduction in any part of it. However,
as was the case of Europe during the famines of the Dark
Ages, there would have been no starvation if there had been
transportation and trade to distribute the available supplies
of foodstuffs. While there is constant need for food in some
quarters of the world, it does not constitute market demand
since demand also must include ability to pay a negotiable
price for a given product. The complexity of exportation of
farm products makes it impossible to take it up at length
here, but it is an area that has received much attention in
the past and merits continued and concerted study.

Promotional activities of certain product interest groups
have been useful. For example, the information dissemi-
nated by such groups as the National Live Stock and Meat
Board, the American Dairy Association and other similar
bodies has served to educate the public on the values of
the products involved. Besides the advertising put out by
these special interest groups, that of some of the large food
chains has helped to move farm products in the form of
foods.

As the population grows—there should follow a larger
field of buyers and consumers of food. However, the continued rate of increase of production could well keep in
step with the growing population and thus perpetuate the
farm problem.

The idea of farmers finding new ways of making money

from their land could help the individual farmer line his pocketbook. For example, some farmers have found that by growing Christmas trees, they have developed an additional source of income. The prospect of setting up recreational facilities on farms has been advocated. Of course it would be impractical—in fact impossible—for every farmer to attempt to boost his income in these ways. The average farm is not a natural Christmas tree garden or a playground for folks on vacation. However, such ideas could lead to other kinds of ingenuity to improve some farmers' incomes.

Considering the trend of farm population shrinking and the average size of farms getting larger, it would be fairly safe to say that the population shift from farm to town will continue. Ways of making the transition easier and more workable include farmers' taking part-time employment in urban areas until they get the feel of the new job. An impressive number of farmers have resorted to this kind of "moonlighting" in off-seasons when farm chores do not require the operator's entire attention. By getting some experience in industry, the farmer would know what kind of "city job" he could do and probably would be much more comfortable in making the switch. But in most cases, it still would not be an easy change.

What role can farm organizations play in helping to solve the farm problem? The older farm organizations have scored great lists of accomplishments in the fields of marketing, education and legislation. However, their inherent differences on policy and practices have sometimes cost great sums of money because these organizations have at times become embroiled in expensive campaigns against each other's programs. If the farm population continues to shrink and if it becomes such a small minority population-wise, it is possible that the farm organizations would be forced to work more closely together as trade associations. While some critics might scoff at Oren Lee Staley's observation that through organization, farmers will be able to compete with other tightly-knit segments of the American

economy—such as organized labor and organized business—it seems reasonable that farmers, too, may have to
compete as an industry against the other industries rather
than as farmers competing with all other farmers and all
other industries to boot.

This short chapter has made no attempt to offer a blue-
print of how to solve the farm problem. Many studies and
heaps of volumes have been written on farm policy and approaches to the problem. For the impatient person who
asks with irritation, "Why don't they do something about
the farm problem?" this should serve notice that the farm
problem is a kind of Gordian knot for which no one has
been able to hone a knife—or devise a practical solution—
sharp enough to cut through easily.

14

REVIEW AND GUIDELINES TO EVALUATION

THE RISE of the National Farmers Organization came, as had some of the earlier agricultural movements, from the discontent of Midwestern farmers in the grip of an economic squeeze. Government programs following the Korean Conflict had not kept their promises of prosperity and the first farmers to join the new NFO in 1955 were bent on petitioning the government for emergency action. Thousands hopped on the NFO bandwagon during the first six months of its existence and membership soared to 180,000. But the protest action of petitioning the government with a list of gripes brought no results.

In its search for a different approach, the NFO adopted a program of collective bargaining. The old idea of the farm strike was thus revised and was destined to make NFO a term of infamy among agricultural market interests. The NFO plan for action was simply that of organizing farmers so that they might hold their products off the markets until buyers and processors of these goods were willing to pay the price the NFO demanded. However, before the NFO would sell at its own price, it planned to force the buying interests to the bargaining table to sign contracts to assure that price levels would remain up where the NFO wanted them. It sounded simple and easy.

Three test holding actions and one all out holding action

on livestock proved that the organization's program would not be so simple and certainly was not easy. For many followers, experiences with these actions raised doubts as to whether the program would actually work.

The success of the program hinged on whether the NFO could organize enough farmers to make its kind of collective bargaining effective. If it won in a holding action and got the contracts it sought, then, it said, it could put into effect its plans for production quotas and bring the output of farm commodities into a sensible economic balance of supply and demand. However, history and the independent nature of farmers in general indicated that the movement would face a tremendous challenge before success could be expected.

In a few short years the NFO did become one of the major farm organizations, even though it was the smallest by a considerable degree. But compared with the history for the Grange, the Farmers Union and the Farm Bureau, the NFO was a different breed of farm movement. While some outsiders called it radical, militant and unrealistic, the NFO preferred to think of its policy and actions as new, liberal and imaginative. However, all success depended on the use of coercive moves to control the markets.

Every twenty to thirty years, over the past century, a "radical" or at least loudly protesting farm movement has risen and fallen with almost predictable regularity. Those that got a foothold generally lasted about a decade or less before becoming extinct. The first, for example, did not actually materialize into a farm movement because of the temporary prosperity brought by the Civil War. This was the Centralia Convention in 1858, which advocated that producers should be the rule rather than the exception in filling public office. The Farmers Alliance and Populist movements of the 1880's called for extreme economic and legislative action to improve the farmers' lot. However, their third-party ideology was eventually absorbed by the two major political parties.

More extreme radicalism was apparent in the story of

the Society of Equity which started in 1902. The idea of collective bargaining was applied to the marketing of wheat and for one year seemed to be effective. A more forceful plan was applied to the marketing of tobacco and a large transaction was completed with the American Tobacco Company after many farmers were forced or threatened into supporting the effort. The violence that accompanied this action disillusioned the membership and this approach to the farm problem was abandoned. The Equity, after attempts for success in other fields, died.

Farmers got their backs up over low farm prices in the late 1920's and the worst of that movement came in 1932 when the Farmers Holiday Association threw up blockades around Omaha and Sioux City. In the wake of violence and other wild-eyed mischief, the Farmers Holiday had its siege and disappeared.

In each instance, these farm movements reflected a great deal of discontent and were efforts of farmers attempting to help themselves by taking immediate and drastic action. In nearly every case they failed because their goals were too extreme to win the favor of enough farmers to be successful. Was the NFO another of these periodic farm revolts that occurred with enough regularity that a new generation was involved each time?

Recalling that some of the surviving major farm organizations had started on a radical tone and had to modify policies and take up new lines of endeavor, there was some reason to doubt the NFO could survive long unless it did unquestionably win some of its battles. Other contemporary farm organizations were active in several fields—legislation, education and cooperative business, including farm marketing agencies. When defeated in one area they could, so to speak, change the subject and alibi by stressing how well they were maintaining a position in another area of interest. But if the NFO sustained a definite setback, it was comparable to a man with a single-shot shotgun. Once a barrel was fired, he'd have to stop and reload. Other farm groups had learned that they had to have at least "double-barrels" to keep up interest within their memberships. It was easier to maintain a number of so-called crises that would flare up occasionally rather than to keep one crisis hot in order to keep a following fired up.

Thus the NFO was committed, not only by consent of the membership but under legislation that so specified, to one course of action—its program of collective bargaining. This obviously posed problems of keeping the "opposition" under siege with a single-shot shotgun. Even though the NFO leadership included a number of spellbinders who could arouse a crowd, there was room for doubt that the emotional approach to keeping farmers organized could endure for long.

Reports of internal strife in the NFO indicated that unless there were some changes in policy and possibly in officers, too, the organization would not last. When informed sources said that 75 per cent of the NFO's leadership were purged in one year (at the end of 1962), it seemed a reasonable assumption that if this kind of action were repeated very often, there would be no intermediate leaders to keep the movement forging ahead.

Were the existing marketing agencies as outmoded and inefficient as the NFO implied? If they were, it would seem that the market interests themselves would have suffered business failures simply because they were not doing the job they were cut out for. But in fact, they were still very much in business. Perhaps rather than attempting to revolutionize the agricultural marketing system, NFO members would have been better off by trying rationally to live with it and make use of its advantages. If the economic principle of supply and demand meant anything, it would seem wiser to limit production within the realm of healthy supply and market demand rather than blame outside traders for the results of overproduction. Since the average farmer has to be informed on many kinds of production skills, as well as marketing, it would seem at least convenient for farmers to take advantage of the services of the market interests. This does not mean that the farmer should ignore market developments, but it is usually to his advantage to use the advice and skills of those in central markets and other areas where prices are established.

While on the topic of marketing, it is significant to point out that NFO educational programs did help to alert farmers to the need of knowing more about the markets that were available to them. They focused attention on the importance of careful planning for farm marketing.

IN ITS first eight years of existence, what had the NFO accomplished? President Oren Lee Staley said:

"I think that it [the NFO's record of accomplishments] keeps the buyers of farm commodities on edge and keeps the prices of farm products higher than if farmers were not organized. It also emphasizes the farm problem, that there is a problem. Our program gives the farmers an opportunity to move together as a unit to meet their problems as an industry."

Because of the many variables influencing the markets, it would be difficult to prove or disprove the claim that NFO's efforts had improved the farm price situation.

Examined objectively, the NFO record did not show too many constructive accomplishments. Because it involved conflict and controversy, the NFO's activities had netted a great deal of attention in the news media. This was in a way useful since many non-farm persons had no idea of the farmer's plight. At the same time, much of this publicity distorted the farm problem and implied that all farmers were in a state of poverty. However, controversy is one criterion of what is news and the NFO promoted plenty of controversy. Thus some segments of the popular press turned some NFO activities into "big stories" that they perhaps did not deserve to be.

Staley claimed each successive holding action was more of a success than the last, but all were basically failures. Had any produced lasting results? Perhaps the only lasting

feature was the ill will stirred by differences of opinion over
the NFO program for action. The sporadic violence that accompanied the all out holding action of 1962 reflected
poorly on all farmers, regardless of who was responsible,
and farm-city relations were in some instances hurt by
these developments.

Many NFO members were proud of the sincerity they
saw in their leaders. There was no doubt that those who
labored long and hard to further the NFO cause were doing
so with the conviction that what they were doing was
morally and economically right. The occasional speculation
that the NFO was a "communist front" organization was significant only as an indication of how suspicious a few anti-
NFO interests could be. NFO bylaws prohibited anyone with
a subversive record from joining the organization or remaining a member if he subsequently turned subversive.

The sincerity and general forthrightness displayed by
most NFO leaders commanded the personal respect of
many persons, whether or not they agreed with NFO policy.
There was due admiration for these farmers who wanted to
get government out of agriculture and who at the same
time were working for a program which they believed would
allow the farmer to solve his own problems. And although
many were not in sympathy with the economic theories and
political tactics of the NFO, all agriculture was in favor of
obtaining what the NFO called its goal—which in essence
was the raising of farm prices to parity and thus giving
prosperity to all farmers.

What did the future hold for the NFO? Would there
be more all out holding actions? With his re-election to a
ninth term, President Staley committed himself and the
organization to this approach to collective bargaining for
agriculture.

Would there be changes in NFO policy? There seemed
to be indications that there would be no changes as long as
Oren Lee Staley was at the helm of the movement.

In view of some of the internal opposition to Staley and

his camp of supporters, could it be assumed that Staley would be replaced? Considering the fact that Staley ruled with an iron hand, plus the reports of vast purges of those who opposed him, it was conceivable that the whole organization might fold up before Staley would be unseated. This, of course, was an extreme speculation.

"Only time will tell my future," Staley had said. "I didn't start in this battle for the fun of it. I'll be there as long as the people want me to help them lead the battle and if they can find someone else better, I'll assist that. . . . Only time will tell."

APPENDICES

Appendix A

NFO'S PRIMARY CONTRACT

MEMBERSHIP AGREEMENT

Date _____

Name _____ or _____
           Print or Type

County _____ Township _____ State _____

ARTICLE I—AUTHORIZATION

I authorize the National Farmers Organization (hereinafter referred to as the N.F.O.) its agents or representatives to act for me as my exclusive representative in collective bargaining in respect to all commodities marketed from my farm, with the exception of those commodities presently covered by other marketing contracts, and to enter into contracts with the processors of products I own and control covering the selling prices and other conditions of disposal, and establish marketing procedure. I further authorize the said organization to act as my exclusive representative in the presentation, prosecution and adjustment of any complaint that I may have against the processor of the commodities of my farm, in accordance with and subject to the rights and privileges granted me by the By-laws of the N.F.O.

This authorization and direction shall be irrevocable for a period of three (3) years from the date appearing above. I agree and direct that this authorization and direction shall be automatically renewed and shall be irrevocable for successive periods of three (3) years each unless written notice is given by me to the N.F.O. not more than twenty (20) days and not less than ten (10) days prior to the expiration of each three (3) year period. This authorization is made pursuant to the provisions of the Capper-Volstead Act enacted February 18, 1922.

ARTICLE II—NATIONAL N.F.O. COMMODITY DEPARTMENTS

Sec. 1—The Board of Directors of the N.F.O. shall create National Commodity Departments for Dairy, Grain, and Meat. Miscellaneous commodities may be assigned by the Board of Directors to any one of the three established Commodity Departments.

Sec. 2—The President of the N.F.O. shall appoint a Department Head who shall be known as a Director, and staff for each of the National Commodity Departments, subject to the approval of the Board of Directors. The Board of Directors shall have the power to remove a director or staff members of a Commodity Department.

Sec. 3—The National Commodity Departments shall be under the direction of the President and responsible for carrying out the intent of this Agreement and administrative policy established by the Board of Directors.

Sec. 4—The National Commodity Departments shall have the responsibility of assisting the Marketing Area Bargaining Committees in their negotiations with the processors and coordinate the activities of all Area Marketing Committees.

Sec. 5—The National Commodity Departments shall at the direction of the Board of Directors make plans for effective marketing procedures to be submitted to the Marketing Area Bargaining Committees for their consideration.

ARTICLE III—MARKETING AREAS

Sec. 1—The President and the Board of Directors shall establish marketing areas for each commodity based on area of supply of key markets.

Sec. 2—Bargaining with processors in each marketing area shall be done by elected Marketing Area Bargaining Committees under the supervision of the Executive Board and with the assistance of the National Commodity Departments.

Sec. 3—Contracts consummated with processors shall cover only members of the marketing area who have signed membership contracts with the N.F.O.

Sec. 4—Marketing areas may from time to time be changed to provide better service for the membership.

ARTICLE IV—MARKETING AREA BARGAINING COMMITTEES

Sec. 1—When in the opinion of the Board of Directors of the N.F.O. sufficient contracts have been signed covering a specific commodity to be effective in collective bargaining, the President shall call a meeting of the members of County Bargaining Committees who represent the commodity in each zone of the marketing area for the purpose of electing a member of the Area Bargaining Committee and an alternate member who shall serve as a member of the Area Bargaining Committee when the regular member is unable to serve.

Sec. 2—The Board of Directors shall divide each marketing area into seven (7) geographical zones for the purpose of distribution of bargaining committee representation.

Sec. 3—Each Marketing Area Bargaining Committee shall be composed of seven (7) members, one from each of the geographic zones of the marketing area.

Sec. 4—The term of office of the bargaining committee members and alternates shall be for a period of one year.

Sec. 5—The Marketing Area Bargaining Committee shall be responsible for the bargaining with the processor for the commodity they represent within their marketing area under the direction of the Board of Directors and the assistance of the National Commodity Department.

Sec. 6—The Marketing Area Bargaining Committee shall meet and counsel with the County Bargaining Committees as provided herein and at other times that they deem necessary.

ARTICLE V—COUNTY BARGAINING COMMITTEES

Sec. 1—Each county organized under the N.F.O. shall call meetings and elect a bargaining committee composed of a chairman and four members for each commodity represented by the N.F.O. in the county, such committees to be for Dairy, Grain, and Meat.

Sec. 2—Anyone who is an N.F.O. member producing farm products for which a bargaining committee is established is eligible to vote for members of the bargaining committee. However, in order to be elected to a bargaining committee, a member of the N.F.O. must be able to furnish ample proof that a substantial part of his farm income is derived from the commodity that the bargaining committee represents.

Sec. 3—County Bargaining Committees shall gather information and determine fair prices for the agricultural commodities which their committee represents.

Sec.4—The Marketing Area Bargaining Committee shall, before entering into negotiations with a processor, call a meeting of the County Bargaining Committee for the commodity they represent, and by a two-thirds' vote of those attending this meeting shall determine the fair price for the commodity to be bargained for with the processor.

Sec. 5—From time to time, Marketing Area Bargaining Committees may call meetings of the County Bargaining Committees to report on the status of negotiations and seek their advice.

Sec. 6—The County Bargaining Committee shall be responsible for organizing farmers in their counties who produce the commodity they represent.

Sec. 7—The County Bargaining Committees may at times be called by the Area Marketing Committee to represent the organization in collective bargaining with processors of their commodity.

ARTICLE VI—RATIFICATION OF MARKETING CONTRACTS

Sec. 1—No contract consummated with a processor shall be effective or binding until it has been ratified by a two thirds' vote of members in a marketing area who have signed contracts with the N.F.O. for the commodity, attending a meeting called for that purpose by the Marketing Area Bargaining Committee and has been approved by the Board of Directors of the N.F.O.

Sec. 2—If a marketing procedure is formulated for a marketing area, it will require the same ratification as contracts with processors.

Sec. 3—It will be the responsibility of the Marketing Area Bargaining Committee to give at least ten days' notice to members who have signed marketing contracts, by first class mail, to the address

shown on this contract, giving date, time and place of meetings on
any issue requiring ratification of N.F.O. members.

ARTICLE VII—MARKETING REQUIREMENTS

Sec. 1—Until such time as a contract has been consummated
with the processor for a commodity I own or control in accordance
with the provisions of this agreement, or until a marketing procedure
has been established for a commodity and ratified in accordance
with the terms of this agreement, a member shall be free to market
his commodity as he chooses.

Sec. 2—When a contract has been consummated in accordance
with the terms of this agreement covering a member's commodity,
and he sells this commodity to a processor other than the one specified by the agreement, the member shall be assessed 10% of the gross
sale of the commodity for liquidated damages.

Sec. 3—A member may request his Marketing Area Bargaining
Committee to waive provisions of this agreement in instances arising
that were unforeseen at the time of the signing of this agreement.
The Area Marketing Committee must make a complete report on all
such cases to the N.F.O. Board of Directors, on waivers granted. The
Board of Directors shall have authority to revoke a waiver if, in their
opinion. the waiver is not justified.

ARTICLE VIII—QUOTAS

Sec. 1—If quotas should become necessary on members under
contract, they will be determined by the same democratic procedure
that the fair price formula was determined and shall require the
same procedure of ratification, membership and approval of the
Board of Directors as the contract with the processor before becoming effective.

Sec. 2—If quotas are established they will be based on contracts
with processors for a specific quality and quantity of products and
quotas will be based on quality, bushel and poundage basis and good
land practices and ratio instead of crop history, and administered by
the establishment of pools based on quality.

Sec. 3—This to be financed, if necessary by additional deductions at the processor level from commodities marketed.

Sec. 4—To implement the provisions of the other Sections of
this Article, approval must be obtained from the members affected,
in accordance with Article VI of this agreement.

Sec. 5—By a two-thirds' vote of N.F.O. members attending county
meetings of which due notice has been given by the County Bargaining Committee at least ten days in advance of the meeting to the affected member giving date, time and place and purpose of meeting,
an additional surplus disposal amount shall be checked off at the
processor level, either for buying farm products and channeling to
needy worthwhile organizations, or to form welfare agencies or
others the N.F.O. may find necessary to keep production in balance
with consumption.

ARTICLE IX—MEMBERSHIP DUES AND FEES

Sec. 1—The membership dues of the N.F.O. shall be $5.00 per
year, or such amount as may hereafter be established by the N.F.O.,
which shall be due and payable to the Treasurer of the member's
county organization, at the date of making application for member-

ship in the N.F.O., and yearly thereafter, as prescribed by the By-laws of the organization.

Sec. 2—A member shall be assessed $20.00 at the time of signing this contract and yearly thereafter by the N.F.O. which shall be used as directed by the Board of Directors to defray expenses incurred in carrying out a program of effectuating collective bargaining with the processor, and other activities in the best interest of the membership of the organization to be determined by the Board of Directors of the N.F.O.

Sec. 3—When a marketing contract has been consummated by the N.F.O. covering a member's commodity, it shall provide that the processor check off 1% of the gross sales of the commodity for the N.F.O. This amount shall then become the member's dues and shall replace the dues and fees otherwise prescribed above in Sections 1 and 2.

ARTICLE X—RESPONSIBILITY OF THE N.F.O.

Sec. 1—The N.F.O. shall not become legal owner or engage in business activities but must remain within the framework of a service organization bargaining for its members who have signed marketing contracts.

Sec. 2—The Board of Directors of the N.F.O. shall decide on all questions involving interpretation of this agreement and make decisions on matters arising not covered by this agreement between conventions.

ARTICLE XI—RESPONSIBILITY OF MEMBER

Sec. 1—I agree to be bound by the terms of this agreement as herein provided, and further agree to comply with the decisions made by the membership and Board of Directors of the N.F.O., as herein provided.

Sec. 2—I agree to process any complaint I have against the N.F.O., its officers or members in accordance with the terms of the By-laws of the N.F.O.

ARTICLE XII—MODIFICATION

It may become necessary during the life of this agreement to change or modify certain Articles, or make amendments to it. In the event this becomes necessary, it will require a two-thirds' vote of members in attendance at marketing area meetings called for that purpose, which notice has been given in accordance with Article VI, Section 2 of this agreement.

Witness_____

Member's Legal Signature_____

Mailing Address_____

State_____

WHITE
National N.F.O. Copy
CANARY
County N.F.O. Copy
PINK
Member's Copy

Appendix B

CAPPER-VOLSTEAD ACT OF 1922

BE IT ENACTED BY THE SENATE AND HOUSE OF REPRE-
SENTATIVES OF THE UNITED STATES OF AMERICA IN CON-
GRESS ASSEMBLED, That persons engaged in the production of
agricultural products as farmers, planters, ranchmen, dairymen, nut
or fruit growers may act together in associations, corporate or otherwise, with or without capital stock, in collectively processing, preparing for market, handling, and marketing in interstate and foreign
commerce, such products of persons so engaged. Such associations
may have marketing agencies in common and such associations
and their members may make the necessary contracts and agreements to effect such purposes: PROVIDED, however, That such
associations are operated for the mutual benefit of the members
thereof, such producers, and conform to one or other of the following requirements:

First. That no member of the association is allowed more than
one vote because of the amount of stock or membership capital he
may own therein, or,

Second. That the association does not pay dividends on stock or
membership capital in excess of 8 percentum per annum.

And in any case to the following:

Third. That the association shall not deal in the products of
nonmembers to an amount greater in value than such as are handled
by it for members.

Sec. 2. That if the Secretary of Agriculture shall have reason to
believe that any such association monopolizes or restrains trade to
interstate or foreign commerce to such extent that the price of any
agricultural product is usually enhanced by reason thereof, he shall
serve upon such association a complaint stating his charge in that
respect, to which complaint shall be attached or contained therein,
a notice of hearing, specifying a day and place not less than thirty
days after the service thereof, requiring the association to show
cause why an order should not be made directing it to cease and
desist from monopolization or restraint of trade. An association so
complained of may at the time and place so fixed show cause why

[274]

such order should not be entered. The evidence given on such a hearing shall be taken under such rules and regulations as the Secretary of Agriculture may prescribe, reduced to writing, and made a part of the record therein. If upon such hearing the Secretary of Agriculture shall be of the opinion that such association monopolizes or restrains trade in interstate or foreign commerce to such an extent that the price of any agricultural product is unduly enhanced thereby, he shall issue and cause to be served upon the association an order reciting the facts found by him, directing such association to cease and desist from monopolization or restraint of trade. On the request of such association or if such association fails or neglects for thirty days to obey such order, the Secretary of Agriculture shall file in the district court in the judicial district in which such association has its principal place of business a certified copy of the order and of all the records in the proceeding, together with a petition asking that the order be enforced, and shall give notice to the Attorney General and to said association of such filing. Such district court shall thereupon have jurisdiction to enter a decree affirming, modifying or setting aside said order, or enter such other decree as the court may deem equitable, and may make rules as to pleadings and proceedings to be had in considering such order. The place of trial may, for cause or by consent of parties, be changed as in other causes.

The facts found by the Secretary of Agriculture and recited or set forth in said order shall be prima facie evidence of such facts, but either party may adduce additional evidence. The Department of Justice shall have charge of the enforcement of such order. After the order is so filed in such district court and while pending for review therein the court may issue a temporary writ of injunction forbidding such association from violating such order or any part thereof. The court may, upon conclusion of its hearing, enforce its decree by a permanent injunction or other appropriate remedy. Service of such complaint and of all notices may be made upon such association by service upon any officer or agent thereof engaged in carrying on its business, or on any attorney authorized to appear in such proceeding for such association, and such service shall be binding upon such association, the officers, and members thereof.

Senator Capper in discussing the bill said:
Mr. President, the cooperative marketing bill as it was offered in both the Senate and House seeks simply to make definite the law relating to cooperative associations of farmers and to establish a basis on which these organizations may be legally formed. Its purpose is to give to the farmer the same right to bargain collectively that is already enjoyed by corporations. The bill is designed to make affirmative and unquestioned the right which already is generally admitted, but which, in view of the Sherman law, is subject to nullifying interpretation by those whose interests are not identical with those of the farmer, and who for one reason or another may be in a position to obtain an interpretation advantageous to themselves and embarrassing or detrimental to the members of cooperative organization.

Mr. Volstead, in discussing the bill said:
The objection made to these organizations at present is that they

violate the Sherman Antitrust Act, and that is upon the theory that each farmer is a separate business entity. When he combines with his neighbor for the purpose of securing better treatment in the disposal of his crops, he is charged with a conspiracy or combination contrary to the Sherman Antitrust Act. Businessmen can combine by putting their money into corporations, but it is impractical for farmers to combine their farms into similar corporate form. The object of this bill is to modify the laws under which business organizations are now formed, so that farmers may take advantage of the form of organization that is used by business concerns. It is objected in some quarters that this repeals the Sherman Antitrust Act as to farmers. That is not true any more than it is true that a combination of two or three corporations violates the act. Such combinations may or may not monopolize or restrain trade. Corporations today have all sorts of subsidiary companies that operate together, and no one claims they violate the act.

Appendix C

NFO'S PROPOSED MASTER CONTRACT

FOREWORD
During the month of September, 1961, all NFO county organizations held meetings of their members to discuss terms to be included in a proposed draft of a master contract to be offered to processors.

The attached copy of a proposed draft of a master contract is based on the information forwarded to the national office recording the conclusions reached by the members. An explanation will be given after each point of the proposed draft of a master contract. Each point is to be thoroughly discussed by the members in each county at their regular county meeting during the month of October.

Most points in the proposed draft of a master contract are to be decided by NFO members. However, everyone must bear in mind that final details on some points involving services to processors must be decided at the bargaining table as these services must be performed in a way most suitable to the processors, as long as they are carried out in a legal manner and not causing difficulty for the members of the NFO.

After discussing the proposed draft of a master contract, each county will report back to the national organization on the conclusions reached by its members. If the members desire any changes or additions, then they will be included in the final draft of a master contract that will be offered to the processors.

These steps are in preparation for actual bargaining in many areas. The actual bargaining will be carried out under the provisions of the membership agreement.

Now that we have reached at least two-thirds of the necessary strength to bring the processors to the bargaining table we will continue to prepare for a all-out holding action at the earliest possible date, but in the meantime we will be offering the processors an opportunity to bargain in good faith. If they do not choose to bargain in good faith, then the NFO will proceed accordingly. After having studied the policies of those processors who do not agree to the terms of the master contract, the NFO will initiate a "no sell, no buy" campaign against those processors whose policies we feel are jeopardizing the future welfare of our members as family type farmers.

[277]

If, through our bargaining efforts, the processors do not agree to sign the master contract then they will have to accept the responsibility and consequences of an all-out holding action. In other words—a battle to a finish. The NFO is preparing to follow either course.

Farmers have the legal right and moral responsibility to price their products. Farmers have more bargaining power than industry and labor combined. The NFO will use whatever strategy is necessary to achieve justice at the market place.

PROPOSED DRAFT OF A MASTER CONTRACT
CAN BE ADAPTED TO ALL COMMODITIES, BUT WE WILL USE PORK AS
AN EXAMPLE. VARIATIONS WILL BE EXPLAINED FOR OTHER
COMMODITIES.

CONTRACT

OF

_____, A CORPORATION

WITH

NATIONAL FARMERS ORGANIZATION, INCORPORATED, of Corning, Iowa

WHEREAS _____, hereinafter referred to as Processor is desirous of contracting with the National Farmers Organization, Incorporated, hereinafter referred to as NFO for a supply of hogs, and

WHEREAS NFO is a farmers' organization many of whose members are engaged in the production of hogs, and

WHEREAS NFO is authorized to contract for the sale of hogs of its members subject to provisions of the membership agreement signed by said members.

NOW, THEREFORE, this Agreement Witnesseth:

1. NFO hereby agrees to act and function as a procurement agent for the purpose of furnishing Processor with hogs to be delivered at its plant or at receiving stations operated by Processor or in any other manner that may be agreed upon.

(*EXPLANATION:* As stated up to this point the contract will go in effect under the provisions of the membership agreement. The NFO will act as procurement agency. The points of delivery will be designated so NFO members will know where they would be expected to deliver their products before they vote on approval of a contract with the processor. The existing marketing facilities for meat, grain and dairy products will be used where ever possible. It will be the responsibility of the processor to pay for the operation of delivery points. Additional price allowance for transportation on delivery shall be allowed producers.)

2. Processor hereby agrees to pay members of NFO for hogs an average price of twenty-two dollars and seventy-five cents ($22.75) per hundred pounds based on No. 1 or No. 2 hogs weighing 190 to 210 pounds each or the market price thereof, whichever is higher, but it is understood that the price for hogs to be paid members of NFO at any given time shall be a price (but not less than the prevailing market price) to be adjusted seasonally from time to time by NFO based on production costs and approval by the members concerned of NFO as provided in its membership agreement.

(*EXPLANATION:* We have used the holding price here as an example of the bargaining price. It is evident from the reports from county meetings held in September that our members realize the necessity of varying prices seasonally. If this was not done everyone would want their sows to farrow in the warm months, feed cattle during the most favorable feeding periods, have their cows all freshen about the same time of the year, or sell their grain all at harvest time. In order to avoid this the main factor to be considered in variations of price will be the variations in cost of production.

Undoubtedly the NFO will be projecting months ahead in order to balance production and delivery of products to meet high and low consumption periods and develop orderly marketing. You can do this by adjusting the average price to what ever point is necessary. You can accomplish these objectives when you are pricing your production before it is produced.

For a further explanation of the $22.75 average figure used on hogs you can use for an example—if the price of hogs was allowed to drop to $21.00 at one period of time it would mean that for another equal period of time, NFO members would receive $24.50 thus balancing out the price of $22.75 on specified grades and weights. If you need to have wider variations to accomplish your objectives you could do so.

This clause (but not less than the prevailing market price) would always keep non-members from getting a higher price than NFO members. Later you will find that NFO members based on services rendered will always receive more than non-members. This means for example—that if the price for NFO members under the master contract at that time was $22.75, but for some reason the outside market price went up above this the NFO members' price under this contract would automatically go up the same amount.)

3. The price to be paid by Processors for hogs other than No. 1 or No. 2 hogs weighing 190 to 210 pounds shall be based on relative merit and on market differentials for weights and classes of hogs as provided in its membership agreement, but not less than the prevailing price.

(EXPLANATION: Many farmers are concerned about keeping production in balance with consumption. Points two and three are very important in this respect. Remember in point two you could adjust variation of price throughout the year to even out the production and develop orderly marketing. In point three you could, to a great degree, keep production in balance with consumption by use of price differentials for various weights and requirements of many products.

For example: If the NFO commodity department could foresee that there would be too much tonnage of pork later in the season, they could recommend to lower the price on heavier weights. Remember our prices are based on No. 1 and No. 2 hogs weighing from 190 to 210 pounds. Suppose, for example, that the price on these hogs at the time was $22.75 per hundred weight. And the next weight bracket was from 210 to 230 pounds and the price was 50c lower, and the next weight bracket was from 230 to 260 pounds and the price was another 50c lower. If the price on the latter two weight brackets was going to be considerably lower than this a little later, then everyone would want to sell in the 190 to 210 weight range. Think of the decreased tonnage this would bring about. If the same thing were done on other commodities the over-all tonnage would certainly be greatly reduced.

In the past this would have probably taken care of any over production in meat. If you had the greater percentage of the total production under the NFO membership agreement and a master contract signed, this principle applied to other commodities could probably keep production in balance with consumption. It could be applied to all meat products in a like manner. You could apply the same principle to dairy products. Think of the effect this would have in reducing the available supply of milk if the minimum on milk was raised from 3.4 to 3.6. On grain you would use a little different approach. You have the advantage on grain in that you can store and let on the market as needed. The feed grain program will also strengthen bargaining power on grain. If necessary you could always use the surplus disposal part of the membership agreement. Many people do not realize that production has never outstripped usage by more than a few percentage points for a given length of time.

Let us take wheat for example. This commodity has as many production problems as any commodity, but in five years the production has only averaged 8.2% above usage. If farmers had decided $2.50 per bushel was a fair price for wheat and had used the surplus disposal part of the NFO membership agreement, they would still have realized almost $2.30 per bushel net on all the wheat they produced, even if they could have received nothing for the 8.2%. Of course, this would not have been true but if it was, by shipping to under-privileged areas here or overseas, farmers would have served a great humanitarian purpose. It could also have been used to establish new markets.

The establishment of price differentials would, of course, be used when the pressure on all outside markets would be downward and all prices would follow

the price established by NFO. This shows what farmers could do when they
control the sale of their products instead of going to the market place and saying, "What will you give me?" Farmers, as individuals, can not carry out any
of the above procedures. It takes an organized agriculture to be successful in
an organized economy. The pools based on quality section of the membership
agreement could be used in addition to the establishment of price differentials
and the use of the surplus disposal section of the NFO membership agreement.)

4. Processor hereby buys under terms of this contract and NFO
hereby agrees to have delivered to Processor not less than ———
head of hogs during each twelve month period that this contract is
in effect but it is agreed that there may be a tolerance of 20% more
or less as the case may be.
(*EXPLANATION:* This point is one that will be a service to the processor.
It will give him a steady source of supply. Many of the processors operate their
plants at 65% or less of capacity. One of the great services that NFO can
render to the processor is assuring him a steady supply in sufficient quantity in
an orderly manner so as to tremendously increase his efficiency. This will be
true for all processors dealing with the NFO, whether they be dairy, meat. or
grain processors and handlers. On these points that are a service to the processor, it should be the processor that indicates what services will be of greatest
value to him. The NFO members must expect to render services because they
will be getting paid for the services rendered, as outlined in later points. All
services rendered must be done, however, with sufficient protection as not to
cause hardship on the NFO members. The tolerance clause of 20% protects the
organization.
Point four is the type of a point that will have to be worked out over the
bargaining table. Members, of course, under the provisions of the membership
agreement will give final approval before it becomes effective. As in all contracts, undoubtedly, there will be a clause giving protection to both parties
from an act of God or causes due to unforeseen circumstances.)

5. Processor shall consult with NFO from time to time with a
view to promoting the delivery of hogs to Processor by members of
NFO.
(*EXPLANATION:* This point is another point to be worked out in detail over
the bargaining table. It is a service to the processor. It will apply to all commodities. The members can be confident their interests will be protected because
they will know each detail as written in the contract before they give their
approval or rejection.)

6. Processor and NFO shall work together for the purpose of en-
couraging the production of hogs by members of NFO that best meet
the needs of consumers and the demands of the market.
(*EXPLANATION:* This is self-explanatory. It will be an advisory point in the
contract and will be mainly an educational program.)

7. It is understood that NFO is offering a form of contract like
this one to other Processors in the United States; and that this contract shall be in full force and effect from the day that NFO advises
each Processor signing a contract like this one that Processors that
have slaughtered ——————— per cent of the hogs slaughtered
in the United States during the last three years have signed contracts like this one; and this contract (subject to renewal) shall be
in full force and effect from that date for a full twelve months
period; but unless either party hereto gives notice to the other of
its desire to terminate this contract not less than fifteen (15) days
and not more than twenty (20) days before the prescribed termination date, it shall thereby be renewed for another year.
(*EXPLANATION:* This point involves strategy in bargaining. From the
processor's standpoint it gives him the greatest possible protection that his competitors can not buy cheaper because the processors signing the contract are
not bound until a sufficient number of processors whose combined processing
for the previous three years would be sufficient to be the controlling factor in
the market. In other words, the NFO will have to decide what per cent of the
processed production they feel is the controlling factor and then bargain on
that basis. This is the same principle that is followed in all other segments of
our economy.

For example: There is a great number of steel companies, but all of them follow the price pattern of a few. They can not afford to do otherwise. Also, it is only human nature for everyone to try to seek the highest price level.

The determined percentage the NFO feels is necessary to be the controlling factor in the market will not be revealed at this time for strategic reasons. The necessary percentage to be the controlling factor in the market will be some higher than the percentage necessary to be the dominating factor in the market. Many economists and marketing analysts have said 25% of the total supply can be the dominating factor in the market. They base this on the fact that if the marketing system now requires 100% of the total supply to fulfill their needs, then to be the dominating factor in the market you must control a sufficient percentage of the total production so that the present marketing system cannot fulfill their needs from other sources. In other words, if you have a holding action and they run out of their reserve or supply, then they have no alternative other than to bargain.

The percentage necessary to be the controlling factor in the market will be higher, but from a strategic bargaining position this offers the NFO the opportunity of using a tremendous amount of strength against an individual processor or a few processors. In other words, we are saying to the processors that we are preparing for an all-out holding action at the earliest possible date but if they want to bargain in good faith in the meantime they will have the opportunity to do so through the master contract. The master contract provides the tools for using the principle of "divide and conquer." If they do not choose to bargain in good faith, then the NFO will review their policies and if it is felt that their policies jeopardize the future welfare of its members, NFO will initiate a "no sell, no buy" campaign in which the NFO will advise its members not to "sell to, or buy from" those processors named. Then, of course, we will exert tremendous pressure on the processor or processors to correct their policies. Why should one processor fight the battle for other processors?

NFO now has two-thirds of the necessary strength to bring the processors to the bargaining table. We will continue to direct our efforts toward an all-out holding action at the earliest possible date. If the processors have not bargained in good faith in the meantime, then we will call an all-out holding action and hold until they have agreed to terms to stabilize prices and marketing conditions in the future.)

8. Accurate and complete records shall be kept by Processor showing the hogs purchased from NFO members and the prices paid therefor, and Processor and NFO shall cooperate to accomplish this purpose.

(EXPLANATION: This point is self-explanatory. Details will be worked out in bargaining. The purpose of this point is to assure NFO members that there will be accurate records. Everyone knows, of course, that any detail such as this will be agreed upon in negotiations and will be included in a contract subject to approval by members as specified in the NFO membership agreement.)

9. For acting as a procurement agent for Processor and for performing other services under this contract Processor shall pay to NFO an amount equal to _____ per cent of the purchase price of any hogs received from NFO members and shall make any other deductions authorized by NFO. Such payments shall be made to NFO within ten (10) days after the close of each month that this contract is in effect and shall relate to all hogs received by Processor from NFO members during that month.

(EXPLANATION: This point is of great importance to all members. It is the provision that will pay them for their efforts in rendering services over what can be rendered today under all present marketing conditions or by individual producers. In other words, NFO members under this provision would always receive whatever percentage is bargained for above the price received by non-members, because non-members could never get more at the market place. This was taken care of in points two and three.

This percentage should be bargained for in negotiations. Certainly NFO members should be paid if NFO does the procuring, offers an even flow through orderly marketing, offers guaranteed supply, and increases efficiency by increasing per cent of capacity processed by the processor by allowing processor to know ahead the approximate time of delivery, etc.

One of the greatest services rendered will be a great savings in transportation. We have the most inefficient marketing system that could possibly be designed. Under present conditions, livestock may be bought and hauled by a processor several hundred miles. Then another processor will often buy livestock close to the location of the first processor and haul part of it back to about the same area from where the first processor bought his supply. The same type of inefficient movement of grain often happens. In the handling of milk, you see as many as four or five milk trucks go down the same road picking up milk. You have not changed the total supply any, but you have had a costly operation both for the producer and the processor.

The NFO members should and will be paid for services rendered. They will receive their pay from the NFO as will be outlined as a result of bargaining. This again will be approved by members as provided under the membership agreement.)

10. NFO shall endeavor to keep Processor advised in advance as to the approximate number of hogs that NFO expects that its members will deliver to Processor in two weeks period; and NFO shall give such information to Processor within a period of three days before the beginning of each two week period.

(*EXPLANATION:* This is another service so the processor can plan his operations accordingly. It could, if members approve, work like this. Using hogs as an example—NFO members would estimate their production three months ahead, but would not be bound to this estimate in any way. Then as this date approached the member would notify the NFO if he felt his estimate was correct. If it was not correct he could give another estimate. Then he could notify the NFO about two weeks ahead of time what day he would like to market his hogs. There would always have to be provisions for change of mind, etc. There might have to be a day or so change in plans in order to give the best service to the processor, but if the prices were the same for a given period this should not cause any great hardship for the members and it could be a very valuable service to the processor.

This again would be spelled out definitely in a contract presented for approval of the members as specified under the NFO membership agreement. It would not be too difficult to keep the processor informed on milk and grain deliveries.)

11. When a Processor has signed this contract the NFO pledges to supply his needs to the best of its ability until this contract goes into effect.

(*EXPLANATION:* This will be rewarding a processor for his foresight.)

12. The Processor shall take care of all deductions as designated by the NFO.

(*EXPLANATION:* This will take care of any decisions made by the NFO members as specified under the membership agreement.)

13. The NFO and the Processor shall have joint supervision of grading and weighing.

(*EXPLANATION:* Producers lose great sums of money on grades and weights. This point will correct that. The details as to how disagreements will be arbitrated must be worked out in bargaining negotiations. The final approval will be made by NFO members as specified under the membership agreement.)

14. The NFO and Processor shall jointly establish uniform grades.

(*EXPLANATION:* This is self-explanatory. There is a great need for uniform grading. The details as to how disagreements will be arbitrated must be worked out in bargaining negotiations. The final approval will be made by NFO members as specified under the membership agreement.)

IN WITNESS WHEREOF the parties hereto have signed this contract on this _____ day of _____, 19_____.

By _____
Its

NATIONAL FARMERS ORGANIZATION, INCORPORATED

By _____
Its

This proposed draft of a master contract is to be discussed by NFO members in their regular county meetings during the month of October, 1961. After the national office has received a report on the discussions by members, a final draft will be prepared and offered to processors.

NOTES

NOTES

1
Cause for Revolt

1. *Family Farms in a Changing Economy,* USDA, AB No. 171, (Washington, March, 1957), p. 8.
2. *United States Census of Agriculture,* 1959, U.S. Department of Commerce, Vol. II, p. 70.
3. *Keeping Abreast of Change in the Rural Community,* USDA, AB No. 215, (Washington, October, 1959), p. 4.
4. *Ibid.*
5. *Solve Your Own Problems,* National Farmers Organization, Corning, Iowa, promotional pamphlet.

2
Evolution of Enough To Eat

1. E. Cecil Curwen and Gudmund Hatt, *Plough and Pasture,* (New York: Henry Schuman, 1953), p. 22.
2. H. G. Wells, *The Outline of History,* (New York: Doubleday and Company, 1949), Vol. I, p. 159.
3. Fritz Baade, *The Race to the Year 2000,* trans. from German by Ernst Pawal, (New York: Doubleday and Company, 1962), p. 3.
4. Curwen and Hatt, p. 36.
5. *Genesis* 4:1–9.
6. *Marcus Porcius Cato on Agriculture and Marcus Terentius Varro on Agriculture,* trans. from Latin by William Davis Hooper and Harrison Boyd Ash, ed. T. E. Page, (Cambridge: Harvard University Press, 1936).

7. Cato, p. 23.
8. *Ibid.*
9. *Ibid.*
10. Varro, pp. 307–8.
11. "Agriculture, History of," *Encyclopedia Americana,* Vol. I, pp. 256–57.
12. *Ibid,* p. 256.
13. Alfred Stefferud, ed., *Power to Produce,* The Yearbook of Agriculture, (Washington, 1960), p. 11.
14. *Ibid.,* p. 133.
15. *Ibid.,* p. 4.
16. John H. Davis and Kenneth Hinshaw, *Farmer in a Business Suit,* (New York: Simon and Schuster, 1957).
17. *Ibid.,* p. 75.
18. *Ibid.,* p. 134.
19. *Ibid.,* p. 228.

3

A Heritage of Agrarian Movements

1. Theodore Saloutos and John D. Hicks, *Agricultural Discontent in the Middle West,* (Madison: University of Wisconsin Press, 1951), pp. 3–6.
2. David Edgar Lindstrom, *American Farmers' and Rural Organizations,* (Champaign, Illinois: Garrard Press, 1948), pp. 76–80.
3. *Ibid.,* p. 72.
4. *Ibid.,* p. 78.
5. *The Grange Blue Book,* The National Grange, Washington, pp. 24–25.
6. Orville Merton Kile, *The Farm Bureau Through Three Decades,* (Baltimore: The Waverly Press, 1948), p. 5.
7. *Ibid.,* p. 6.
8. Lindstrom, pp. 96–106.
9. *Ibid.,* p. 79.
10. Saloutos and Hicks, p. 32.
11. *Ibid.,* p. 114.
12. *Ibid.,* p. 124.
13. *Ibid.,* pp. 147–48.
14. *National Union Farmer,* Denver, March, 1952.
15. *Ibid.*
16. *Ibid.*
17. *Ibid.*
18. *1962 Policy Statement of the National Farmers Union,* Denver, March 21, 1962, pp. 7–8.
19. Kile, pp. 24–36.
20. *Ibid.,* p. 36.
21. Lindstrom, p. 126.

22. Kile, p. 48.
23. *Ibid.*, p. 51.
24. *Ibid.*, p. 72.
25. *Ibid.*, p. 70.
26. *Farm Bureau Policies for 1963*, Atlanta, Georgia, December 13, 1962, p. 6.
27. *Summary of Legislative Policies and Programs of the National Grange, 1963*, Washington, pp. 3, 5.
28. Saloutos and Hicks, pp. 435–43.
29. John L. Shover, "The Farm Holiday Movement in Nebraska," *Nebraska History*, Vol. XLIII, (March, 1962), p. 53.
30. *Ibid.*, p. 58.
31. *Ibid.*, p. 65.
32. Saloutos and Hicks, p. 449.
33. Shover, *op. cit.*, p. 72.

4
"Let's Call a Meeting . . ."

1. Omaha (Nebraska) *World-Herald*, September 22, 1955.
2. *Ibid.*, September 27, 1955.
3. Dale Cramer, "An Agrarian Tide—Still Standing," *The New Republic*, April 16, 1956, pp. 11–12.
4. Omaha *World-Herald*, September 27, 1955.
5. *Ibid.*, September 23, 1955.
6. *Ibid.*, September 26, 1955.
7. *Ibid.*
8. *Ibid.*, March 19, 1956.
9. *The Stockman's Journal*, Omaha, October 6, 1955.
10. *Ibid.*, October 7, 1955.
11. Omaha *World-Herald*, December 16, 1955.
12. *Ibid.*
13. New York *Times Magazine*, January 22, 1956.
14. Omaha *World-Herald*, March 20, 1956.
15. *The Stockman's Journal*, September 12, 1955.
16. *Ibid.*, April 2, 1963. See tables on p. 3.
17. *Farmer-Labor Press*, Council Bluffs, Iowa, September 27, 1962.
18. *Ibid.*
19. *National Farmers Organization: Its Origin, Aims and Objectives*, Corning, Iowa, mimeographed handout, n.d., p. 3.
20. *Ibid.*, pp. 2–3.
21. Des Moines (Iowa) *Register*, September 10, 1957.
22. Omaha *World-Herald*, September 10, 1957.
23. Des Moines *Register*, September 10, 1957.
24. The Atlantic (Iowa) *News-Telegram*, February 19, 1958.
25. From a handbill posted by NFO members.
26. *Ibid.*

27. The author conducted a lengthy tape-recorded interview with Oren Lee Staley at NFO headquarters in Corning, Iowa, on May 8, 1962.
28. *Ibid.*
29. *The Stockman's Journal*, April 3, 1961.
30. *Ibid.*, April 4, 1961.
31. *Ibid.*
32. *Ibid.*, April 7, 1961.
33. *Ibid.*, April 13, 1961.
34. *Ibid.*
35. *Ibid.*
36. *Ibid.*, April 17, 1961.
37. *Analysis of the NFO's Test Holding Action on Cattle, Hogs and Sheep*, Corning, Iowa, mimeographed handout, n.d., p. 3.
38. *Ibid.*, pp. 12–14. (pp. 3–5 of statement attached to *Analysis* . . .).
39. *Resolutions—National Farmers Organization,* mimeographed copy, distributed at 1961 NFO National Convention in Des Moines, Iowa, December 8, 1961.
40. *Remarks of Secretary of Agriculture Orville L. Freeman before the annual convention of the National Farmers Organization*, Des Moines, Iowa, USDA 4065–61, December 8, 1961.
41. *The Prairie Farmer*, Chicago, January 6, 1962.
42. *Ibid.*, February 3, 1962.
43. *The Stockman's Journal*, August 16, 1962.
44. Omaha *World-Herald*, August 18, 1962.
45. Sioux Falls (South Dakota) *Argus-Leader*, August 23, 1962.

5
The Big Meeting for Action

1. *The NFO Reporter*, Corning, Iowa, Special Issue, August, 1962.
2. The author attended this "meeting for action" as a member of the working press. This account is based on the author's observations, notes and a tape recording of the speeches and ensuing proceedings.

6
The All Out Holding Action of 1962

1. Sioux Falls (South Dakota) *Argus-Leader*, August 30, 1962.
2. *Ibid.*, August 31, 1962.
3. Omaha (Nebraska) *World-Herald*, August 31, 1962.
4. *Ibid.*
5. *Ibid.*

6. *The Stockman's Journal,* Omaha, September 1, 1962.
7. *Ibid.*
8. *Ibid.*
9. Omaha *World-Herald,* August 31, 1962.
10. Sioux Falls *Argus-Leader,* August 31, 1962.
11. Omaha *World-Herald,* September 1, 1962.
12. *Ibid.*
13. Kansas City (Missouri) *Star,* September 1, 1962.
14. Omaha *World-Herald,* September 3, 1962.
15. *The Stockman's Journal,* September 5, 1962.
16. Sioux City (Iowa) *Journal,* September 4, 1962.
17. *Ibid.*
18. *The Stockman's Journal,* September 5, 1962.
19. *Ibid.*
20. Des Moines (Iowa) *Register,* September 5, 1962.
21. *Ibid.*
22. *The Stockman's Journal,* September 6, 1962.
23. Des Moines *Register,* September 5, 1962.
24. Kansas City *Star,* September 5, 1962.
25. *Ibid.,* September 6, 1962.
26. *Ibid.*
27. *Ibid.*
28. *The Stockman's Journal,* September 7, 1962.
29. Omaha *World-Herald,* September 6, 1962.
30. *Ibid.*
31. *Ibid*
32. Des Moines *Register,* September 8, 1962.
33. Omaha *World-Herald,* September 8, 1962.
34. *Ibid.*
35. *The Stockman's Journal,* September 8, 1962.
36. Kansas City *Star,* September 7, 1962.
37. *The Stockman's Journal,* September 7, 1962.
38. *Livestock Market News Weekly Summary and Statistics,* Vol. XXX, No. 37, (USDA, Washington, September 11, 1962), p. 697.
39. *Ibid.*
40. *Ibid.,* p. 694.
41. *Ibid.,* p. 695.
42. *Ibid.,* p. 697.
43. Omaha *World-Herald,* September 9, 1962.
44. *Ibid.*
45. Kansas City *Star,* September 10, 1962.
46. Sioux City *Journal,* September 11, 1962.
47. Omaha *World-Herald,* September 10, 1962.
48. Des Moines *Register,* September 11, 1962.
49. Omaha *World-Herald,* September 10, 1962.
50. Kansas City *Star,* September 12, 1962.
51. *Livestock Market News Weekly Summary and Statistics,* Vol. XXX, No. 38, (USDA, Washington, September 18, 1962), p. 717.

52. *Ibid.,* pp. 714–15.
53. Omaha *World-Herald,* September 15, 1962.
54. *Ibid.*
55. Des Moines *Register,* September 16, 1962.
56. *Ibid.,* September 12, 1962.
57. Livestock Auction Markets Association, Kansas City, news release, September 10, 1962.
58. *Ibid.*
59. American National Cattlemen's Association, Denver, news release, September 12, 1962.
60. Sioux Falls *Argus-Leader,* September 12, 1962.
61. Omaha *World-Herald,* September 16, 1962.
62. *Ibid.*
63. *Ibid.,* September 15, 1962.
64. *Ibid.*
65. Sioux City *Journal* and Omaha *World-Herald,* September 20, 1962.
66. *Ibid.*
67. Omaha *World-Herald,* September 15, 1962.
68. Kansas City *Star,* September 15, 1962.
69. *Ibid.,* September 16, 1962.
70. Minneapolis (Minnesota) *Tribune,* September 12, 1962.
71. *Ibid.,* September 14, 1962.
72. Kansas City *Star,* September 17, 1962.
73. *Ibid.*
74. *The Stockman's Journal,* September 18, 1962.
75. *Ibid.*
76. *Ibid.*
77. Omaha *World-Herald,* September 18, 1962.
78. *The Stockman's Journal,* September 19, 1962.
79. *Ibid.*
80. Kansas City *Star,* September 17, 1962.
81. *Ibid.*
82. *Ibid.,* September 24, 1962.
83. *Ibid.,* September 18, 1962.
84. *Ibid.,* September 20, 1962.
85. Sioux City *Journal,* September 17, 1962.
86. Minneapolis *Tribune,* September 18, 1962.
87. *Ibid.*
88. Des Moines *Register,* September 19, 1962.
89. Kansas City *Star,* September 20, 1962.
90. *Ibid.*
91. Sioux Falls *Argus-Leader,* September 19, 1962.
92. Des Moines *Register,* September 28, 1962.
93. Kansas City *Star,* September 20, 1962.
94. *Ibid.,* September 27, 1962.
95. Omaha *World-Herald,* September 29, 1962.
96. *Ibid.*
97. Kansas City *Star,* September 27, 1962.
98. Sioux Falls *Argus-Leader,* September 24, 1962.

99. Minneapolis *Tribune,* September 26, 1962.
100. Madison (South Dakota) *Daily Leader,* September 25, 1962.
101. Sioux Falls *Argus-Leader,* September 28, 1962.
102. Sioux City *Journal,* October 2, 1962.
103. Des Moines *Register,* September 30, 1962.
104. Sioux City *Journal,* September 28, 1962.
105. *The Stockman's Journal,* October 2, 1962.
106. *Ibid.*
107. Kansas City *Star,* October 3, 1962.
108. On March 21, 1963, the author tape-recorded a second exclusive interview with Oren Lee Staley at NFO headquarters in Corning, Iowa.
109. Des Moines *Register,* January 13, 1963.
110. Sioux City *Journal,* January 15, 1963.
111. *The Stockman's Journal,* February 9, 1963.

7
A Glance at Marketing

1. *Livestock Terminal Markets in the United States,* USDA, MR No. 299 (Washington, January, 1959), p. 2.
2. Alfred Stefferud, ed., *Marketing—The Yearbook of Agriculture, 1954,* USDA, (Washington, 1954), p. 48.
3. *Livestock Terminal Markets in the United States,* p. 31.
4. Stefferud, *op. cit.,* p. 56.
5. *Livestock Terminal Markets in the United States,* pp.3–4.
6. *Livestock Auction Markets in the United States,* USDA, MR No. 223, (Washington, March 1958), pp. 3–7.
7. *Ibid.,* pp. 23–29.
8. *Ibid.,* p. 7.
9. *Ibid.,* p. 14.
10. *Marketing Grain Through a Grain Exchange,* University of Illinois in cooperation with the Chicago Board of Trade, (Urbana, Illinois, November 13, 1961), pp. 2–5.
11. *Grain Marketing Efficiency, the Story of the Kansas City Board of Trade,* Kansas City (Missouri) Board of Trade, (Kansas City, 1961), p. 7.
12. *Hedging Highlights,* The Chicago Board of Trade, n.d., p. 7.
13. *Marketing Grain Through a Grain Exchange,* p. 7.
14. *Ibid.,* p. 8.
15. *Ibid.,* pp. 9–10.
16. *Federal Milk Marketing Orders,* USDA, MP No. 732, (Washington, 1956), p. 4.
17. *Ibid.,* p. 21.
18. *Marketing Margins for White Bread,* USDA, MP No. 712, (Washington, November, 1962), pp. 5–6.
19. *Pork Marketing Margins and Costs,* USDA, MP No. 711, (Washington, April 1956), p. 35.

20. *Marketing Costs and Margins for Fresh Milk,* USDA, MP No. 733 (Washington, February 1959), p. 5.
21. *The Food We Eat,* USDA, MP No. 870, (Washington, September 1962), p. 2.
22. *Ibid.,* p. 3.

8
"Sign on the Dotted Line . . ."

1. Jim Thomson, "Does NFO Have the Answers?" *Prairie Farmer,* Chicago, May 20, 1961, from a reprint.
2. Christopher Kelly, "NFO Demands Collective Bargaining," *Farm Quarterly,* Cincinnati, Ohio, Fall Issue, 1961.
3. Letter from Lyman S. Hulbert, Washington, D.C., to Oren Lee Staley, President, National Farmers Organization, Corning, Iowa, November 13, 1958, from a mimeographed copy distributed by the NFO.

9
Staley's Kind of Organization—I

1. Des Moines (Iowa) *Register,* September 10, 1962.
2. *An Analysis of the Present Livestock Marketing System,* National Farmers Organization, Corning, Iowa, n.d., p. 2.
3. *Ibid.,* pp. 32–36.
4. Christopher Kelly, "NFO Demands Collective Bargaining," *Farm Quarterly,* Cincinnati, Ohio, Fall Issue, 1961.
5. *The NFO Reporter,* National Farmers Organization, Corning, Iowa, May 1962.

10
Staley's Kind of Organization—II

1. Chicago, Omaha, Kansas City, St. Joseph, Sioux City, and Sioux Falls (South Dakota).
2. Transcribed verbatim from a tape recording of Staley's speech.
3. *Ibid.*
4. Des Moines (Iowa) *Register,* December 14, 1962.

11
The NFO's "Big Foe"

1. From a letter to the author from Creston J. Foster, news director, American Farm Bureau Federation, Chicago, April 9, 1963.

3 3 3

2. From a letter to the author from Jack Jackson, director of public relations, The National Grange, Washington, April 2, 1963.
3. *Official Statement of the National Farmers Union Executive Committee*, The National Farmers Union, Denver, September 7, 1962, mimeographed release.

12
The NFO Since 1962

1. Minneapolis (Minnesota) *Tribune*, March 8, 1963.
2. *Ibid.*
3. *The NFO Reporter*, Corning, Iowa, March, 1963.
4. *The Stockman's Journal*, Omaha, Nebraska, August 30, 1963.
5. Des Moines (Iowa) *Register*, June 26, 1963.
6. *Ibid.*, October 22, 1963.
7. From a tape recording of the meeting.
8. Omaha (Nebraska) *World-Herald*, November 15, 1963.
9. Sioux City (Iowa) *Journal*, November 20, 1963.
10. Des Moines (Iowa) *Tribune*, December 5, 1963.
11. Letter to the author from Oren Lee Staley, NFO president, December 13, 1963.

INDEX

INDEX

Agribusiness, 32–34
Agricultural Adjustment Act of 1933, 63–64, 158
Agriculture, history of, 21–29
American Dairy Association, 256
American Farm Bureau Federation
  general history of, 52–58
  policies of, 57–58, 66, 177, 193, 196, 198, 205, 227–29
  relationship to Extension Service, 57
American Meat Institute, 185
American National Cattlemen's Association, 117, 231
American Society of Equity, general history of, 45–47
American Tobacco Company, 46–47
Auction livestock markets, 108–9, 135, 144, 147–51
  costs of, 149
  trading volume at, 149–50
Automobiles, on farms, 31

B

Bakewell, Robert, 28–29
Barrett, Charles, 49–50
Battle Line, 122–23
Beermann, Ralph, 105
Benson, Ezra Taft, 66
Bryan, William Jennings, 44, 45
Burley Tobacco Society, 46–47

C

Capper-Volstead Act of 1922, 73, 167–69, 193
  text of, 274
Casper, Robert, 209, 211–12, 214, 243–46, 248–49
Cato the Elder, 24–25
Centralia Convention, 37–38, 260
Chenaworth, R. B., 30
Citizens of Nodaway County Organization for Free Enterprise, 129–30, 227
Clarke County Citizens Protective Association, 128–29, 227
Clubs for farm boys and girls, 52
Cochran, Dale, 246, 250
Collective bargaining for agriculture
  NFO adopts policy of, 73
Colorado Cattle Feeders Association, 122
Colored Farmers Alliance, 43
Committee for Economic Development
  farm policy statement of, 90–91
  firms deny endorsing CED statement, 92, 97, 204, 255
  reaction to CED statement, 90–91, 94, 97

Commodities Exchange Act, 64
Commodity Credit Corporation, 151, 253
Cooperatives, 254
  dairy, 158, 254
  of Equity Society, 47
  of Farm Bureau, 56–57
  of Farmers Union, 49–51
  of Grange, 41–42
County agricultural agents
  and Extension Service, 57
  and Farm Bureau, 57
  and USDA, 53
"Cow war" of Farm Holiday Association, 61
Curwen, E. Cecil, 21, 22
Crawford, Corbin, 75
Credit Mobilier Scandal, 38

D

Dalton, John, 109, 123
Dartmouth College Decision, 38
Davis, John H., 32–34
Deere, John, 30
Democratic Party, 44
Direct selling to packers, 144–46
"Dollar Wheat Bulletins," 46

E

Education, agricultural, 52
Equity Cooperative Exchange, 47
Everitt, J. A., 45, 46
Exporting farm products, 256

F

Farm cost-price squeeze, 6, 9–10, 65–66
Farm discontent
  general problems causing, 36–38
  geographic area of prevalence, 35
Farm Holiday Association, 261
  general history of, 60–64
Farm organizations, nature of early, 37
Farm population
  aging of, 8
  trends, 6–7, 10, 15, 22
"Farm problem," explained, 8–9
  NFO definition of, 18
Farm production
  in Corn Belt region, 4
  general trend in 1962, 96

increases in, 9
livestock production trends in 1955, 63
planning, 10–11
techniques needed for, 11
utilization research for farm products, 255
Farm strikes, 62
Farm wages, compared with city wages, 3
Federal Bureau of Investigation, 124
Federal Land Bank, 197
Food chain stores, 235
Food consumer, as opponent of NFO, 235–36
Food consumption, 161–62
Freeman, Orville L., 86–87, 104–5, 123

G

Grain commission firms, 152, 252–53
Grain grading, 152
Grain marketing
  cash trading in, 152–53
  cost factors in, 151–52
  futures trading in, 153–55
Gresham, Newt, 48

H

Hall, Caroline A., 39–40
Hatch Act of 1887, 42, 52
Hedging, 153–55; *see also* Grain marketing
Hinshaw, Kenneth, 32–34
Horses and mules, as farm power, 30
Houser, Theodore, 92
Howard, James R., 55–56
Huff, Clarence E., 50
Hussey, Obed, 30

I

Interstate Commerce Commission, 41

K

Kansas Farmers Union, 106
Kelley, Oliver Hudson, 39–40
Kile, O. M., 40, 52
Knapp, Seaman, 53
Knights of Columbus, 195–96
Kriege, Fred, 62

L

LaFollette, Robert, 60
Land Grant Act of 1892, 42, 52
Lindstrom, David Edgar, 36, 38
Livestock Auction Markets Association, 117, 120, 231, 233–34
Livestock commission fees, 140
Livestock commission firms, 103, 141–42, 232–33
Livestock Market News Service, USDA, 78–79, 80, 82, 106, 111, 112, 113, 115, 116, 134–35, 185
Livestock market receipt data, 79, 80, 105–6, 112, 113, 115–16; tables on, 134–35
Livestock and meat imports, 185
Livestock price trends, 71, 113, 114, 116; tables on, 134–35
Livestock transportation costs (by truck), 143–44
Loghry, Jay, 67–69, 217
Lowdown, The, 227

M

Market, definitions of, 138
Marketing margins
of fresh milk, 161
of pork, 160–61
of white bread, 160
McCormick, Cyrus, 30
Meat price trends, 110, 114, 116
Meat supplies, 113
Milk marketing, 157–60
Milk marketing orders, federal, 159–60
Milk prices, 160

N

National Catholic Rural Life Conference, 245
National Farmers Organization
all out holding actions of, 99–100; 1962 action recessed, 131; Staley appraises 1962 action, 132–33; all out holding action on grains, 250–53
area bargaining committees, 165
"character assassination" charges, 243
confusion within the, 241
duties of president of, 178–79, 209
education department of, 184–86
farm-labor conferences of, 220–22
financing of national organization, 181, 204
grain exporting program of, 253
home office, described, 176
labor unions and the, 74, 192, 217–22, 225
marketing quotas proposed by the, 165
mass demonstrations, meetings of, 3, 67, 69, 81, 86, 91–92, 93–102, 120, 121, 124–26, 212, 237, 238, 240–41, 243, 246, 248
master contract of, 86, 105, 110, 169–72, 206, 277–82
meeting for action, 1962, 93–102
member–non-member conflicts of, 189–90
members, examples of, 190–201
membership agreement of, 163–68, 192, 269–73
membership dues and fees, 5, 166, 210, 217
membership figures of, 70, 72, 75, 222
milk dumping, 237–39
milk price bargaining program of, 237–40, 241, 242
"Minuteman System" of, 106, 186–87
national elections of, 69, 209–16, 242–50
national staff organizers, 187–90, 205–6
"no buy—no sell" program, 212
opposition to, 224–36
organizational structure of, 180–81
origin of, 4, 66–68, 71–72
pheasant hunting ban of, 127–28, 133
picketing activities of, 125–26, 240–41

National Farmers Organization (*continued*)
plan for action, 4, 73, 261–65
purges of membership, alleged, 205, 242, 250, 265
"rat battle," 119–20, 231
Reporter, The NFO, 74, 178, 182–84, 205, 211, 224
sabotage charges from, 247–48
service charges to processors, proposed, 171
social activities of, 201
"specific holding action" proposal, 210, 215
"test holding actions" of, 2, 77–78, 82, 85
unrest within, 125, 206–17, 262
violence connected with, 108–10, 120–21, 123–25, 126, 136–37, 225, 244, 247
voluntary grain sales agreement, proposed, 251
"wildcat holding actions" of, 240–42
National Farmers Union
general history of, 47–52
policies of, 51, 61, 66, 74–75, 230–31
National Grange, The
general history of, 39–42, 58–59
policies of, 59, 66, 229, 230
National Livestock Feeders Association, 104, 114, 123
National Livestock and Meat Board, 256
Nave, Forest, Jr., 249
Newbold, Charles, 29
New York State Agricultural Society, 52
Nonpartisan League, 47, 59–60
Northern Farmers Alliance, 42, 43
Northwest Missouri State College, 177

O

Orton, Duane, 67, 71

P

Packers and Stockyards Act, 64, 143, 162, 185
Packing industry, 111, 185, 234–35

"Penny farm auctions," 63
Plows, history of, 29–30
Populist Party (People's Party), 43–45, 260
Price supports, farm, 7, 68, 70, 72, 252–53
Private treaty trading, 138, 141–42

R

Railroads, 38, 40–41
Railway freight rates for grain, 156
Reapers, grain, 30
Red Poll Cattle Club of America, 118
Reno, Milo, 60, 61–62
Republican Party, 71–72, 122–23
Rossiter, Vince, 95–96, 245

S

St. Paul Retail Food Dealers Association, 118
Saloutos, Theodore, 35, 45, 46, 47
Shuffling livestock, charges of, 79, 82, 83
Shuman, Charles B., 87–89, 228–29
Smith-Hughes Act of 1917, 52
Socialist Party, 60
South Dakota Game, Fish and Park Department, 128
South Dakota Grange, 128
South Dakota Motel Association, 128
Southern Farmers Alliance, 42, 43
Staley, Oren Lee
elected NFO president, 126
excerpts of speeches by, 97–100, 214–15
opponents charges against, 202–6, 208–9, 210, 242–46
personality sketch of, 174–78
Steam power, 31
Stockyards activities, 106, 119, 122, 141–42

T

Terminal livestock markets
description of, 140–47
essentials of, 140

volume of trade in, 146
Texas Farmers Alliances, 42
Thatcher, Myron W., 47, 50
Third Power, The, 45
Townley, Arthur C., 59
Townshend, Charles, 28
Tractors, farm, 31
Truth About the Farm Bureau, The, 228
Turner, Daniel, 67–69, 70

U

United Auto Workers (AFL-CIO), 74, 217
United Packinghouse Workers (AFL-CIO), 67, 220–22

U.S. Grain Growers, Inc., 56
U.S. Grain Standards Act, 152

V

Varro Reatinus, 25–26

W

"Walkie-talkies," 213
Weaver, J. B., 45
Wells, H. G., 21
Wheat referendum, 1963 national, 254–55
Woodward, Harold, 209, 210, 214

Y

"Yellow sheet," 185